Mary Pepchinski, Christina Budde (eds.)
Women Architects and Politics

I0092965

This volume includes papers delivered at the conference Women Architects and Politics in the Long 20th Century at the Deutsches Architekturmuseum (DAM) in Frankfurt/Main from January 17 to 19, 2018. Additional chapters include lectures presented within the framework of the exhibition Frau Architekt. Over 100 Years of Women as Architects held at DAM from September 30, 2017 to March 8, 2018 as well as research carried out for this event.

Mary Pepchinski, professor for architecture and society at the Technical University Dresden until 2021, studied at Columbia University in New York and the University of the Arts in Berlin. She researches about architecture and gender, and held guest professorships in women's and gender studies at the Technical University Graz (2002) and the University of Applied Sciences Mainz (2017-18). She was the scientific advisor to *Frau Architekt. Over 100 Years of Women as Architects* at the Deutsches Architekturmuseum (DAM) (2017).

Christina Budde served as a curator for public architectural education at the Deutsches Architekturmuseum (DAM) in Frankfurt/Main until 2020. She studied English and politics at the Goethe University Frankfurt and the University of Warwick (UK). At DAM her curatorial projects and publications focused on contemporary architecture, photography, and cultural education, as well as informal learning processes. In 2017 she co-curated the exhibition and catalog *Frau Architekt. Over 100 Years of Women as Architects* at DAM.

Mary Pepchinski, Christina Budde (eds.)

Women Architects and Politics

Intersections between Gender, Power Structures
and Architecture in the Long 20th Century

[transcript]

The Kulturstiftung des Bundes/German Federal Cultural Foundation provided funding for this exhibition and conference.

The Gesellschaft der Freunde des Deutschen Architekturmuseums e.V. (Friends of DAM) and private sponsors provided funding for the *Frau Architekt* films and for this project.

Bibliographic information published by the Deutsche Nationalbibliothek
The Deutsche Nationalbibliothek lists this publication in the Deutsche Nationalbibliografie; detailed bibliographic data are available in the Internet at http://dnb.d-nb.de

© 2022 transcript Verlag, Bielefeld

Cover layout: Kordula Röckenhaus, Bielefeld
Translation: Mary Pepchinski (chapters by Irene Nierhaus, Wolfgang Voigt, Karl Kiem, Kerstin Renz, Annette Krapp and Christina Budde)
Typeset: Francisco Bragança, Bielefeld
Printed by Majuskel Medienproduktion GmbH, Wetzlar
Print-ISBN 978-3-8376-5630-5
Print-ISBN
PDF-ISBN 978-3-8394-5630-9
https://doi.org/10.14361/9783839456309
ISSN of series: 2702-8070
eISSN of series: 2702-8089

Contents

III. Women Architects in divided Europe 1945-1990

IV. Gender and Global Practice

V. The Politics of Representation (2): Women Architects on Display

VI. Engaging the Academy, Challenging the Profession

Introduction

Mary Pepchinski, Christina Budde

The exhibition *Frau Architekt. Over 100 years of women in architecture* (29.09.2017–08.03.2018) at the Deutsches Architekturmuseum (DAM) Frankfurt-am-Main recounted the history of 20th century architecture from the perspective of women architects, focusing on their past and present, their contributions to architecture, the reality of their lives and their struggle for existence and giving a face and a voice to these previously "invisible" designers. The exhibition was one of DAM's most successful in recent years, not only because it was "long overdue," as was evident from visitor comments, but also because architecture stands *pars pro toto* for the struggles that women still have to negotiate in male domains. Fortunately, this attracted visitors who do not necessarily belong to the regular audience of an architecture museum.

To create an alternate account of modern architecture history in Germany, *Frau Architekt* presented the biographies and buildings of 22 women architects. A profound desire for personal emancipation is at the heart of these stories, although this striving had specific meaning for each protagonist and was particular to her context. As the sociologist, Ulla Bock, observes: "It follows that emancipation can gain a different face for each woman, a specific accentuation in each case, and for one and the same woman it can prove to be something different today than tomorrow."[1] *Frau Architekt* also revealed that the path to emancipation required an engagement with politics, or what the feminist writer and activist Kate Millett identifies as "power-structured relationships, arrangements whereby one group of persons is controlled by another."[2] This includes women who willingly joined movements, embraced political platforms or participated in organized religion; those who found

---

1 Bock (1988), 85.

2 Millett (orig. 1968; 1980), 31–32.

themselves reacting to greater forces that were seemingly beyond their control; or those who benefitted from the seismic shifts in prevailing political, social and cultural norms as they pursued a career in architecture.

Yet the combination of female emancipation, a desire for architectural professionalism and an entanglement with the political currents that upended the long 20th century does not always lead to comfortable answers. On their way to the first-floor gallery in DAM where *Frau Architekt* was on display, visitors would have glimpsed a poster, hanging in the stairway, with a statement followed by the first names of 22 women. A striking graphic, it consists of words that are rendered in bold capital letters against a bright red background.[3] (Figure 1) At the top, the pronouncement, *Die Zukunft der Architektur* (The future of architecture) appears in black characters, followed by the first names of the women featured in *Frau Architekt*, printed in white. Roughly midway along the left margin, a black line is drawn through the center of "Gerdy," a gesture meant to distance it from this group. "Gerdy" is Gertrud Troost, an interior architect and designer who became Hitler's trusted confidant and wielded extraordinary influence during the Third Reich. The poster, ostensibly conceived to acknowledge women's achievement in architecture, could not possibly include such a figure under this pronouncement. Or should it? And if so, how? The degree to which her name should be revealed and/or obscured not only caused much debate among the curators and the graphic artist who created this image, but also pointed to the limits of all-encompassing assumptions when attempting collective biography.

This incident brings us to another issue concerning gender and the writing of history. Since the Second Women's Movement of the 1970s, much of women's history has focused on unearthing forgotten figures to serve as role models to bring about a more equitable future.[4] How is it possible, then, to include women in the historical record whose actions or political convictions are abhorrent? Or, as Despina Stratigakos asks about Gerdy Troost and other women who were actively involved in the Nazi cause, "could they be considered feminists in any sense?"[5]

***

---

3 The designer, Bernd Kreutz, generously contributed the design of this poster, and also printed posters and postcards with this graphic for the exhibition.

4 Lerner (1993), 274.

5 Stratigakos (2016), 145, especially footnote 139 and the literature referenced there.

Figure 1: Poster Die Zukunft der Architektur (The future of architecture)
(Design: B. Kreutz); Stairway at DAM (Deutsches Architekturmuseum),
October 2017. Source: M. Pepchinski.

Indeed, the renewed turn towards "politics"—or rather "power structures"—
also can be understood as a reflection of our turbulent times. Anyone who
lived through late 1960s and early 1970s might be excused for feeling a sense
of *déja vu*, as forces that champion long-held beliefs about the acceptable
course of private and public life clash with those seeking to eliminate them
or identify other ways of being in the world. Recent elections and referen-
dums, from Brexit to the US elections of 2016 and 2020, exert impact well
beyond the borders of the nations where their ballots were cast. Grass roots
activism, including the Black Lives Matter protests; the Fridays for Future

demonstrations; the #MeToo movement; the Occupy protests for economic justice and many others, now inspire people to speak out and take action. And, as we complete this volume, the COVID-19 pandemic continues its rampage, forcing elected leaders to make wrenching decisions with far-reaching consequences about public health, while war in Ukraine is causing untold destruction and displacement.

In conjunction with *Frau Architekt*, an international conference, "Women Architects and Politics in the Long 20th Century," took place at DAM in January 2018. Speakers and moderators from Austria, Belgium, Germany, Great Britain, Hungary, Ireland, Israel, Sweden, Switzerland and the USA explored the lives, careers and activism of women architects in relation to emancipation movements; hegemonic cultural and social norms; the dictates of organized religion; as well as contemporary institutional structures and professional practices. The great, overwhelmingly positive response to this event encouraged us to document the conference and to take stock of the current debate on gender equity in architecture. Several texts that were delivered at other events in conjunction with *Frau Architekt* or that were authored by colleagues who contributed to this project in various capacities were included too.

Chapters by Irene Nierhaus and Elke Krasny introduce themes that we hope will resonate with readers not only as they peruse these contributions but also when they pore over other texts about architecture. They pose the question: How do we critically engage with the inherited conceptual "power structures" that restrict, define and convey knowledge? Irene Nierhaus recalls her friendship with Margarete Schütte-Lihotzky, started years before the latter evolved into a feminist icon and the ultimate symbol of a committed political life. She argues for the enduring validity of memory drawn from personal experience to reflect upon the past and warns against the temptation to (over) interpret historical figures, which can skew and even obscure the true essence of their lives and legacy. Drawing upon the work of political theorists Joan C. Tronto and Maria Puig de la Bellacasa Fischer along with architecture historians Catherine M. Soussloff and Despina Stratigakos, Elke Krasny urges a "radical rethinking" of the practice of architecture, away from a knowledge-based endeavor fixated on individual accomplishment, novelty, the dictates of capital and systems of oppressive hierarchies, to one that holds dear the disvalued, "racialized and sexualized" labor of preserving and nurturing life, or "care" work, as a professional paradigm. By extension, "care" work serves as a conscious, critical ideal for the committed, gendered architect. The notion of architecture as "care" also prompts us to reconsider the telling of (feminine) biography, possibly to abandon the strict division between the private tasks of nurturing (tending to a family or preserving the legacy of a teacher or partner) and the public activity of designing and building to accept all life-sustaining labor as an integrated and continuous condition.

Case studies in the following two sections explore how "power structures", such as class and religion, along with the experience of war, migration, exile and the socio-political landscape of post-war Europe, shaped the lives of women architects. For many of the women architects in this collection, it is not surprising that their perception of the world was profoundly bourgeois. The social status quo, male supremacy and patriarchy were not really questioned and equal treatment with male counterparts was hardly claimed. At the same time, the implicit acceptance of this gender hierarchy also excluded women from the historical record—and continues to do so.

In her chapter about the Zionist architect Gertrud Goldschmidt, Sigal Davidi shows that in Mandatory Palestine, which offered refuge to many architects who fled from Nazi Germany and gave women far more freedom of action than old Europe, the work of female designers was often attributed to male partners or colleagues. Furthermore, the Zionist movement envisioned a physically strong and robust "New Man" to offset the negative stereotype of the "weak" Jew but lacked a clear counterpart for a Zionist woman. As Sigal Davidi observes, a "New Woman" in this context "emerged independently of the Zionist utopia."[6] Edina Meyer-Maril describes the odyssey of another Jewish woman, Judith Stolzer-Segall. Unlike Goldschmidt, Stolzer-Segall was a staunch communist. She spent her youth and young adulthood in different cities in Eastern and Central Europe before going into exile in Mandatory Palestine in the 1930s. Along the way, she took advantage of various professional opportunities, often with remarkable success. After 1945, she returned to West Germany and received her long-sought German citizenship, yet her engagement with architecture abruptly ceased. It is as if the arduous years in flux were more vital and productive to her career than the attainment of her ultimate personal goal, namely a place that she iden-

---

6 Compare Sigal Davidi's chapter in this collection.

tified as "home." Was this lack of "roots," or the constant state of upheaval and dislocation, a requirement to sustain a desire for architectural practice?[7]

Turning to the period of National Socialism in Germany, Wolfgang Voigt recounts architectural education at the Technical University of Stuttgart under the architect Paul Schmitthenner during the final year of the Second World War. At that moment in time, women, foreigners and "war-disabled" male students were in the majority in many classrooms. Although Schmitthenner had joined the Nazi party, he eventually distanced himself from it for complex professional and personal reasons. A passionate educator whose status had been diminished, this period of crisis and the unusual composition of the student body presented him and his students with a brief opportunity to reinvent the deeply entrenched, power-based binary structures used to disseminate architectural knowledge. In a departure from the typical focus on women architects who hailed from the middle and upper classes, Karl Kiem explores the life of Princess Victoria zu Bentheim und Steinfurt, whose long life appears riddled with contradictions: A member of the German high aristocracy and a prolific architect, she was an early member of the Nazi party who successfully cleared her name after the war. Her class status kept her private life and professional endeavors isolated from the constraints of those "power-structured relationships" that her bourgeois counterparts could not easily escape.

Kerstin Renz recounts a journey undertaken by the young architects Maria-Verena Fischer and Dorothee Keuerleber to the USA in the early 1950s under the auspices of the Cultural Exchange Program, a part of the re-education of West Germany. Both women were fascinated by this nation's innovative school architecture, such as buildings that were flooded with light and air and were touted as the embodiment of democratic ideals. In actuality, these schools were reserved for white children only and the newly built neighborhoods surrounding them enforced a system of social segregation and racial separation. Such facts did not concern these women and went unchallenged and without reflection in their accounts. Although deeply influenced by their American sojourn and committed to careers in architecture, upon their return to the conservative atmosphere, which permeated the post-war years in West Germany, a clear-cut path to professional fulfillment was difficult to find.

7   Compare Ahmed (1999); Otsuka (orig. 2011; 2019).

Indeed, positioning oneself in the public sphere as a woman was highly unusual, even undesirable in West Germany. Most women, anchored in the bourgeois notions of class and gender, would not have thought of claiming it for themselves. As Annette Krapp demonstrates, even Maria Schwarz, the partner of the architect Rudolf Schwarz in both life and work, tacitly accepted that her professional endeavors for the Roman Catholic Church remained subordinated to those of her husband.

Not only West Germany, but much of Western Europe in the post-war years clung to traditional feminine ideals, and several nations, including Switzerland, only granted women suffrage in the 1970s and 1980s.[8] In their chapter about *SAFFA 1958*, a vast, open-air exhibition focusing on the life and work of Swiss women held in Zürich, Katia Frey and Eliana Perotti show how contemporary architecture served as a medium to communicate ideas about gender and national identity. Whereas this event's innovative construction and progressive design masked the conservative model for women that was propagated in Switzerland at that time, it paradoxically launched the careers of hundreds of professional women who contributed to its production and dissemination.

Meanwhile, the socialist nations of Eastern Europe identified gender equality as an intrinsic component of their ideology. Although this bold intention did not lead to parity, it ushered women into the workforce and opened up some opportunities in public life.[9] Mariann Simon examines this ambiguous legacy and reviews the entrance of women to the profession of architecture in post-war Hungary. During the rapid modernization of the 1950s, the growing economy required a well-educated workforce, and women made impressive gains in the professions, notably architecture. In the ensuing decades, however, as the economy slowed, more traditional attitudes towards gender emerged and were amplified by legislation which encouraged young mothers to take a respite from their careers. Combined with the stubborn persistence of traditional attitudes towards women, gender equality remained elusive.

---

8 Women received the right to vote in Switzerland in 1971; in Portugal in 1974; and in Liechtenstein in 1984. See: https://de.wikipedia.org/wiki/Frauenwahlrecht_in_Europa, accessed on April 12, 2021.

9 For women architects in Socialist Europe, see the chapters in: Pepchinski/Simon (2016).

In the last decades of the twentieth century, global architectural culture has emerged. Supported by elite cultural institutions, it propagates the ideal of a small coterie of internationally active, overwhelmingly male "star" architects whose pronouncements and projects have world-wide impact. In her chapter about Zaha Hadid and Denise Scott Brown, Kathleen James-Chakraborty analyses the careers of these influential women architects and explores how they won access to elite architectural practice. By examining their formative years on the periphery of the British empire, the influence of their families upon their careers as well as their performance and orchestration of professional identity, she considers the extent to which these two extremely different women were able to secure a place on the ultimate platform of architectural power and influence.

As more women—along with many others who have been traditionally excluded from architecture—are studying this discipline or establishing themselves in practice, they question its premises and reimagine its parameters. In doing so, they articulate a critique of disciplinary power structures; for them, the status quo is no longer accepted as an immutable, authoritative standard but a point of departure to be questioned, challenged and reimagined in order for a more inclusive and socially responsive profession to arise.

The profession of architecture has long been considered a masculine domain, and the institutions that have been created to support it tend to perpetuate this idea. How is it possible for long-established architectural institutions to acknowledge a feminine presence and accept women as equals? The chapters by Elizabeth Darling and Lynne Walker along with those by Christina Budde and Mary Pepchinski address this situation and describe the representation of the feminine architect within the framework of a leading school of architecture, the Architectural Association in London[10] or a well-regarded museum, DAM in Frankfurt-am-Main.[11] Pursing diverse approaches at two European universities, Donna Drucker recalls the introduction of a course in Gender Spatial Theory at the Technical University of Darmstadt and Torsten Lange and Gabriele Schaad describe their seminars, "Architectures of Gender," at the ETH Zürich. Both demonstrate that this content is an integral to architectural knowledge. Lange and Schaad also remind us that the recent interest in gender studies at architecture faculties

---

10 Darling/Walker (2017).

11 Pepchinski/Budde/Voigt/Schmal (2017).

is not new. They note that illustrious institutions, including the ETH Zürich, successfully pioneered such educational offerings in the 1990s, only to have their efforts be forgotten or "made invisible." Demanding access to such courses and avenues of study requires a challenge to institutional structures, which marginalize and dismiss anything related to a gender framework to consider architecture.

Finally, Harriet Harriss and Ruth Morrow look back upon the process of compiling their co-edited volume, *A Gendered Profession*,[12] which sought to identify solutions to make architectural labor and education more socially responsible and equitable. They encourage us to question the universally accepted rules that govern architectural practice, such as attitudes towards time. For example, a feminine life has a temporal dimension, which can require taking a leave from work to bear children or care for a family. Yet such extended absences from a drawing board are viewed as being incompatible with the long hours that young architects are expected to invest in their careers. Furthermore, the assumption that an architect must devote lengthy, exhausting days to architectural work to demonstrate professional commitment is neither productive nor advantageous to one's health. Another unchallenged notion concerns technology, and Harriss and Morrow encourage us to think about the need to invent new processes and products to allow architecture to accommodate a feminine presence. They conclude that change requires activism on many levels if "power-structured relationships, arrangements whereby one group of persons is controlled by another" can be put aside in favor of equity and access to architecture by all members of society.[13]

The chapters in this collection are not intended as universalizing statements about the relationship between gender, architectural practice and political structures. Written by straight and queer, overwhelmingly cis-gender, Caucasian authors hailing from Europe, Israel and North America, the contributions are a brief historical collage with digressions into the present and the current gender discourses in architecture. There is still much to investigate, and we hope the ideas presented here inspire interest, criticism and revision, particularly by those who investigate the woman architect in

---

12   The other two editors are James Brown and James Soane. See Brown/Harriss/Morrow/
      Soane (2016).

13   Brown/Harriss/Morrow/Soane (2016).

diverse geographical and social contexts in addition to grappling with other constructions of power and authority.

Finally, we thank the many people who helped make this publication become a reality. We are grateful to the staff and direction of DAM for their help and encouragement, as well as the scientific advisory committee to *Frau Architekt*, Fritz Backhaus, Hilde Heynen and Gorch Pieken, who encouraged us to sharpen our arguments and not shy away from the issue of politics. Hilde Heynen, Helena Mattsson, Mary McLeod, Tanja Scheffler, Sandra Schuster, Despina Stratigakos and Ines Weizman participated in the 2018 symposium, and we are grateful for their insightful comments and criticism. In the process of making this publication a reality, many people and institutions lent their support. We thank Annika Linnemann at transcript publishers in addition to: *Fürstliches Archiv*, Burgsteinfurt; Stephan Rethfeld; Taylor and Francis Publishers for allowing us to publish an excerpt of Donna J. Drucker's "Bringing Gender and Spatial Theory to Life at a German Technical University" (2016); Denise Scott Brown; Thomas Carpenter; Marie-Theres Deutsch; Diller Scofidio and Renfro; Yen Ha; Anna Heringer; Andreas Siekmann; Alexander White of RIBA Publishing; Womxn in Design: Junainah Ahmed, Brittany Giunchigliani, Shira Grosman and Malia Teske; and Désirée Edschmid for her generous help in editing the final text. Lastly, our deepest gratitude extends to both the *Kulturstiftung des Bundes* (German Cultural Foundation) and the *Gesellschaft der Freunde des Deutschen Architekturmuseum e. V.* (Society of Friends of the German Architecture Museum) for their generous support of the *Frau Architekt* project in general and this publication in particular.

Literature

Ahmed, Sara (1999), "Home and away. Narratives of migration and estrangement," in: *International Journal of Cultural Studies*, December 1, 1999, https://doi.org/10.1177/136787799900200303, accessed on April 13, 2021.

Bock, Ulla (1988), *Androgynie und Feminismus. Frauenbewegung zwischen Institution und Utopie*, Weinheim und Basel: Beltz.

Brown, James/Harriss, Harriet/Morrow, Ruth/Soane, James (eds.)(2016), *A Gendered Profession. The question of representation in placemaking*, London: RIBA Publishing.

Darling, Elizabeth/Walker, Lynne (eds.)(2017), *AA Women in Architecture 1917-2017*, London: AA Publications.

Lerner, Gerda (1993), *The Creation of a Feminist Consciousness*, New York/Oxford: Oxford University Press.

Millett, Kate (orig. 1968; 1980), *Sexual Politics*, New York: Ballantine Books.

Otsuka, Julie (orig. 2011; 2019), "'Come, Japanese!'," in: Ahmad, Dora (ed.): *The Penguin Book of Migration Literature*, New York: Penguin, 23–34.

Pepchinski, Mary/Simon, Mariann (eds.)(2016): *Ideological Equals. Women Architects in Socialist Europe*, London: Routledge.

Pepchinski, Mary/Budde, Christina/Voigt, Wolfgang/Schmal, Peter C. (eds.) (2017), *Frau Architekt. Seit mehr als 100 Jahren: Frauen im Architekturberuf/ Frau Architekt. Over 100 Years of Women in Architecture*, Ausstellungskatalog/Exhibition Catalogue, Deutsches Architekturmuseum (DAM), Frankfurt-am-Main (30.09.2017-08.03.2018), Tübingen/Berlin: Wasmuth.

Stratigakos, Despina (2016), *Hitler at Home*, New Haven/London: Yale University Press.

Nicht zuschütten[1]
A personal remembrance
of Margarete Schütte-Lihotzky

Irene Nierhaus

From my experience in gender research, I have become cautious about descriptions of identity, which is the subject of any kind of biographical writing. So it is necessary for me to emphasize that I am writing a personal memoir of Margarete Schütte-Lihotzky in which biographical details of the remembered are intermingled with the autobiographical circumstances of the one who is doing the remembering. Here I am constructing a/my narrative about *die Schütte* (as she is known in Vienna) from a specific perspective that occurred at a specific place and point in time. While living in Vienna in the late 1970s, I met Grete, when she was in her late 70s, a woman with a rich life and full of verve as she conveyed her version of history, architecture and politics and recalled her activities in the resistance, the women's movement and with internationalism. In my 20s at the time, I was curious about these topics and constantly in search of alternatives to those available to me in my life and the courses that were offered at the local institutions of high learning. Because the Department of Art History at the University of Vienna was extremely conservative, I studied for a year at the University of Rome. There, I was introduced to a civically and culturally oriented, socio-historical contextualization of art and architectural history by professors such as Carlo Giulio Argan, the art historian and then communist mayor of Rome.

Back in Vienna and in search of a critical and socially relevant method of writing art history, I first met Grete through the women's movement

---

1 In this context, *nicht zuschütten* means "don't bury [her]" or "don't obscure [her]". The title is a wordplay on the first part of Margarete Schütte-Lihotzky's last name. The German verb *zuschütten* means to cover up, to bury or to obscure.

and left-wing political circles. At the university, I mainly took courses with the architectural historian Renate Wagner-Rieger, who was a very devout Catholic and quite conservative regarding personal issues, yet was liberal, open-minded and supportive when it came to academic pursuits. She was my political counterpart to Grete, yet I deeply appreciated her because of her generosity towards me and my fellow students regarding our desire to experiment and explore new lines of thought. I don't remember the first time I met Grete. She had not become the *die Schütte*, the famous or much talked about person, so I just got to know her little by little. She was living history and, seen from today, also something like a *role model* who impressed me and, I would like to think, had an influence on my life. (Figure 1)

Her influences on me include: her contextualized means of thinking about space; her willingness to take a clear-eyed stand in relation to current political matters (except for her attachment to an ossified communism); her unwavering engagement for the emancipation of women, social classes and all people; her understanding of the world at large and her cosmopolitanism; her concentrated, objective and precise way of working; her conviction that life-long, educational offerings to impart knowledge are necessary; her awareness of social appearances, her humor and her charm; her confident elegance; and, last but not least, her ability to act independently and with a slight detachment in any given situation, as well as the manner in which she carried this out. The latter quality appealed to me because I perceived it as an expression of her autonomy and self-reliance, especially when compared to the prevailing notions of appropriate feminine behavior at the time, like the eternal smile, the constant pressure to establish cordial relations and preserve harmony. Grete always countered such gender stereotypes with humor, recalling the memory of a discussion by the jurors of a student competition during her years at the School of Arts and Crafts in Vienna. The jurors tried to guess which project had been submitted by the lone female participant and assumed it was a romantic "design with flowers." But to everyone's astonishment it was "of all things the most rational project" that came from none other than herself. We liked to laugh about such gender missteps; at the time, such assumptions only fueled my arguments against the much-debated, feminist "female aesthetics," based on differential feminism with ideas of an inherent gender difference and that were commonplace then. (Today, however, I would probably take a second look at this story.)

Figure 1: Margarete Schütte-Lihotzky, 1980s. Source: Ronald Zak.

Grete's reflections on housework and the necessity of changing how it is perceived as women's work responded to the pressing concerns that occupied myself and my fellow feminists in those years, particularly as we discussed alternate ways of living in communal apartments and households, although to some extent these notions were not radical enough for us. Nonetheless, such issues directly affected our daily lives and found an echo in our thoughts about the future. Other models, such as the boarding house and the "single-kitchen" apartment block seemed particularly desirable. While the design of the Frankfurt kitchen appealed to me from the beginning, I had my misgivings about its potential to improve women's lives due to its integration into the single-family household. It was only through conversations about the real political conditions and historical context of Weimar Germany that Grete was able to make the concept of this built-in kitchen comprehensible to me. As a result, I gave my first public lecture as an art historian on the Frankfurt kitchen at the first German-speaking conference of women art historians (Marburg an der Lahn 1982, publication 1984[2]), where we claimed gender as a category of analysis for art history. Today, the kitchen is now a part of international architectural history, demonstrating how spatial thinking about activity and use is translated into built form with integrated furnishings and informs the layout, function and aesthetic appearance. Grete

---

2 Nierhaus (1984).

even installed a mini-version of this kitchen, which, as she said, „*alle Stückl'n spielt*" (plays all the pieces) in her own small apartment in Vienna.

I also experienced the kitchen's structuring of the analytical, combinable and specific in other areas of Grete's life. She always took great care to prepare herself for events and speeches, being well aware of the impact that her presentation had when she engaged in the public sphere. She skillfully and sympathetically combined eloquence, hard work and charm. Careful planning in advance rather than leaving anything to chance was a motto that could be applied to different parts of her life, and she regularly had a Bulgarian doctor give her life-strengthening injections. And—thanks to her long life—she was able to take the writing of her biography into her own hands too. I find this determination to stand up for herself as well as her championing of the feminist cause all the more relevant today, because within the feminist movements the relationship to empowerment (and power) was often judged negatively and has often been discussed in opposition to powerlessness as an intentional "otherness."

For me, Grete, or rather *die Schütte*, was someone who "is" history. Even until today, when I stroll through the park of the Schönbrunn Palace, among other venues, I am reminded of her recollections of taking long walks through such places to evade her persecutors and make contact with the political underground—her stories sneak into one's experience of the city, like the way the memory of the expelled and murdered Jewish citizens abruptly edges into consciousness when coming upon the so-called *Stolpersteine* while wandering the streets.

While collaborating on the publication of the second edition of the *Erinnerungen aus dem Widerstand 1938-1945*,[3] I learned about the many facets of her life under National Socialism. Turning to the book's extensive appendix, I was overcome with existential dread when I read her dispassionate account, like a hero's memorial, that enumerated and recorded the biographical data, political functions and judgments that were handed down against her fellow resistance fighters and prisoners. In her characteristic severity, she only spoke about herself with reserve, recalling the danger that she had faced

---

3 Nierhaus (ed.)(1994). The title is translated as "Memories from the Resistance". This memoir first appeared in 1985 at the East German publisher *Volk und Welt* and the West German publisher *Konkret Literatur Verlag*.

and the necessity of developing a requisite self-discipline, like an acquired "armor", for example, to be able to survive prison.

Taking notes, recording and communicating—she undertook such acts of documentation with conviction and as the explicit obligation of a survivor. And she did this in Austria, during a period when few people were willing to confront the era of Nazism, while the mainstream—as evidenced by the "Waldheim Affair"[4]—denied and disavowed it. (Ruth Beckermann recently explored the prevailing attitudes at this time in her film *Waldheim's Waltz*.[5])

In addition to the matter-of-fact Grete, there was the charming, jocular and elegant Grete, who always attached great importance to wearing well-tailored blouses in fine materials with appealing colors and to displaying a carefully arranged coiffure. She loved good food and dancing, and praised Kemal Atatürk, whom she had met at a reception during her years in exile in Turkey. I remember her telling me: "He was an excellent dancer!" When she was almost 100 years old, *die Schütte* was still dancing with her friend and fellow architect, Hubert Hofmann. One of the most beautiful moments that remains fixed in my memory is of a joint celebration with her, the painter Georg Eisler (son of the composer Hanns Eisler) and the historian Eric Hobsbawn, and with whom I felt, at the end of the 20th century, to have finally arrived at a moment in this century that was finally felt "right" to me. Don't bury history. This goes for all those who, as they sift through the layers of her life, want to redesign the archaeology of *die Schütte* to uncover someone else.

Translated by Mary Pepchinski

---

4 The "Waldheim Affair" refers to the scandal surrounding former UN General Secretary Kurt Waldheim (1918-2007). Specifically, this refers to his lack of remorse and unwillingness to accept his complicity, as a *Wehrmacht* officer and a member of the National Socialist Student League, regarding crimes committed by these organizations during the Second World War, including the Holocaust. He also omitted his activities during the Third Reich from his official biography. A controversy arose in 1986 when this information was made public as he was preparing his candidacy for the office of the president of Austria, a largely ceremonial position. Although he did go on to this role, he remained isolated on the international stage.

5 *Waldheim's Waltz* (2018) by Ruth Beckermann (Director) is a documentary film that probes the social and political conditions in Austria that enabled details of Kurt Waldheim's career during the Second World War to be obscured in the post-war years and into the present.

Literature

Nierhaus, Irene (1984), „Die Fabrik des Hauses: Die Küche für den Arbeiter-
   haushalt," in: Bischoff, Cordula/Dinger, Brigitte/Ewinkel, Irene/Merle,
   Ulla (eds.), *FrauenKunstGeschichte: Zur Korrektur des herrschenden Blicks*,
   Gießen: Anabas, 1984, 158-166.
Nierhaus, Irene (ed.) (1994): *Margarete Schütte-Lihotzky: Erinnerungen aus dem
   Widerstand. Das 'kämpferische Leben einer Architektin von 1938-1945*. Wien,
   Promedia, 1994.

Film and Internet Sources

Beckermann, Ruth (2018), *Waldheim's Waltz* (German: Waldheims Walzer),
   Österreicher Rundfunk (ORF), 2018, 93 mins.
Waldheim Affair http://www.demokratiezentrum.org/en/knowledge/stati
   ons-a-z/the-waldheim-affair.html, accessed on February 11, 2021.
Waldheim Affair https://de.wikipedia.org/wiki/Waldheim-Affäre, accessed
   on February 11, 2021.

Care Trouble
Thinking through gendered entanglements in architecture

Elke Krasny

Is architecture a form of care? How to think, practice, build and write architecture as care? The following reflections are indebted to my growing concern that architecture today, very much dominated by the form-follows-capital mantra, must be more fully understood as a care practice. A closer look reveals that there is virtually no limit to care in architecture. This includes architecture in all its different phases and stages, from the organisation of shared work in an architectural office to the completion of a building, from interactions with clients and contractors to labor conditions on construction sites, from considerations of material flows in architecture to maintaining or repairing existing buildings, from educating future architects to writing about architecture.

Yet historically there has been a separation between architecture and care structured around the axes of gendered symbolic, political and knowledge power and its concomitant division of labor. Since care is crucial for architecture in all its manifestations, it is important to gain a critical understanding of the discursive process through which architecture was historically separated from the work of care. This process is deeply rooted in the binary system of traditional Western thought with its cultural, epistemological, material, philosophical, political, social and technical consequences of organising difference as a structure of gender hierarchy which devalued its feminine part.

This essay sets out to explore care trouble in architecture and invites a radical rethinking that suggests architecture can be practiced as care. Relatedness, interdependence, co-implicatedness and connectedness, both on the ontological as well as the political level, have been central to feminist theorising. Looking at the fundamental task of architecture, which, in the broadest definition possible, is the provision of shelter, we come to see that architecture and care are deeply implicated in one another. Such care provided through architecture is indispensable to human life and survival. Despite the obvious care function of protecting humans from sun, wind, snow or rain and giving the support necessary for the vital functions of everyday living, architecture has been firmly associated with autonomy and not with dependency. Unlike other binary oppositions like nature-culture, private-public or reproduction-production, the architecture-care divide has never been named as such. My analysis of central moments in canonical architectural discourse in antiquity, in the Renaissance period and the Enlightenment era, renders legible the discursive manoeuvres underpinning the architecture-care divide. I am particularly interested in thinking through the entanglements of architecture, care and gender using a cross-disciplinary approach that brings together feminist care perspectives in political theory and science-and-technology studies along with feminist art and architecture history. I build on the work of care thinkers like Joan C. Tronto and Maria Puig de la Bellacasa in addition to the scholarship of critical art and architecture historians Catherine M. Soussloff and Despina Stratigakos. A comprehensive and comparative analysis of the architecture-care divide goes beyond the scope of this essay and awaits further discourse analysis and historical-materialist research.

Even though philosophy, cultural studies and, more recently, science-and-technology studies have brought new perspectives to traditional architectural history, in the wake of the work of Gilles Deleuze and Michel Foucault, concerns such as biopolitics, control, power and representation have overshadowed a critical engagement with care. Only very recently, practitioners, researchers, thinkers and scholars in architectural history and theory have turned to care and reproduction in architecture. Such recent work can be found in the volume *Social Reproduction in Architecture. Politics, Values, and Actions in Contemporary Practice*, edited by Doina Petrescu and Kim Trogal in 2017, the curatorial research project *Care + Repair* (2017-2019), curated by Angelika Fitz and Elke Krasny and the contributions in *Caring Architecture. Institutions and Relational Practices*, a volume edited by Catharina Nord and Ebba Högström in 2017, which adopts a narrower view on care than the essay here and specifically examines institutions of organized care such as hospitals or assisted living. What we see taking shape across the contributions mentioned above is a new perspective on architecture as care.

This essay traces the architecture-care divide historically. It aims to contribute to the recent efforts of thinking about architecture as care, efforts that are urgently needed today to counteract austerity impositions and hyper-competitive, neoliberal capitalism that pits architecture and care against each other in the most brutal ways.

The architecture-care divide

With shelter central to human life and survival, architecture is without a doubt a most important form of care. The following normative definition of care provided by Berenice Fisher and Joan Tronto in 1990 is useful to my purpose here as it supports the claim that architecture is a form of care. This is their broad and general definition of care and involves

> "everything that we do to maintain, continue, and repair our 'world' so that we can live as well as possible. That world includes our bodies, ourselves, and our environment, all of which we seek to interweave in a complex, life-sustaining web." (Fisher and Tronto 1990: 103)

Taking this definition to look at the functions performed by architecture, we see that architecture not only gives the support necessary to maintain and sustain human bodies, but it is also intricately intertwined with the environment. Thus, we can conclude that architecture has obligations regarding care, namely, to contribute to living in the best way possible. Even if we assume agreement, on the most general level, with the notion that architecture constitutes a form of care, the hierarchical symbolic, political, economic and knowledge power that is traditionally associated with this discipline suggests that the idea of care is profoundly troublesome. The kind of work that is identified as care has historically been sexualized and racialized. The subject positions assigned those who (must) perform care labor come with the burdens of political exclusion and the economic realities of un(der)paid labor.

For the analysis of the gendered dimension and uneven distribution of power between architecture and care, I look to political philosophy as it developed public sphere theory and care theory, which must be understood as interdependent. Beginning with Aristotle's *Politics*, care has been assigned to the private sphere. (Tronto 2013: 25) This allocation has had an impact upon the organization of gender along the public-private axis. Historically, this divide barred women's access to the public sphere, in cultural, political, social, economic, material and educational terms, because as dependent figures who were identified with care work, they were denied access to this realm. (Tronto 2013: 25)

Canonical architectural discourse reveals that the knowledge power of architecture was organized along the public-private axis. Not only were architects considered to be important players in the public sphere, but they were the ones who gave shape to this divide by articulating the differences between the public sphere and the private sphere in spatial terms. Indeed, this has always included the realm of care, namely the making of the private sphere. Because architects had to have intimate knowledge about the home to conceive the best possible spaces for it, the design of the private sphere was included in the portfolio of the art of building. We see that architecture was always implicated in care. Yet discursively and ideologically, canonical writings on architecture and the professionalization of architectural education did everything possible to separate architecture from the threat of feminization posed by care work.

Care was kept at a distance, very much leading to "women's absence in architecture." (Stratigakos 2016: 1) Looking for care trouble in architecture renders legible these gendered entanglements. For example, the canonical architectural discourses guaranteed this discipline's dominant position in traditionally gendered binaries. When considered in relation to autonomy, citizenship, creativity, knowledge and power, architecture and care occupied very different positions. Even though it was always taken as a given that architecture does in fact provide care, the discursive orientations I will trace here circumvented care to refute its threatening association with dependency, feminization and denigration.

The following three sections of this essay provide an analysis of canonical formations central to architectural discourse. My first example is the distinction made in antiquity between the building of huts in imitation of nature and the acquired expertise distinct to the art of building as described in Vitruvius' *Ten Books of Architecture*. The second example looks at the establishment of architecture as an independent art that is different from necessity-driven craftsmanship in the Renaissance era. This is found in Leon Battista Alberti's *De re aedificatoria. On the Art of Building in Ten Books*. In his-torical-materialist terms, such a distinction was the condition for the emer-gence of the concept of the artist-genius. The third example concerns the birth of the modern architect during the period of the Enlightenment, which was based on the introduction of a new, systematic educational model that linked architecture to the idea of free and equal citizenship. Taken together, these examples allow us to see the ideological maneuvers that resulted in architecture as separate from care; they also render legible the complex ways in which gendered entanglements are entwined in architecture and care.

The analysis here is based on a close reading of the three, above-men-tioned moments that are central to the definition of architecture and the idea of the architect. It will reveal that architecture defined as the *art of building* carried out by the independent *artist-genius*, and later by *free and equal citizens*, was effectively organized around the gendered divide between architecture and care. The idea of a woman architect is absent from the canonical writ-ings of Vitruvius and Alberti. When women are mentioned, it has to do with their bodies inspiring architectural elements, their bodies inflicted by mat-ters of pregnancy or with the gendered division of public and private spaces. Women are mentioned fifteen times in Vitruvius' *Ten Books on Architecture*. They are statuary hewn in marble (4), have ill-health during pregnancy (58) and their footprints translate into the proportions of the slender columns for a temple to Diana (103). In addition, they are mentioned regarding the spa-tial arrangement of gender-separated, yet jointly heated, rooms at the baths (157). (Vitruvius 1960: 4, 58, 103, 157) Women are mentioned eighteen times in Alberti's *On the Art of Building in Ten Books*. Again, much of it has to do with bodily matters. What is of interest to us here is that Alberti describes the division of space according to gender. Whereas men were forbidden from entering the private quarters of women in a home (Alberti 1755: 343), it was a criminal act for a woman to go into temples associated with masculine sacrifice, such as the Temples of Martyrs. Likewise, men were prohibited access to temples linked to femininity, like the Temples of the Virgin Saints. (Alberti 1755: 370) Women were not considered as potential students when the *École Polytechnique* was established during the French Revolution. This Enlightenment institution with its model public education that gave birth to the modern architect only accepted women students in the second half of the twentieth century. No mention is made of women architects in these canonical moments in architectural discourse. Yet these discourses are very much concerned with drawing a line between the provision of structures needed to sustain everyday life, i.e., care, and the independent creation of lasting, beautiful and useful architecture. Care trouble in architecture points to gendered knowledge power, the division of labor underlying the architecture-care divide as well as the historical exclusion of women from the concept of the architect.

The art of building: More than shelter

Among the most influential writings on architecture dating back to antiquity are *The Ten Books of Architecture* written by Vitruvius in 30 BCE. In his mytho-historical account *On the Origin of the Dwelling House*, presented as the first chapter of the second book, Vitruvius constructs a narrative leading to the development of human dwelling. (Vitruvius 1960: 38–41) First, the fire was discovered. Then, humans gathered around it. Finally, this gave rise to the construction of shelters. The knowledge required for building was acquired through mimesis. According to Vitruvius, this activity followed a specific order. Constructing shelters was first learned through imitating nature, that is, by observing how birds build their nests. Then, humans gradually learned the techniques of construction by imitating each other, and them made improvements and refinements to optimize their shelters. (Vitruvius 1960: 38)

Constructing dwellings is a part of everyday life, carried out as needed by everyone who is fit to do it. The narrative depicting the origins of dwelling and its provision of shelter was thus firmly conceived as something natural. Dwelling knowledge was learned from nature and therefore a part of it.[1] This account lays the foundation for a nature-culture binary that separates

---

1   Even though my focus here is on the discursive mechanisms as they pertain to gender, we can easily discern here another power knowledge effect of the nature-culture divide. Centuries later Bernard Rudofsky named this anonymous architecture or architecture without architects. This introduces a hierarchical and colonial distinction between authored and signatured architecture based in culture and non-authored, anonymous or indigenous architecture rooted in nature. Bernard Rudofsky published his book *Architecture without Architects: A Short Introductioin to Non-pedigreed Architecture* in 1964 on the occasion of an exhibition by the same name he curated at the Museum of Modern Art in New York.

protective dwelling from architecture. This discursive move can clearly be tracked in Vitruvius' chapter on the *Education of the Architect*, which can be found in the first part of the first book of his treatise.

Vitruvius defines architecture as the result of the coming together of all the arts. (Vitruvius, 1960: 5–14) This definition not only clearly renders architecture legible as culture, but from the onset assigns a position of hierarchy to architecture among the other arts. Had the knowledge required to perform the work of an architect been learned via imitating nature, this would have presented a profound challenge to the independence of their creators and their production of aesthetic surplus value. Vitruvius goes beyond the nature-culture divide, as he employs metaphorical language that links the knowledge power of architects to warfare. And it also marks a point in his treatise where the gender of the architect is made explicit. Men who engage in architecture are armed with knowledge, and this includes expertise about all the arts. Education gives men this armature of erudition. Vitruvius describes the kind of knowledge necessary for making architecture, distinguishing between those who have manual skills but lack academic learning and those who are only versed in theory and abstract ideas. He concludes that architects need both kinds of expertise, "like men armed at all points, have the sooner attained their object and carried authority with them." (Vitruvius 1960: 5) No language could be further removed from care than the language of war. And, this knowledge power, which fortifies architects to master architecture, must bridge the divide between theory and practice. Only the combined efforts of manual skills and theory can equip the architect to achieve works of culture. Vitruvius goes on to list in detail the education necessary that will supply the architect with his armor of knowledge. This includes drawing, geometry, history, philosophy, music, even medicine, law and astronomy. (Vitruvius 1960: 5–6)

Imitating nature is, of course, not included as a strategy to acquire knowledge to create dwellings. Instead, Vitruvius reveals the kind of person who is best suited to become an ideal architect. Not only must an individual have a thorough education, but also be endowed, indeed armed, from the onset with a unique disposition: "Neither natural ability without instruction nor instruction without natural ability can make the perfect artist." (Vitruvius, 1960: 5)

What opens up between *The Origin of the Dwelling House* and *The Education of the Architect* is the deep schism that separates nature from culture. Care, provided by dwellings in the form of shelter, is a mere imitation of construction knowledge that everyone can find in nature. Architecture, on the contrary, reconciles practice and theory because it unites all the arts with the combined knowledge power of astronomy, geometry, jurisprudence, music and philosophy. Architecture is learned through culture. And we begin to comprehend that a profoundly gendered and hierarchical knowledge power regime is being established here with the making of dwellings and the art of building placed on their respective sides of the nature-culture divide. Yet the politics of gender do not stop at this point, because human nature comes into play too. A specific type of person, identified as the artist-genius during the early modern period, is introduced into the equation. The contours of this individual, who requires both natural ability and profound knowledge gained through education, were first outlined in antiquity as part of the conditions that must be met to become the perfect artist. This is instructive when regarding the long durée of the *genderinflicted* and *genderconflicted* entanglements of architecture and care. It is through Vitruvius' natural ability argument that care was essentially behind the discursive as well as the concrete historical and material boundaries that prevented women from being regarded as capable of becoming architects. Historically, women were not only considered to be part of nature, and not culture, but they were also believed to have an "essential, caring [...] nature." (Kirk 1997: 347) Taken together, these assumptions about women did not make them obvious candidates who could be educated to become perfect artists as described by Vitruvius.

Before moving on to the next influential episode in the architecture-care divide, I want to focus attention on care trouble in architecture. While the nature-culture divide appears as a clear-cut separation that distinguishes mere protection from the art of building, the three qualities named by Vitruvius as being necessary to architecture are not easily divorced from care. Taken together, "[...] durability (*firmatis*), convenience (*utilitas*) and beauty (*venustatis*)" result in architecture. (Vitruvius 1960: 17) What is of interest to me in identifying the traces of care trouble in canonical architectural discourse is the Latin term *utilitas*, which can be translated as convenience or usefulness. Both suggest a closeness to care. Let me join *utilitas* with *venustatis*. This brings us to convenient beauty or beautiful convenience, useful beauty or beautiful usefulness. Joining them together shows the effort with which architectural discourse sought to resolve the troublesome nature of

care in architecture. There was clearly an awareness of architecture's impli-
cation in use, including its everyday use, to provide the support necessary
that we can live as well as possible. Yet durable, lasting architecture had to go
beyond the merely useful. Beauty elevated the care provided through architecture to the *art of building.*

Architect-genius: More than a craftsman

The early modern period of the Renaissance witnessed a continuation of the
influential Vitruvian discourse. This is evidenced by Leon Battista Alberti's
choice of a title for his treatise: *De re aedificatoria. On the Art of Building in Ten
Books.* Written during the 1440s and 1450s, in 1485 it became the first book on
architecture ever to be printed. Like Vitruvius' enduring influence, Alberti's
writings shaped thinking about architectural practice, history and theory for
centuries to come. Even though Vitruvius and Alberti focus on the historic
legitimization and definition of architecture, the same concept of the architect can be traced through their discursive operations.

   With the nature-culture binary fully articulated since antiquity, and
with architects considered agents of culture, the Renaissance period built
on this existing dualism and added a significant new component to it: the
dichotomy between *mestiere*, craftsmanship, and *arte*, architecture. This
hierarchizing split negotiates the tensions between necessity and autonomy,
dependence and independence, learned skill and creative genius.

   In the preface to his treatise, Leon Battista Alberti slightly pauses the
flow of writing and inserts a definition of the architect. I will quote him here
to tease out the implications for the knowledge power regime underlying the
concept of the architect-genius and its historical-materialist consequences.
Distinguishing the architect from the "carpenter" or the "joiner," Alberti
insists that only a person who by "sure and wonderful Art and Method" in
combination with "Thought and Invention" can imagine and realize architecture. (Alberti 1988:3) According to Alberti, the distinction between the
skilled workman and the architect is determined by the latter's intellect and
creativity, qualities that enable him to be a master. Unlike the skilled workman, the master-architect is freed from having to bow to necessity. This distinction serves to prevent a work of architecture from being reduced to mere
necessity or simple purposefulness. While the architect is elevated to the

position of the thoughtful and inventive master, the craftsman is demoted to serving as the master's instrument. The architect and the craftsman are not considered equals because the architect occupies a position of authority.

Before I go on to locate this separation in the material conditions of the modern period in Italy, I examine Alberti's continuation of Vitruvius' line of argument, which keeps care trouble in architecture at bay. Again, it is the marriage of beauty and utility that is used to elevate architecture to its foremost status. The value of beauty that transcends mere necessity is argued to be of general use to mankind. The usefulness of beauty is thus firmly linked with autonomy and independence as opposed to necessity and dependence, qualities that are conventionally associated with the labors of care. The architect is conceived of as the master endowed with intellectual and imaginative abilities, who is able to create the "greatest beauty" for the "uses of mankind." (Alberti 1988: 3)

The *mestiere-arte* divide is not merely an ideological construct. It reflects material and economic reverberations in the organization of knowledge power regimes and the distribution of work during the early modern era. Art historical scholarship has identified fourteenth century Italy, when Alberti's treatise was written, as the period that witnessed the *mestiere-arte* separation. What is of importance in our context here is that architecture took the lead in this historical process of separation, becoming the first artistic discipline to align primarily with creative genius, or *arte*, and distance itself from craftsmanship, or *mestiere*. (Soussloff 1997: 67)

Read through a historical-materialist lens, independence is not only a concept constitutive to the individuality of the modern subject, who was historically gendered male and embodied in the most exemplary way in the figure of the genius, but also as the result of shifts in knowledge power regimes and economic struggles. The independence of architects was based on their rejection of the stranglehold of the guilds that had previously kept as an exclusionary secret the knowledge power of craftsmanship, thus regulating access to the professions. This independence from the kind of knowledge, that had been handed down through generations and was protected and prescribed by the guilds, is rooted in the architect's work. According to Alberti, this work goes beyond tasks that have a purely practical nature to engage in those that require extraordinary mental activity, or the efforts of genius. (Alberti 1755: 687)

Independence, a much-glorified idea in the Western history of consciousness, is the precondition that allows for the genius to be in possession
of abilities such as intellectual strengths and creative capacities. (Alberti
1755: 3) Regarding the specific conditions of fourteenth and fifteenth century
Italy, this meant breaking away from the rules of tradition and convention
that were upheld by the guild system. So, independence became associated
with another trope of early modernity, the trope of the new. The credo of this
conceit is that only independent thought, which is not bound by tradition,
can move forward and overcome the limitations of the past. Independence,
the opposite of dependence, also must be read literally as a condition for
genius. It is helpful to turn to political theory to raise awareness regarding
the gendered exclusion of women and all other dependents from the concept
of the genius. The independent-dependent opposition is connected to the
binary of public and private. Tracing the impact of this split and its gendered
dimension back to Aristotle, Joan C. Tronto writes: "The way that franchise
was conceived was to exclude those who were dependent." (Tronto, 2013: 25)
This not only organized public and political life, but equally the classed, gendered and racialized division of labor. Furthermore, independence, and not
dependence, determined who could become a genius-architect. Independence therefore meant freedom from the mundane reproductive labors of
care. Architects and architecture had to repudiate care on the level of those
who performed the labor of this discipline and, on the level of building, the
work that is produced. Necessity tied to purpose is characteristic of care, that
is, something we need to thrive and to survive, something we want to "get
us through the day," like the buildings we live in, which give us the support
required to maintain, restore and repair ourselves. Meanwhile, such need-
based necessity is transcended by architecture through the notion of the
greatest beauty for the *uses of mankind*. (Bellacasa, 2017: 87) Free from these
constraints, architecture makes its claim to a kind of beauty that can be used,
a beauty made useful by architects who think and invent independently.
Nothing, therefore, could be further from genius than care. While care
speaks of dependency and thinks of subjects as interdependent from the
start on both the ontological and the political level, autonomy stands for subjects who are assumed to be independent. The care trouble in architecture,
which comes with the idea of the architect-genius, points to a deep problem
regarding the conception of the modern subject. Whereas independence is
understood as the ideal condition of the modern Western subject that exists

in opposition to the subordination and neediness of dependence, the concept of interdependence has neither been central to the historical trajectories of political thought nor to formative ideas in architecture.

Furthermore, architecture was not only integral to the discursive formations that gave rise to the independent subject of the artist-genius but is central to these arguments. In *The Absolute Artist. The Historiography of a Concept*, art historian Catherine M. Soussloff explores the genealogy of the idea of the artist-genius. She argues that the first full-fledged biography to portray the artist-genius is Antonio Manetti's *Life of Filippo Brunelleschi*, written in the 1480s. (Soussloff 1997: 43) "Thus the concept of 'the artist' emerges concurrently with the elevation of the media, architecture and painting, and their originator, Brunelleschi." (Soussloff 1997: 67) It is no surprise that an architect, Brunelleschi, was the subject of the quintessential biography that gave rise to the concept of the artist-genius.

Biography, a Greek composite meaning life-writing, is the literary form that gave birth to the artist-genius, who could also have been called the architect-genius. Yet this "professional genre" could not have been further removed from everyday life and its drudgeries. (Soussloff 1997: 24) According to Alberti, he was independent of practical, necessary tasks, thus distinguishing the architect-genius from that of the craftsman and the daily labor of reproduction. (Alberti, 1755: 687)

We clearly see here the central axes of the regime of gendered knowledge power and the division of labor that rendered the architect-genius an independent figure by freeing him from the toil of repairing, maintaining and preserving daily life. It has barred women's entry into architecture precisely because of the social conventions that made them dependent and associated with the necessities, duties and responsibilities of care. Placing architecture above care, and consequently "men above women," kept the existing "gendered hierarchy" intact. (Tronto, 2013: 79)

Modern architects: Free and equal citizens

The institutionalization of modern architectural education takes us to the period of the Enlightenment. In 1794, with the opening of the *École Polytechnique* in Paris, the first school for modern architectural education was inaugurated. Architectural education, much like other academic training in the sciences, technology and practical arts, comprised part of the political and economic reordering that was rooted in the Enlightenment concept of the modern subject. In his monograph, *The Making of the Modern Architect and Engineer*, Ulrich Pfammater traces the rise of modern architectural education. There are two observations concerning his study, which includes the formation of modern and systematic architectural education, that matter to the concerns here: the gendered idea of citizenship and the notion of welfare as distinct from care. Firstly, the equality and freedom mantra of the French Revolution not only defined the status and the privileges that come with citizenship, but it also rendered women and people of color, that is, those who were excluded from the idea of citizenship and consequently from the legal status conferred onto subjects through it at that time, unequal and unfree. Therefore, the gendered and racialized concept of citizenship made the new educational model that shaped the modern architect an exclusive one. As citizenship historian William R. Brubaker points out, not only the formal institution, but also the political imaginary of citizenship was shaped by the French Revolution and its 1789 *Declaration of the Rights of Man and of the Citizen*. (Brubaker 1989: 30)

No mention is made of women. They remained outside of the political idea of citizenship. The historical gendering and racializing of citizenship, both ideologically and state institutionally, resulted in the exclusion of those identified through bodies other than male and white. "Slaves, wage-earners and women were initially ruled out of active citizenship [...] Even when dependency was redefined, [...] (in 1848) women remained unacceptable as citizens." (Scott, 2005: 37)

Therefore, bodily differences formed the foundations of the idea of citizenship, rendering it deeply gendered and racialized. Even though the Western history of ideas has celebrated the French Revolution as giving birth to the concept of abstract and universal citizenship, the opposite was the case. Citizenship was very much embodied, and not an abstract ideal. According to gender historian Joan Wallach Scott, "[...] the difference of sex was not considered to be susceptible to abstraction" for the French Revolutionaries. (Scott, 2005: 37)

The body identified as male was constitutive to the notion of citizenship. And, by extension, the body identified as male was prerequisite to being granted access to higher education and consequently to the modern professions, such as architecture. Therefore, architecture defined as a profession of "free and equal citizens" was clearly not open to women who, because of their bodies and their dependency, were excluded from citizenship.

Secondly, the idea of general welfare defined care in such a way that gender hierarchies were reinforced, even though architecture was considered important to the general well-being of society. Let us look at how the period of the Enlightenment rendered architecture as a form of "men's caring," that is socially and politically different from women who "care 'naturally'." (Tronto 2013: 70) Because architecture was considered relevant to general welfare and individual happiness, we clearly see that architects had a social obligation to perform a kind of care work. While the political and philosophical discourse of the period did assign architecture the task of welfare, the ideological orientations of this discourse insured this was never confused with the kind of caring labor that is performed by women daily in the private realm.

General welfare clearly provides and requires care. This form of care, which the Enlightenment era saw as a public responsibility in democratic societies, was simply not identified as care to uphold the gendered ideal of masculinity, thus establishing "men's caring" as "non-caring care." (Tronto 2013: 72–73) This formulation articulated the Enlightenment version of the public-private binary in existence since antiquity. General welfare was expected to carry out tasks to support daily life, but to do so at a distance or an indirect manner, and not in the first-hand way that is normally associated with the work of care. (Tronto 2013: 70) Tronto uses the example of the eighteenth century formation of the police to illustrate how men's caring was defined by the notions of "protection" and "production." (Tronto, 2013: 70) The two terms are useful here to identify architecture's contribution to general welfare, and to see how the care provided by architecture was thoroughly gendered masculine. Protection is a central function of architecture, with architecture providing it in the form of useful and convenient beauty. Production can be aligned with the earlier idea of the independent architect-genius and, when examined through a historical-materialist lens, it fully conforms with the advances of capitalism and its values during the eighteenth century.

The institution of a new model of architectural education was an integral component of the work of protection and production. And as Pfammater points out, the need to be systematic and learned lent a high social status to the profession of the modern architect. He also helps us to tease out how care trouble in architecture was negotiated in the Enlightenment concept of the modern architect. "Through the ideas developed by the new culture of education, the modern architect and engineer attained a similarly respected status in France in the 19th century as that of the scholar in the *Ancien Régime*." (Pfammater 2000: 98)

Public welfare is linked to individual living conditions. This renders the venue where direct and intimate care is given a task for architecture. Therefore, the disassociation of architecture from the feminine, and ultimately feminized, underpaid, undervalued and exploited forms of care had to be fully ensured. General welfare was a public function which included the provision of the private living conditions of individuals. Architects had to be experts about caring domesticity yet remain independent from it.

Equally important to the politics of the architecture-care divide is that caring duties, specifically the dirty work of daily reproduction, were not included in the idea of general welfare. The provision of care was not associated with the status of citizenship, while the provision of architecture was clearly linked to the status and privileges of free and equal citizens.[2] The concept of citizenship was closely connected to ideas about general welfare and perpetuated the gendered knowledge split concerning power and the division of labor in the architecture-care divide.

The institutionalization of Enlightenment architectural education resulted in extending the concept of the architect to include the free and equal citizen who made important contributions to the general welfare and ideals of a democratic society. Even though older models of architectural education were already part of the Beaux Arts tradition in seventeenth century Paris, Pfammater argues that the birth of the modern architect is linked to the introduction of polytechnical education at the Parisian *École Polytechnique* in 1794/95. (Pfammater, 2000: 8)

Women students were not allowed to enrol. Therefore, women were excluded from the early and formative years at this institution, which shaped the making of the modern architect. They were equally excluded from being

---

2 In her 2005 essay, "Care as the Work of Citizens. A Modest Proposal," Tronto has suggested to consider carrying out care work as a basis to receive citizenship. (Tronto 2005: 131) This not only counteracts the long-held tradition in political theory to separate care from public life, but her proposal also presents a political move in times of a precarious, globalised care workforce very often denied the status and privilege of citizenship in their countries of work.

of service to the general public. Pfammater expresses his puzzlement over women's exclusion given that women in France were actively engaged in both philosophical circles and Enlightenment endeavors. (Pfammater, 2000: 248) Yet he fails to make the connection to the gendered and exclusionary concepts of citizenship, general public and welfare. Thus, the *École Polytechnique* remained an all-male institution for 176 years until 1970, when changes in the law granted entry to women. (Pfammater, 2000: 248) This so-called universal educational model was based upon exclusionary concepts of citizenship, equality and freedom, and resulted in the deeply gendered concept of the modern architect.

Women architects

When women first appeared as architects at the end of the nineteenth century, public discourse by fellow architects immediately constructed them as a threat to the profession. Despina Stratigakos has lucidly analysed this in her 2016 book, *Where Are the Women Architects?* Meanwhile, the architecture-care divide, as I aim to tease out in the following section, unsettled the profession's gendered foundations.

A 1911 article by German architect Otto Bartning raises the question: "Should Women Build?" (Stratigakos 2016: 8) He puts forward a strong argument for the architect's autonomy, which he sees undermined by meddlesome housewives who interfere with it by bringing their "often troublesome wishes" to the design process. (Stratigakos 2016: 8) An even worse scenario arises when women, assigned the gender role of caring labor at home, should desire to become architects themselves. In the German architect's view, protection against feminization was in order, as "not female architects but rather supremely manly men" were now required. (Stratigakos 2016: 8)

With women beginning to enter the profession, new discursive ammunition targeted the trouble surrounding care, trying to keep it at bay and ensure that the profession stayed masculine. One line of argument was to relegate women to designing those spaces in the home that are clearly marked as sites of reproductive labor, from "the non-public housekeeping areas of the home" to "kitchens and cellars, and closet-rooms and servants' sleeping rooms." (Stratigakos 2016: 6) What we have here is a design program for women architects made up of the most narrowly defined spaces that are used exclusively by those who perform the caring labor within private homes. This explicitly spells out the architecture-care binary as it underlies the gendered division of labor in architecture.

In lieu of a conclusion: Toward *carearchitectures*

While the thrust of this analysis was epistemological and historical in orientation and sought to reveal how care trouble in architecture underpinned this profession's deeply gendered foundations, my interest is to move beyond the architecture-care divide to find ways of repairing its harmful and damaging effects. My goal is to encourage more caring architectural practices that ultimately overcome and de-binarize this split.

Inspired by Donna Haraway's non-dualistic concept of "emergent nature-cultures," I want to express my hope that it is possible to move toward *carearchitectures* in as many stages, phases and directions of architecture imaginable. (Haraway 2003: 1) Much scholarly work will have to be done to trace multiple architectural histories of care that go beyond the hegemonic architecture-care divide. Today, *carearchitectures* are much needed to do everything possible *to maintain, sustain and repair our "world" so that we can live as well as possible*. Such *carearchitectures* would include more than human worlds extending their care to humans, non-humans and the environment alike. This is crucial to arrive at a more even distribution of the protection and support that *carearchitetures* can provide. For example, Maria Puig de la Bellacasa has drawn attention to work "that foregrounds the importance of repair and maintenance of technology infrastructures as practices of care supports." (Bellacasa 2017: 43) Care most certainly includes the repair and maintenance of architecture as part of what we call infrastructure. But I would go beyond that and claim that *carearchitectures* always embody the idea of how they can be better sustained, repaired and maintained to provide lasting and ongoing support. Understanding architecture and care as being intrinsically entwined is as much a scholarly endeavor as it is a political project.

I will end with a quote by Alberti to make his view of architecture useful for present and future *carearchitectures*: "For it is certain, if you examine the Matter carefully, it is inexpressibly delightful, and of the greatest Convenience to Mankind in all Respects, both public and private." (Alberti, 1755: 3)

Literature

Alberti, Leon Battista (1755 [1485]), *The Architecture of Leon Battista Alberti in Ten Books*, trans. Leoni, J., London: Printed by E. Owen.

Brubaker, William Rogers (1989), "The French Revolution and the Invention of Citizenship," *French Politics and Society*, 7(3), 31–49.

Fisher, Berenice/Tronto, Joan C. (1990), "Toward a Feminist Theory of Caring," in: Abel, Emily K./Nelson, Margaret K. (eds.), *Circles of Care. Work and Identity in Women's Lives*, Albany: State University of New York Press, 35–62.

Haraway, Donna (2003), *The Companion Species Manifesto: Dogs, People, and Significant Otherness*, Chicago: Prickly Paradigm Press.

Kirk, Gwyn (2007), "Standing on Solid Ground. A Materialist Ecological Feminism," in R. Hennessy, Rosemary/Ingraham, Chrys (eds.), *Materialist Feminism. A Reader in Class, Difference and Women's Lives*, New York and London: Routledge, 345–363.

Nord, Catharina/Högström, Ebba (eds.) (2017), *Caring Architecture. Institutions and Relational Practices*, Newcastle upon Tyne: Cambridge Scholars Publishing.

Petresca, Doina/Trogal, Kim (eds.) (2017), *The Social (Re)Production in Architecture. Politics, Values, and Actions in Contemporary Practice*, London and New York: Routledge.

Pfammater, Ulrich (2000), *The Making of the Modern Architect and Engineer: The Origins and Development of a Scientific and Industrially Oriented Occupation*, trans. Ferretti-Theilig, M., Basel, Boston, Berlin: Birkhäuser.

Puig de la Bellacasa, Maria (2017), *Matters of Care. Speculative Ethics in More Than Human Worlds*, Minneapolis and London: University of Minnesota Press.

Rudofsky, Bernard (1964), *Architecture without Architects. A Short Introduction to Non-Pedigreed Architecture*, New York: The Museum of Modern Art.

Scott, Joan Wallach (2005), "French Universalism in the Nineties," in: Marilyn Friedman (ed.), *Women and Citizenship*, New York: Oxford University Press, 35–51.

Soussloff, Catherine M. (1997), *The Absolute Artist. The Historiography of a Concept*, Minneapolis and London: University of Minnesota Press.

Stratigakos, Despina (2016), *Where are the Women Architects?* Princeton and Oxford: Princeton University Press in association with Places Journal.

Tronto, Joan C. (2005), "Care as the Work of Citizens. A Modest Proposal," in: Friedman, Marilan (ed.), *Women and Citizenship*, New York: Oxford University Press, 130–148.

Tronto, Joan C. (2013), *Caring Democracy. Markets, Equality, and Justice*, New York and London: New York University Press.

Vitruvius (1960 [30 BCE; trans. 1914]), *The Ten Books on Architecture*, trans. Morgan, M. H., Mineola, New York: Dover Publications.

Gertrud Goldschmidt
Architect and Zionist

Sigal Davidi

Introduction

It was only by pure chance that I became aware of the work of architect Gertrud Goldschmidt. I was searching for information on the first women architects in pre-state Israel and contacted Ya'akov Goldschmidt because I knew that he was friendly with the family of one of these architects. When I finished describing my research to him, he said casually, "You know, my mother was also an architect in the 1930s." That was how I first learned about Gertrud Goldschmidt.

In the 1930s architecture was not acknowledged around the world as a woman's profession, and Mandatory Palestine, or Eretz Israel, was no exception.[1] Although architecture was not an obvious profession for women at that time, during the late 1930s, seventeen women architects were already practicing there. Most of them were new immigrants, graduates of German and Austrian technical universities (called *Technische Hochschule* or TH), and four had completed their studies at the Hebrew Technion in Haifa, established in 1924. Among them were Genia Averbuch, Yehudit Chlenov, Dora Gad, Anna Klapholtz, Elsa Gidoni Mandelstamm, Lotte Cohn, Gertrud Krolik, Zipora Neufeld-Cherniak, Helene Roth, Yehudit Stolzer Segall, Paula Szwif and, last but not least, Gertrud Goldschmidt.

These women architects were involved in every kind of architectural specialization and carried out projects of different scales. They designed urban

---

1 In the period discussed in this article, namely, from 1920 to the establishment of the State of Israel in 1948, Palestine under the British Mandate was also referred to as Palestine or Eretz Israel (Land of Israel), one of its biblical names.

quarters—new neighborhoods and city squares—as well as educational and social welfare facilities, apartment buildings, single family homes and interiors. They worked to realize the Zionist vision of developing a Jewish national home. And finally, they all played an important role in promoting modern architecture in Eretz Israel.[2]

Gertrud Goldschmidt was one of the first modern architects in Mandatory Palestine. Despite that, her name and works are missing from the local historiography of 20th century architecture. This article describes Goldschmidt's life and her work during the early 1930s, which primarily involved commissions from middle-class Zionists with a capitalist orientation.

Early life in Germany: Becoming a Zionist and an Architect

Gertrud Goldschmidt (1898-1997), daughter of Emma and Siegfried Kochmann, was born and raised in the Silesian town of Jauer, formerly in Germany, now in Poland (Jawor) (Figure 1). Her parents ran a successful business in the town where there were few Jewish families. Although she grew up in a non-Zionist environment, she later joined *Blau-Weiss*, a Jewish youth movement established in Germany in 1912.[3] The rise of the Zionist movement, which aimed to establish a national home for the Jewish People in Eretz Israel, greatly influenced the course of Goldschmidt's life. This national awakening set off several waves of Jewish immigration to Palestine, beginning in the late 19th century. The recently arrived immigrants strove to embody the "New Jew," namely a strong and robust figure, who was a farmer and a fighter. They were determined to realize that ideal in reaction to the way Jews had been perceived until then—physically weak, landless, rootless and spiritual in nature. Goldschmidt's life took a turn with the growing popularity of the Zionist Movement in Germany,

---

2 Davidi (2017).

3 The movement's members were children of assimilated German Jewish families who wished to enter a youth movement but, being Jewish, were rejected by the German nationalist youth movements. In 1922, the movement adopted a Zionist platform and encouraged its members to specialize in agricultural or professional work before they emigrated to Eretz Israel.

Figure 1: Gertrud Goldschmidt, 1920. Source: Courtesy of the Goldschmidt family, Ramat HaSharon, Israel.

Figure 2: Goldschmidt House, Tel Aviv, 1931. Source: Courtesy of the Goldschmidt family, Ramat HaSharon, Israel.

in particular, the ideas of the Zionist leader, Kurt Blumenfeld.[4] He was typical of the second-generation Zionists who assumed leadership positions after World War I. They had joined the movement because they had come to the realization that German society would never fully accept them. They clung to Zionism to satisfy a deep need for a modern Jewish identity. These young Jews found what they were looking for in "practical Zionism," that is, a means for living in the present and the future that was more comprehensive and engaged than Theodor Herzl's political-philanthropic, first-generation Zionism. Blumenfeld urged Zionist youths to immigrate to Eretz Israel. In 1912 he initiated a resolution at the Zionist Congress stipulating that every Zionist should strive for immigration to Eretz Israel. This idea made a great impression on Goldschmidt. Before enrolling in academic studies, she consulted Otto Warburg, the prominent Zionist leader, about the profession she should choose to assist the nascent Jewish society there.[5]

Warburg, a botanist and a researcher, was a pillar of German Zionism and president of the World Zionist Organization (1911-1921). He was a great supporter of "practical Zionism," which was becoming very popular in Germany due in part to his backing and initiatives.[6] As might be expected, Warburg told Goldschmidt that the only profession that could help develop Eretz Israel was agriculture. Despite being more inclined to study architecture, Goldschmidt decided to study botany. In 1919, she enrolled in this subject at the University of Würzburg, but her passion for architecture triumphed, and she quit after one semester.[7] In May 1920, she was accepted as an architecture student at the *Technische Hochschule* in Munich.[8]

---

4 Kurt Blumenfeld (1884-1963) was president of the Zionist Federation of Germany from 1924 until he immigrated to Palestine in 1933.

5 Interview with Ya'akov Goldschmidt, Ramat HaSharon, October 23, 2007.

6 Warburg went to Eretz Israel on a long research tour (1899-1900), which yielded invaluable information on ways to develop agriculture there, thus greatly assisting "practical Zionism." He emigrated to Palestine in 1920.

7 "Winter-Semester 1919/20 Personalbogen", February 11, 1920. University of Würzburg (JMU), Archive.

8 Technical University of Munich (TUM), Archive.

Goldschmidt studied under the renowned architect Professor Theodor
Fischer, who had taught many of Europe's leading modernist architects,
including Hugo Haring, Ernst May, Bruno Taut and Jacobs Johannes Peter
Oud. The celebrated Jewish architects Richard Kauffmann and Erich Mendelsohn, both of whom later immigrated to Eretz Israel, were among his
students. Beginning around 1907 the *Technische Hochschule* in Munich had
accepted women as guest students in architecture, yet few female students
were officially enrolled.[9] The first woman completed her diploma in 1915, and
by 1924 there were a total of 5 female and 288 male students at the architecture faculty.[10] Goldschmidt received her diploma in August 1923.[11] She initially
remained in Germany and worked at the Bavarian Settlement Department in
Nürnberg and for an architect named Meyer.[12] In January 1924 she acted upon
Blumenfeld's dictate and immigrated to Eretz Israel. Goldschmidt was the
second woman architect in practice there, after Lotte Cohn who had arrived
three years earlier from Berlin. They became good friends.[13]

Settling in Palestine

During her time with the *Blau-Weiss* movement, Gertrud met Martin Goldschmidt, her future husband, who was studying hydraulic engineering at the
same university in Munich. Martin immigrated to Eretz Israel in 1923 and the
two were married a year later. They settled in Tel Aviv, which was the modern urban center and heart of the burgeoning Jewish community. It was a
middle-class stronghold and amid a public and private building boom. Upon
her arrival in Mandatory Palestine, Goldschmidt immediately joined the

---

9 Maasberg/Prinz (2012), 637; Stratigakos (1999), Appendix 1, 389–390.

10 Maasberg/Prinz (2012), 638 footnote 34.

11 Gertrud Kochmann, Diploma, TUM. Ya'akov Goldschmidt, private archive.

12 Registration form for the "Architects' Association of Eretz Israel", 1924. Central Zionist Archives, J116/7 (Hebrew).

13 Goldschmidt carried out her first project in Mandatory Palestine in collaboration with
Lotte Cohn. In 1931 Goldschmidt and Cohn won a planning competition for a workers'
neighborhood in northern Tel Aviv. Eight proposals had been submitted. They shared the
first prize with the office of Genia Averbuch and Sha'ag. They did not realize the project as
another architect received the commission. Lavon Institute for Labour Research, IV-208-
1–284A.

"Architects' Association of Eretz Israel" to make contacts and meet colleagues who shared her professional interests.[14] Many women architects worked for public planning departments after immigrating to Palestine, and she was briefly employed at the Public Works Department (PWD) of the Mandatory Government.[15] She waited until the early 1930s to establish an independent architectural office because she was raising her three children, who born in 1925, 1927 and 1929.

To understand the buildings of Gertrud Goldschmidt, it is worth taking a closer look at the local architectural context in Eretz Israel. During the 1920s and 1930s, Jewish architects in Mandatory Palestine—men and women alike—were looking to create an architectural language that would represent the young Jewish community. In the 1920s their designs covered a wide range of styles, including Orientalism, Eclecticism and even Neoclassicism. The influx of young architects, who had studied and worked in Europe in the 1920s and early 1930s, accelerated the introduction of modern architecture into Eretz Israel. These architects had an up-to-date professional education, had been exposed to Western values, and had experienced dramatic political and social upheavals. The functionalism, stylistic simplicity and freedom from historical bonds that characterized modern architecture found an echo in the Zionist's notion of the "New Jew." With the massive construction that was required to accommodate an expanding immigrant community, modern architecture gained prominence in the early 1930s. Whereas many local architects, such as Yehuda Magidovitch, Ze'ev Rechter, Josef Berlin and even Lotte Cohn, began by designing in an eclectic style and integrating elements such as arches and domes into their designs, all later embraced modernism.

In 1931 Goldschmidt carried out her first independent project, a house for her family in a new workers' neighborhood in northern Tel Aviv. (Figure 2) The small residence included an office for herself.[16] Unlike many of her fellow architects in Mandatory Palestine, Goldschmidt embraced modern architecture from the start of her career. The design of her home is typical of the early

---

14 The association was founded in 1923 by local Jewish architects, among them Lotte Cohn. Under the British Mandate, architects were not required to join the "Architects' Association of Eretz Israel" to become registered in Mandatory Palestine.

15 Jewish architects and engineers employed at the PWD did not plan buildings for the Mandatory government. Rather, they drafted and developed construction plans.

16 Documentation in the Tel Aviv Municipality Building Archive.

modern style that the Jewish community of Eretz Israel adopted at this time. It did not display the complexity and dynamism of the International Style that would invade Tel Aviv just a few years later. Her house was a simple composition of undecorated masses, adjusted to the local climate. The northern façade had a covered balcony accessed through the living room's wide glass door. (Figure 3) Adopting the spatial practices of the eastern Mediterranean, she installed a stairway that led to a roof terrace, where one could relax in the cool evening sea breeze in the manner of the local Arabs. To shade the western and southern windows, she designed horizontal cornices that ran the width of the building. Shading cornices were typical features of Richard Kauffmann's work, as seen in his design of the Kruskal House (1931), considered the first modern building that Kauffmann planned in Tel Aviv, and one of the city's first examples of modern architecture.[17] The similarity between these two early modernist buildings by Goldschmidt and Kauffmann, both students of Theodor Fischer, is noteworthy.

After the Nazi rise to power in 1933 and the subsequent anti-Jewish laws and persecution, immigration to Mandatory Palestine increased. Martin's parents were among the newly arrived immigrants. Gertrud Goldschmidt added a second floor to the family home, where she designed a two-room apartment accessed from the outside by external stairs. The completion of her family home marked the beginning of an intensively productive period for this architect. In the following years, she planned a factory, urban villas and an apartment building in Tel Aviv and worked in the neighboring towns of Ramat Gan, Kfar-Saba and Rehovot. Members of the German immigrant community commissioned many of these buildings, which were designed in the International Style.

An all-female factory in Tel Aviv

In 1933, Gertrud Goldschmidt received an offer to plan the Hadar-Scheflan factory in Tel Aviv which produced cardboard boxes and paper cups. In the early 1930s this was the only factory of its kind in the Middle East. It was

17 Levin (1984), 10 (Hebrew); *Tel Aviv's Modern Movement* (2004), 73.

originally established in Berlin in 1899 and moved to Tel Aviv in 1924.[18] Chaya Scheflan, the founder's widow, who was then the owner and manager of the factory, decided to construct a new facility to increase production and to provide the employees with more amenable working conditions. It is worth noting that this was an all-female project: A woman ran the factory, a woman architect designed the building and 65 women employees comprised much of the workforce. Goldschmidt arranged the spacious production halls in an L-shaped plan and included ample fenestration to provide light and ventilation. She included a separate building in the central yard with toilets, showers, dressing areas and a recreation room for the staff. The factory's logo featured a schematic representation of the building, highlighting its modern, functional design.

However, collaborative projects with women acting as both client and architect were seldom in Eretz Israel and always involved friends or relatives of the architect. Nonetheless, a few examples are worth noting. Goldschmidt also planned a residence for a female acquaintance (Rebecca Dosik House, 1934). Lotte Cohn designed the prestigious "Pension Kaete Dan" on the Mediterranean in Tel Aviv for her good friend Käte Dan in 1932 and completed the Cohn residence in Jerusalem's Rehavia neighborhood for her sisters Helene and Rosa Cohn, which became the "Helene Cohn Boardinghouse" in 1933.[19] To the best of my knowledge, Goldschmidt was the first woman architect to build a factory in Eretz Israel. Nonetheless, women architects in Mandatory Palestine, Goldschmidt included, had far greater professional opportunities than women architects elsewhere at that time. In the early 20th century, for example, many European women architects engaged mainly in domestic architecture, which was considered their "natural" domain.[20]

There is nothing trivial about the fact that women architects in Eretz Israel were able to achieve a level of professional equality with their male colleagues. Their success could be attributed in part to the special circumstances that developed in Mandatory Palestine in the 1930s. The waves of immigra-

18 Hadar-Scheflan factory. https://sites.google.com/a/tlv100.net/tlv100/old_east/shfln (Hebrew), accessed on Sept. 22, 2020.

19 The most significant collaboration was that of Lotte Cohn, Elsa Gidoni Mandelstamm and Genia Averbuch with Zionist women's organizations. It significantly contributed to the professional advancement of women architects and to their public visibility. See: Davidi (2016), 217–230.

20 Walker (2017), 11–25; Stratigakos (2001), 90–100.

tion resulted in a significant increase in construction, which offered abundant possibilities to men and women architects alike. Significantly, architecture, like many other professions, was newly established in Eretz Israel, and was not as set in its ways as it was in many European countries. This may have resulted in a less condescending attitude towards women, which enabled them to explore their talents and abilities more fully. In Eretz Israel, the drive to build a "Jewish National Home" created unique professional opportunities that proved beneficial to the immigrant women architects, expanding their scope of activity beyond the domestic sphere.

Beit Haikar – Winning an architecture competition

Goldschmidt's plan for the Miller House, a private villa in Rehovot (1933), shows her to be a mature modern architect, well versed in the International Style. (Figure 4). Rehovot was then a small town, mostly inhabited by farmers who cultivated the lands around it. Civil engineers planned most of the private houses. Yet starting in the early 1930s, modern architecture was introduced and quickly flourished. Goldschmidt's sophisticated education and her nearly decade-long acquaintance with the local climate helped her formulate a modern architectural vocabulary that was sensitive to regional conditions. For the Miller House, she designed a dynamic façade with a dominant curve, long horizontal windows with shading cornices and numerous balconies, some shaded by pergolas. Following the local trend towards home farming, she also included a vegetable patch for domestic use in the yard.[21]

Her client, Yesha'yahu Miller, was the brother of Tuvia Miller, one of the most prominent public figures in Rehovot. Without doubt, this striking building enhanced Goldschmidt's professional reputation in the town. In 1934, she was invited to take part in a prestigious architectural competition to design the farmers' administration building, *Beit Haikar* (Farmers' House), which was also to be their social and cultural center. Five architects and engineers participated, and Goldschmidt, the only woman, won.[22]

---

21 Site plan. Ya'akov Goldschmidt's personal archive, Ramat HaSharon, Israel.

22 Documentation in: The Farmers' Federation of Eretz Israel Archive, Rehovot, Israel.

Figure 3: Interior, Goldschmidt House, Tel Aviv, 1931. Source: Courtesy of the Goldschmidt family, Ramat HaSharon, Israel.

Figure 4: Miller House, Rehovot, 1933. Source: Courtesy of the Goldschmidt family, Ramat HaSharon, Israel.

Most of the women architects in Eretz Israel worked in partnership with a male colleague, either an architect or an engineer, as it was probably helpful when navigating the male-dominated architecture and construction industries. Goldschmidt was no exception. The official letterhead of her firm, which was identified as an "engineering office," displayed the names of both Gertrud and Martin. However, not all the plans that she submitted for approval to the Tel Aviv municipality bore Martin's name as the engineer of record. After winning the competition for the Farmers' House, Goldschmidt invited her cousin, the architect Chanan (Heinz) Pawel, who had just immigrated from Stuttgart, to be her associate.[23]

The Rehovot Farmers' Federation was part of the "Civil Circles," which consisted of associations of middle-class Zionists with a capitalist orientation, such as farmers, merchants, industrialists and professionals, who formed a group distinct from the workers on the left of the political spectrum and the orthodox on the right. The Farmers' House stood in the center of town, on the main road to Rishon LeZion and Tel Aviv. The competition committee's choice of a distinctly modern design reflected the farmers' desire to have their representative building stand out in the town's landscape.

Presumably, the competition committee did not have the advancement of women architects in mind when it selected Gertrud Goldschmidt.[24] As long as they could rely on her to design the building to their satisfaction, they were not concerned about entrusting the planning of such an important project to a woman architect. An overall review of the work of women architects during the 1920s and 1930s in Mandatory Palestine reveals that most of their commissions came from the "Civil Circles" and private clients, rather than from the dominant socialist organizations such as the *Histadrut* (the General Organization of Workers in Eretz Israel) and the kibbutzim. The frequent commissions given to women architects by members of the centrist middle class indicates that this segment of society greatly appreciated their professional work.

---

23 Chanan (Heinz) Pawel (1909-1976) was born in Stettin, Germany (now Szczecin, Poland). He studied at the *Technische Hochschule* in Stuttgart and worked there for one year before immigrating to Palestine in 1934. He was Goldschmidt's professional associate from 1934 to 1937.

24 See, documentation in: The Farmers' Federation of Eretz Israel Archive, Rehovot, Israel.

Gertrud Goldschmidt's winning design displayed the formal vocabulary of modern architecture. (Figure 5) Her plan was a composition of rectilinear forms that drew attention to a hierarchy between the different functions of the building. The management office, the most pronounced element, was prominently positioned on the front façade above the entrance. A balcony lent additional emphasis to this room and, with a flagpole placed in its middle, imparted a sense of respectability and stateliness. Goldschmidt placed a large assembly hall adjacent to the management office and along the street. The comments that she attached to the drawing reveal that she intended the hall to be very elegant and serve as the cultural center of Rehovot. In her mind, that small agricultural town was an urban center that needed a formal room for dances and celebrations, and she designed the assembly hall to serve these purposes as well. In practice, however, the assembly hall offered modest cultural activities that were quite different from her vision. It became more of a local community center than the grand space that she suggested in her notes and drawings. The Farmers' House hosted professional agricultural lectures that were attended by the region's farmers, Shabbat ceremonies and festive holiday events, as well as chamber music concerts.

The move to Jerusalem: Agriculture triumphs

During their early years in Mandatory Palestine, although Martin Goldschmidt took on freelance projects planning irrigation systems for citrus orchards, Gertrud Goldschmidt's architectural work provided the main source of income for her family. Ya'akov Goldschmidt recalled that his mother worked late and hired other women to do the household chores and care for the children during the day.[25] Tel Aviv and its environs proved to be a fortuitous place for a woman to work in architecture at this time, and even to prosper. Nevertheless, despite winning the competition for a public building, by the late 1930s Goldschmidt was unable to pursue her professional career. In 1937, the British Government offered her husband a position in Jerusalem, and the family subsequently relocated there. As a result, she was obliged to give up her architectural practice. Her final project was the family residence in Beit HaKerem, a modern garden neighborhood on the western outskirt

25 Interview with Ya'akov Goldschmidt, Ramat HaSharon October 23, 2007.

Figure 5: Beit Haikar, Rehovot, 1930s. Source: Myra Warhaftig (1996),
Sie legten den Grundstein: Leben und Wirken deutschsprachiger
jüdischer Architekten in Palästina, 1918-1948, Tübingen: Wasmuth.
Courtesy of saai | Archiv für Architektur und Ingenieurbau am
Karlsruher Institut für Technologie (KIT), Karlsruhe, Germany.

Figure 6: Goldschmidt House, Beit HaKerem neighborhood,
Jerusalem, 1937. Source: Courtesy of the Goldschmidt family,
Ramat HaSharon, Israel.

of Jerusalem that had been planned by Richard Kauffmann in early 1920s. (Figure 6)

Moving to Jerusalem was fatal to Gertrud Goldschmidt's career as an architect. 1936 marked the beginning of the Arab Revolt against the Mandatory Government and Jewish immigration. The local Arabs went on a general strike that escalated into an armed struggle. The journey from the mountains of Jerusalem to Tel Aviv took several hours, and the roads were unsafe. Her need to find a new circle of clients in Jerusalem coincided with the beginning of an economic depression and a slowdown in new construction. After 1939 and during the Second World War, building came to a complete halt due to a scarcity of construction materials.[26] All these circumstances combined to force Goldschmidt to abandon architecture after seven years of intensive work. She handed over her clients to her good friend Lotte Cohn, who had moved from Jerusalem to Tel Aviv in the early 1930s.

Once she stopped working as an architect, Goldschmidt dedicated her energies to her family and to agricultural work. She became an enthusiastic farmer, planting an orchard and a vegetable garden in addition to tending a chicken coop on the 4,000 square meters of land that surrounded the family home. Most of the produce was used at home, and the surplus was sold. The Goldschmidts also supported Martin's parents and sister. To increase the family's income during the Second World War, Goldschmidt prepared meals for summer vacationers in Beit Hakerem's local guesthouses, cared for their children, and designed gardens for the houses of families in the neighborhood—all traditional, domestic women's tasks. Despite her past determination to study and, most of all, to practice architecture, Goldschmidt finally realized Otto Warburg's Zionist vision, devoting the rest of her life to agriculture. The only exception came in 1949 after the establishment of the State of Israel, when she submitted a design to a prestigious competition for the Jerusalem International Convention Center, *Binyenei Ha'Umah*.[27]

---

26 A report from 1939 by the Jerusalem Branch of the Association of Architects and Engineers revealed that 40% of its members were unemployed with scant chances to find jobs in their profession. Lavon Institute for Labour Research, IV-250-36-1-237.

27 Ya'akov Goldschmidt, personal archive. The competition's initiator was the Jewish Agency, who wished to build a center that would host Zionist and various other conventions. Architect Ze'ev Rechter won the competition.

Forgotten architects

In researching the careers and lives of women architects in Mandatory Palestine, one must consider their personal circumstances to understand their
professional success and commitment to family and home life. The traditional
Jewish-conservative view of gender permeated the Zionist utopia. The Zionist
movement made no effort to transform the patriarchal nature of Jewish society. It was only intent on shaking off the weak image of the diaspora Jew and
proving that he could take part in building a "Jewish National Home." [28] Nevertheless, a "New Woman"—who was educated, professional and economi-
cally autonomous—emerged independently of the Zionist utopia.

First-generation women architects embraced this feminine ideal, breaking from the "female helpmate" stereotype that dominated Zionist ideology.
They were educated, highly motivated and ran their own architectural firms
with complete dedication. For many, this devotion to professional work
involved choices that affected their private lives and their ability to com-
mit to marriage and raising a family. It is not surprising that many women
architects in Mandatory Palestine, such as Lotte Cohn, Elsa Gidoni Mandelstamm, Dora Gad, Helene Roth and Judith Stolzer Segall, remained single or,
if they married, never had children. Those who did have children eventually
abandoned their profession or had their working life come to a standstill, as
was the case with Gertrud Goldschmidt and her colleagues Gertrud Krolik
and Zipora Neufeld-Cherniak. Martin Goldschmidt pursued a successful
career and was eventually appointed head of the Mandate Government's
Water Commission. When the State of Israel was established, he set up the
hydrological service within the Ministry of Agriculture and is regarded to
this day as Israel's pioneer hydrologist. Gertrud Goldschmidt, a promising
and groundbreaking architect, relinquished her architectural practice in
favor of her husband's professional endeavors. She fell into oblivion.

Over the years, Gertrud Goldschmidt's name has been omitted from the
historiography of architecture in Eretz Israel. Most architectural historians
are not familiar with her work, which explains why she is never mentioned as
one of the earliest modern architects in Israel. In 2015, a comprehensive book
was published on the history of architecture in Rehovot. The book, *[One] Hun-*

---

28 Naveh (2007), 117–123.

dred Houses in Rehovot, was sponsored by the Rehovot municipality.[29] Both the Miller House and the Farmer's House are described in detail, but the name of Gertrud Goldschmidt is missing. Likewise, the "Tel Aviv—100 years" website that documents Tel Aviv's history initially did not mention her as the planner of the Hadar-Scheflan factory. When I commented on this omission, the website was corrected.

In documenting and researching the work of women architects in Mandatory Palestine, we are correcting a historical injustice. The inclusion of their names and buildings produces a more detailed and accurate picture of modern architecture in Eretz Israel, with its multi-faceted processes and many achievements. It broadens the accepted historical insights that have been gained so far about this period and highlights the achievements of pioneering women architects here.

Literature

Davidi, Sigal (2016), "By Women for Women: Modernism, Architecture and Gender in Building the New Jewish Society in Mandatory Palestine," *Architectural Research Quarterly*, vol. 20, no. 3, 217-230.

Davidi, Sigal (2017), "German and Austrian Women Architects in Mandatory Palestine, 1920-1948," in: Pepchinski, Mary/Budde, Christina/Voigt, Wolfgang/Schmal, Peter C. (eds.), *Frau Architekt. Seit mehr als 100 Jahren: Frauen im Architekturberuf/Frau Architekt. Over 100 Years of Women in Architecture*, Ausstellungskatalog/Exhibition Catalogue, Deutsches Architekturmuseum (DAM), Frankfurt-am-Main (30.09.2017-08.03.2018), Tübingen/Berlin: Wasmuth, 49-57.

Levin, Michael (1984), *The White City: The architecture of the international style in Israel*, Tel Aviv: Tel Aviv Museum of Art. (Hebrew)

Maasberg, Ute/Prinz, Regina (2012), „Aller Anfang sind wir—Wege von Architektinnen im 20. Jahrhundert," in: Winfried Nerdinger (ed.), *Der Architekt—Geschichte und Gegenwart eines Berufsstandes*, Munich: Prestel, 2012, vol 2, 635-650.

Naveh, Hannah (2007), "Gender and the vision of Hebrew masculinity," in: Tzaban, Yair/Yovel, Yirmiyahu/Shaham, David (eds.), *New Jewish Time:*

---

29 Ravid (2015).

Jewish Culture in a Secular Age - An Encyclopedic View, Tel Aviv: Keter, 2007, vol. 3, 117-123. (Hebrew)

Ravid, Baruch (2015), *[One] Hundred Houses in Rehovot: Architecture in the Colony 1890-1950*, Rehovot: Rehovot Municipality, 2015 (Hebrew).

Stratigakos, Despina Maria (1999), *Skirts and Scaffolding. Architects, gender, and design in Wilhelmine Germany*, Dissertation Bryn Mawr College, Bryn Mawr, Pa. USA; Ann Arbor [Mich.]: University Microfilms 1999.

Stratigakos, Despina (2001), "Architects in Skirts: The public image of women architects in Wilhelmine Germany," *Journal of Architectural Education*, 55(2), 2001, 90-100.

Tel Aviv's Modern Movement: The White City of Tel Aviv, a World Heritage Site (2004), The Helena Rubinstein Pavilion for Contemporary Art, Tel Aviv Museum. Exhibiton Catalogue, Tel Aviv: Yafo Municipality, 2004.

Walker, Lynne (2017), "An Irresistible Movement," in: Darling, Elizabeth/ Walker, Lynne, *AA Women in Architecture, 1917-2017*, London: AA Publications, 11-25.

Internet Sources

Hadar-Scheflan Factory https://sites.google.com/a/tlv100.net/tlv100/old_east/shfln (Hebrew), accessed on Sept. 22, 2020.

Archives

Central Zionist Archives, Jerusalem, Israel

Lavon Institute for Labor Research, Tel Aviv, Israel

saai | Archiv für Architektur und Ingenieurbau am Karlsruher Institut für Technologie (KIT), Karlsruhe, Germany

Technical University Munich (TUM) Archive, Munich, Germany

Tel Aviv Municipality Building Archive, Tel Aviv, Israel

The Farmers' Federation Archive, Rehovot, Israel

University of Würzburg (JMU) Archive, Würzburg, Germany

Ya'akov Goldschmidt, private archive, Ramat HaSharon, Israel

"A small flock of female students"
Paul Schmitthenner's *Meisterklasse* in Tübingen, 1944-1945

Wolfgang Voigt

Today, in the Federal Republic of Germany (FRG), the enrollment at architecture faculties reveals a conspicuous trend. The number of women students has risen steadily over the past decades, and now they are in the majority, a development that clearly demonstrates progress towards gender equality. Although we are accustomed to thinking of this change as a phenomenon of the 21st century, this is not quite correct. Throughout the 20th century, there have been other instances when women have made up more than half of a student body or had a strong presence at faculties of architecture or design. For example, as modernism was emerging around 1914 in the German Empire, large numbers of women were in attendance at some schools which offered courses in furniture, crafts and interior decoration, such as the Grand-Ducal School of Arts and Crafts in Weimar under the direction of Henry van der Velde.[1] For women, training in the applied arts was appealing, as they were not required to have an *Abitur*, that is, the rigorous high school diploma that was a prerequisite for entrance to a university. Although women were admitted to all German universities by 1909, few had the opportunity to attend an academic high school to receive the prerequisite education. As a result, for much of the 20th century, the universities were almost completely the preserve of men. Nonetheless, in 1919 and 1920, during the first two years of the Weimar Bauhaus, when fine arts and crafts took precedence and the administration did not conspire to keep their numbers low, women and men were enrolled in equal numbers.[2] And by the 1980s in the

---

1 Schulte (1992) 95–117, esp. 113–116; Hüter (1992) 285–340, esp. 320–324.

2 Rössler/Blümm (2019), 9; Droste (1991, orig. 1990), 40.

German Democratic Republic (GDR), female students outnumbered males at architecture faculties.[3]

Paul Schmitthenner and the *Stuttgarter Schule* during the Second World War

Another example occurred during the Second World War. At that time, the number of women studying architecture at German universities was relatively high. This came about for two reasons: young men had been drafted into the army and, beginning in 1936, restrictions placed on women students after the First World War were eased and their ranks increased.[4] In the 1944 spring semester at the *Technische Hochschule* (TH or technical university) in Stuttgart, just as many women as men were studying architecture. In the following winter semester 1944-45, although there were probably more male than female students, there was one class that was almost exclusively populated by women, a situation which appears worthwhile to look at more closely today.

Particularly in the interbellum period, the highly respected *Stuttgarter Schule* (Stuttgart School) attracted many students—almost all men, with many foreigners among them. The designation references both the location where the most prominent practitioners held professorships and the kind of architecture, based on regional forms and materials, that they propagated. At the end of 1918 and a few months before the founding of the Bauhaus in Weimar, the two leading protagonists, Paul Bonatz (1877-1956) and Paul Schmitthenner (1884-1972), took advantage of the political vacuum of the November Revolution to introduce radical educational reforms. The credo of the *Stuttgarter Schule* was simple: handwork was given a high priority in instruction and architecture should not result from abstract, aesthetic notions about design. Instead, it should arise from what Schmitthenner called *gebaute Form* (built form), namely that the means of construction must be adequate to the material used and that a building should always be developed with regards to a specific context, such as the landscape and local

---

3 Engler (2016), 8; Scheffler (2017).

4 Compare, the chapter by Annette Krapp about Maria Lang Schwarz and especially footnote 8 in this collection.

means of construction. Thus, experience was given preference over experimentation and practice was more highly valued than theory. The idea of an international architecture, as propagated by Walter Gropius, was an anathema to the *Stuttgarter Schule.*[5]

In the final year of the Second World War, this faculty of architecture, which had embraced Nazi doctrines willingly, lay in ruins, both physically and metaphorically. After extensive aerial attacks in the summer of 1944, only the exterior walls of the main building of the TH Stuttgart remained standing. The professors experienced the apocalypse as a double blow, as not only their university but also the majority of their private homes had been either destroyed or were badly damaged.[6] Their numbers had been reduced and the institutes of some tenured professors had been abandoned, due in part to injuries sustained in the war or because staff members had been drafted into the army.[7] In the summer of 1944, the last, prominent German emigrant, Paul Bonatz, left for Turkey. Although he did not join the NSDAP and had experienced difficulties due to a courageous and critical statement about Hitler, he nevertheless participated in the planning of important projects for the Nazi regime. In the final year of the war, the Turkish government offered him a contract to erect several schools, an opportunity which enabled him to flee his homeland and avoid the anticipated inferno there.[8]

In Stuttgart, the ranks of male students dwindled. Masculine youth born after 1918 were drafted and sent to the front lines; many were killed or were captured by the allies. Only "war disabled" men were allowed to study. As long as they were not forced to take a job in the armaments industry or related employment elsewhere, women could also attend universities. The desolate situation notwithstanding, Stuttgart was one of the few German architecture faculties that continued to offer instruction during the last year

5 For the *Stuttgarter Schule*, see: Voigt (2003); May (2010); Philipp (2012).

6 See: Executive Board of the Faculty of Architecture: Letter to the architecture students in the armed forces of the Technical University of Stuttgart, Stuttgart in February 1945, in the University Archive, Technical University of Stuttgart (hereafter: UaS), SN 64 Nr. 165. By November 1944 the residences of professors Bonatz, Janssen, Schmitthenner, Schmoll von Eisenwerth, Stortz and Wetzel were destroyed; the apartments of professors Hanson and Keuerleber were damaged; and only von Tiedje's house was intact. See: Faculty meeting on November 9, 1944, UaS.

7 Ibid.

8 Voigt (2010).

of the war. Substitute quarters were found in a school at the edge of the city that Paul Schmitthenner had completed in 1930.[9] Under increasingly difficult conditions, the few remaining professors took up instruction in the fall semester 1944-1945.

Paul Schmitthenner's own residence was destroyed in a bombing raid in September 1944. Built in 1922 and situated on a hill overlooking the city, the house was known as the legendary "Noah's Ark over Stuttgart" and was familiar to professionals and laypeople alike.[10] He fled the city taking only some salvaged household goods. In the village of Kilchberg on the outskirts of the old university city of Tübingen, he was able to rent a few rooms in a small castle to use as an apartment.

For Schmitthenner, the loss of his own house, which had seemed like an isolated idyll far removed from the political storms of the past two decades, was the final blow in his experience of war that had been marked by a growing estrangement from the Nazi regime. In the beginning of the 1930s, when he had hoped to be entrusted with the reform of German architectural education on a national level, he ostentatiously made a point of joining the Nazi party and appeared to his colleagues as being headed on the path to becoming the leading architect in Germany.[11] But when the desired career did not materialize because his deliberately unassuming design for the German Pavilion for the 1935 World Exposition in Brussels was not favorably received, his gradual aversion to the regime took its course.[12] In the summer of 1940, the architect received the news of the death of his younger son, Martin Schmitthenner, who had been drafted into the army during the campaign in France. In his youth, he was a follower of the poet Stefan George and had befriended Claus Count von Stauffenberg who attempted to assassinate Hitler in 1944. Shortly before his death, Martin Schmitthenner left a political testament which brutally described the bare truth about National Socialism and the nature of the war. Paul Schmitthenner printed an excerpt of this statement and sent it to a select group of friends. Shortly thereafter

9 The *Horst-Wessel-Schule* in Stuttgart-Zuffenhausen was built between 1927-30 by Paul Schmitthenner as the *Hohenstein Schule*. Compare faculty meeting, November 9, 1944, UaS.

10 For Paul Schmitthenner's own house, built in 1922 (Am Kriegsbergturm 27, Stuttgart), see: Voigt (2003), 133–134; Schickele (1927).

11 Voigt (2003a); Voigt (1985).

12 Voigt (2003a).

he became aware of the systematic murder of mentally ill patients under the secret "euthanasia" program and composed a personal memo expressing his outrage at it.[13]

In 1938, with war imminent, Schmitthenner, wrote to a friend about the necessity of preserving one's true nature and artistic predilections for the aftermath of conflict.[14] Starting in 1942, as more and more cities were devastated by the aerial war and many of his own buildings were destroyed or damaged, he sensed the complete eradication of what he valued in architecture, where the ethic of handwork was central. The physical substance was annihilated, but he wanted to keep its values alive for the future. "Now would be a great opportunity," he wrote to a colleague, "that young people, from well-situated backgrounds do that, what one has previously considered to be a step downward, and take a step up to handwork, which one can raise to the level of art. That would be a renewal of the very nature of our people."[15]

By late 1944, he understood the total destruction as an opportunity, although the thought of continuing to hold university classes in the destroyed city of Stuttgart was absurd.[16] Considering the growing problems that the students faced, such as the need to find housing in the bombed-out city, he proposed that all classes be relocated to the countryside. In doing so, those students who had been injured in the war and now populated the lecture halls would be protected from the last phase of the air strikes. Each of the four remaining professors for architectural design should take a group of 25 to 30 students and settle in a small city in the region. The intact buildings and structures there were better objects of study than the rubble of Stuttgart. Instruction in additional subjects, such as architecture history, structural design and urban planning, was to be carried out in rotation by professors who would visit a group for four weeks. All professors were to meet with one another once a month to exchange information and compare experiences.[17]

---

13 Ring binder „Persönliche Dinge. Notizen 1938-1940," Undated entry, probably October 3, 1940. Archive Paul Schmitthenner (APS).

14 Paul Schmitthenner to Wilhelm Schäfer, September 30, 1938, in: Wilhelm Schäfer Papers, Heinrich-Heine-Institut Düsseldorf.

15 Paul Schmitthenner to Hermann Hampe, April 26, 1946, APS.

16 Paul Schmitthenner to Max Laeuger, November 16, 1944, saai | Archiv für Architektur und Ingenieurbau am Karlsruher Institut für Technologie (KIT).

17 Paul Schmitthenner: „Ein Vorschlag," undated (Fall 1944), UaS, SN 64 Nr. 165.

For Paul Schmitthenner, the crisis could enable a better kind of education to come into being: "When I oversee a seminar with 25 students, to whom I can totally devote myself and who, for their part, must focus on the teacher, the result is what a seminar always should be, the *Meisterklasse*."[18] By this time, he was living in the countryside near Tübingen and taking care of details, such as finding rooms at the University of Tübingen to be used as classrooms and dormitories for the students. In the end, of the four remaining professors for architectural design in Stuttgart, he was the only one who carried out this plan.

"A small flock of female students" in Tübingen

Interestingly, the authority responsible for university education in Stuttgart, the Baden-Württemberg Ministry of Culture, agreed to this proposal but with a stipulation about gender. Whereas men would be instructed in Stuttgart, Schmitthenner was allowed to establish a special course, mainly for women students, to continue until May 1, 1945 and the completion of the final diploma examination.[19] Nothing has been handed down to explain why the genders were separated.

Faced with the coming Herculean task of rebuilding the country, the younger professors may have had doubts about the continuing relevance of Schmitthenner's approach to architecture. The guidelines issued by the Reich Commissioner for Social Housing or the information that was contained in Ernst Neufert's *Bauordnungslehre*[20] (architectural graphic standards) emphasized other methods of planning and construction, such as industrial prefabrication and standardization,[21] and gave no consideration to Schmitthenner's appreciation for handwork and the honest use of materials. Furthermore, when considering the disregard that women in the profession of architecture encountered, men probably did not trust them to be able to carry out the hard work needed in the immediate post war years. Viewed in this light, they were shunted off to Schmitthenner's class. Certainly, he

---

18 Ibid. *Meisterklasse* is translated as master class.

19 Compare the faculty meeting, November 17, 1944, in: UaS, SN 64 Nr. 165.

20 Here the reference is to the edition from 1943.

21 Voigt (1999); Harlander/Fehl (eds.)(1986).

did not view the "old-fashionedness" of his teaching to be a shortcoming, but rather, a particular strength.[22]

The archival materials from the *Technische Hochschule* in Stuttgart are fragmentary, and only schematic information about the composition of the class is known.[23] References to this class, in the form of drawings that are kept in Paul Schmitthenner's papers, record that nine women and four men, including one from Turkey and one from Holland, who participated without the goal of completing the diploma examination, took part in it. There may have been more students, but the fact of an almost women-only class has been orally handed down.[24] Furthermore, an official document refers to "our female diploma students" and to "a small flock of female students" in Tübingen.[25]

In the 1920s, Schmitthenner taught in a classical lecture format to over-filled auditoria. Now the small group permitted an intimate, interactive seminar: First "a general discussion [should] take place, and about the things that only have a direct connection to architecture. During this exchange, I let each person have enough space, get an impression of their way of thinking and level of education. As far as possible, collaboration should take place."[26] The facilities and equipment were poor: students drew on blocks of trans-parent paper, "without drawing boards and T-squares, [and] the blackboard had a surface area of 1½ square meters and a hole in the middle from a shell."

---

22 The conditions of Jože Plečnik in the 1950s at the University of Ljubljana are somewhat similar to the situation in Tübingen under Schmitthenner during the last year of the Second World War. See: Potočnik (2016).

23 List of students at the diploma course in Tübingen, Winter Semester 1944/45, in: UaS, SN 64 Nr. 165. The list, apparently compiled before the start of the course, records 14 women and 10 men. Concerning the men, only 4 participated. Documentation exists of nine women participants. Drawings in the Schmitthenner papers confirm the presence of seven women (Gerti Gonser, Ursula Heim, Margarete Köster, Marga Jäger, D. Langenbach, Wal-traud Wing, V. Zarnik); the drawings in UaS indicate an additional female participant (Le-onore Rosshirt). In addition, there are the recollections of a contemporary witness, Elisa-beth Prüss Schmitthenner. Drawings in the Schmitthenner papers show three men (Henk de Bie, Mukkader Cizer, Hubert Roth) were in attendance, and drawings in the Archive of the Architekturzentrum Wien indicate that another man (Norbert Heltschl) participated.

24 Interview by the author with Elisabeth Schmitthenner, March 1, 1984.

25 Letter to the students in the armed forces; See, UaS, SN 64 Nr. 165.

26 Paul Schmitthenner, „Gedanken zum Unterricht in Tübingen," handwritten notes, Fall 1944, APS.

Because the rotation of the teaching staff remained a mere idea, Schmitt-henner more or less taught all the courses alone. "I personally occupied all the professorial chairs, from architectural history to statics," he reported to Paul Bonatz, who was now living in Istanbul, when the long-interrupted mail service was resumed. "I was my own best student, and my teaching 25 years ago appears to me today like the mere attempt of a beginner."[27]

Schmitthenner's course in Tübingen offered instruction in applied arts, architectural typology, construction detailing, the measuring of historic monuments, the reconstruction of buildings and urban planning. Only one portfolio, containing examples of one exercise with 12 projects, nine by women and three by men, has survived. The theme was a "garden house" and, in light of the extreme need for housing for those who had been bombed out, could hardly be seen as relevant. It should be noted that the need for "temporary buildings" also appears in the course concept and the concern for the homeless was addressed elsewhere.[28]

"The tasks that remain, that allow us to keep living, lie in the depths and silences, ..."

For the "garden house" exercise, the external dimensions and the plan were specified. Although the two-story pavilion should house a hermit and accommodate his small parties, the hedonistic purpose was not the most important problem to be addressed. Rather it was a variation of Schmitt-henner's "constructive architectural design" which formed the core of his pedagogy. Depending on the means of construction and building materials (natural stone or stucco over brick or exposed brickwork or timber), all the relevant details of a simple, small building were drawn up. In the spirit of Schmitthenner's concept of *gebaute Form*, it was possible to learn how every building material required a suitable method of construction, and that works of architecture that are fabricated from different materials should be distinct from one another. Hence a drawing of a façade is accompanied by the most important details, for example, how a wall and roof are connected or

---

27 Paul Schmitthenner to Paul Bonatz, May 8, 1946, APS.
28 Paul Schmitthenner, See, UaS, SN 64 Nr. 165.

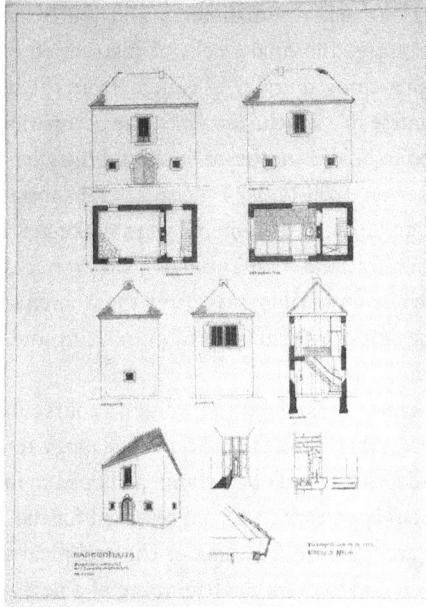

Figure 1: Ursula Heim, Garden House Exercise, TH Stuttgart under the direction of Prof. Paul Schmitthenner, 1944-45. Source: Archive Paul Schmitthenner, München/Johannes Schmitthenner.

how a window is placed into a wall.[29] The extant "garden house" projects follow this example and reveal a series of variations with great aesthetic appeal, as each student tried to give his or her design its own character. (Figure 1) Schmitthenner encouraged those who were not from Germany to develop a design based on the building traditions of their native country. We observe the work of V. Zarnik, who may have hailed from Yugoslavia, and who drew a house with a round-arch loggia and a flat, hipped roof that recalled architecture from the Mediterranean region; or one by Henk de Bie from the Netherlands, who designed a northern Holland brick building with curved gables.

It seems curious that the almost all women class in Tübingen took place during the last year of the war. Yet the course can be seen as a means to escape both the present, marked by need and violence, and the impending military defeat followed by a post-war period, which Nazi propaganda

---

29 Drawings of the *Gartenhaus* (garden house) exercise, APS.

painted as having barbarian punishments and the extermination of the German people in store. The final weeks of instruction took place within earshot of the approaching thunder of canons from the west. Schmitthenner brought the course to a conclusion when the occupation of Tübingen by the Allies appeared to be in a matter of days, and the women received their diploma certificates on April 15, 1945. Because transportation to Stuttgart had been severed and official documents were no longer available, the certificates were drawn by hand.[30] In Tübingen, the war ceased when French troops entered the city on April 19, 1945. How the women students survived the first days of the occupation, marked by plundering and violence, has not been handed down.

Paul Schmitthenner considered the women's course in Tübingen as an attempt to transition "his" *Stuttgarter Schule* pedagogy to a new phase. By testing a more in-depth method of teaching, he hoped to introduce the elite model of the *Meisterklasse*, that had been reserved for the art academies in Germany, to the architecture faculties at the technical universities. Furthermore, Tübingen was to mark the beginning of a new approach to architecture, which now had to divorce itself from the gigantism as propagated by Albert Speer. "The tasks that remain, that allow us to keep living, lie in the depths and silences, and have to be approached differently than the big things without foundations that were planned and built," he wrote in February 1945 to his friend Theodor Heuss, who would become the first president of the Federal Republic of Germany a few years later.[31]

But this experiment quickly came to an end. Due to his pro-Nazi stance from 1932 to 1934, the American occupation forces suspended Schmitthenner from his university professorship in the autumn of 1945. Like all those who had been a member of the Nazi party, he was required to undergo a denazification process which he successfully absolved, in part due to his open opposition to the death sentences handed down by the Nazi People's Court. Nevertheless, he was not allowed to return to the university, and the women's class in Tübingen became Paul Schmitthenner's final activity as a teacher. At his former university, newly recruited staff, such as Richard Döcker, the chief site supervisor at the 1927 Weissenhof Housing Estate, ensured that a second *Stuttgarter Schule*, now based on modernism, would take hold.

---

30 Sketch for the diploma of Ursula Heim, APS.
31 Paul Schmitthenner to Theodor Heuss, February 22, 1945, APS.

Power and pedagogy: The legacy of the Tübingen experiment after 1945

We can assume that the women in Tübingen, who received their diplomas and were taught by a professor, who was known for the theatrical posturing of an urbane gentleman, were daughters of bourgeois families. The extant archival materials about the women who studied architecture during the war years reveals that their fathers were architects, engineers, businessmen, factory owners, etc. The attraction of "New Tradition," that is, the kind of moderate, craft-based architecture that Schmitthenner and Bonatz propagated, for these female students is obvious. They were not adherents of modern, urban culture, but rather hailed from small or mid-sized cities and intended to build architecture that was suited to their social and professional circles once they returned home. Presumably, they had little interest in radical visions and the internationalism of Bauhaus-inspired design.[32]

Of the nine women students that are documented, little is known about them in later years. They probably left the profession of architecture for familiar reasons—marriage and motherhood—or perhaps they did not practice at all. There are, however, two notable exceptions. Elisabeth Prüss (1921-2017) was one of those courageous women who opened her own office and, with great tenacity, established herself professionally. Her family was critical of the Nazis and, in 1949, she returned to her hometown, Neustadt on the Baltic Sea, where she became a self-employed architect.[33] She was not readily welcomed in a profession that was dominated by men. At the time, the 28-year-old was also a single mother. One can hardly imagine the hostility that she endured in that remote provincial town. During her studies and the early post-war years, she had worked at Paul Schmitthenner's architecture office. Together they produced the images and texts to accompany the book *Gebaute Form.* (Figure 2) Her collaborations are identified with the abbreviation "P" which appears on many drawings. Initially this monograph remained unpublished. In 1959, she became Elisabeth Schmitthenner, the second wife of

---

32 Compare the discussions about the women students of Heinrich Tessenow at the Technical University of Berlin during the 1920s and 1930s in: Bauer (2003).

33 Ardito (2013); Norbert Becker, interview with the contemporary witness Dipl.-Ing. Elisabeth Schmitthenner on April 3, 2014 in Munich, transcribed by Katja Nagel. Typescript, file in: UaS; Voigt (2018).

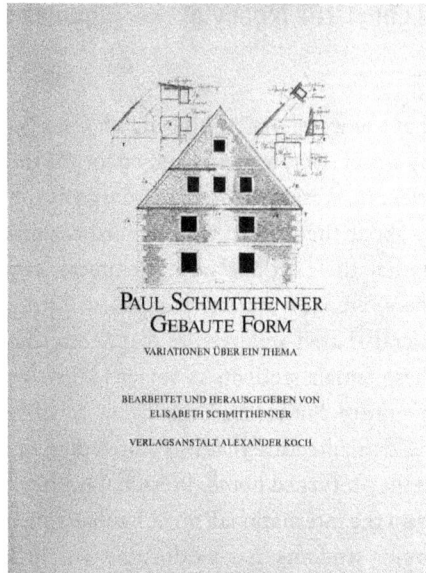

Figure 2: *Paul Schmitthenner, Gebaute Form. Variationen über ein Thema. Bearbeitet und herausgegeben von Elisabeth Schmitthenner (Paul Schmitthenner. Built Form. Variations on a Theme. Compiled and edited by Elisabeth Schmitthenner). (1984). Source: Gebaute Form (1984)/Johannes Schmitthenner.*

Paul. After his death, she sensitively edited the materials and supplemented the texts. In 1984 she published *Gebaute Form*, first in German and a few years later in Italian.[34] Although she never put her contribution in the foreground, the final publication is a wholly collaborative endeavor. (Figures 3–4)

The other woman from the Tübingen course who went on to practice is Gerti Gonser (1921-1997). To become an architect, she had to overcome resistance on the part of her family. Her father, an architect in civil service, did not think much of this idea. Because she did not have his official approval, she traveled to Berlin in 1940 to meet with officials at the Reich Ministry for Sciences and National Education and was able to secure admission to the TH Stuttgart. During her studies, she worked as a ticket collector in the Stuttgart streetcar system, a typical job for women during the war.

---

34 Schmitthenner (1984)(ed.); Schmitthenner/Frank (eds.)(1988).

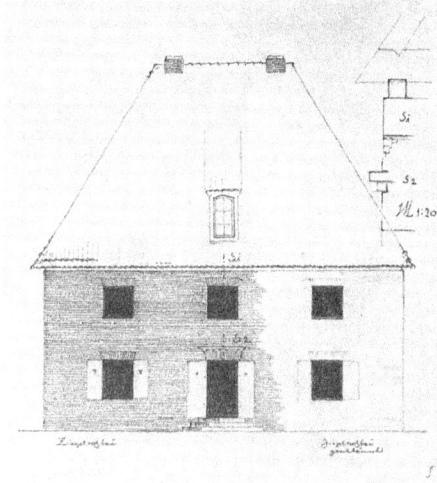

Figure 3: Paul Schmitthenner, Ziegelmauerwerkbau, aus Gebaute
Form (brick masonry house, from Built Form) (1984). Source: Archive
Paul Schmitthenner, München/Johannes Schmitthenner.

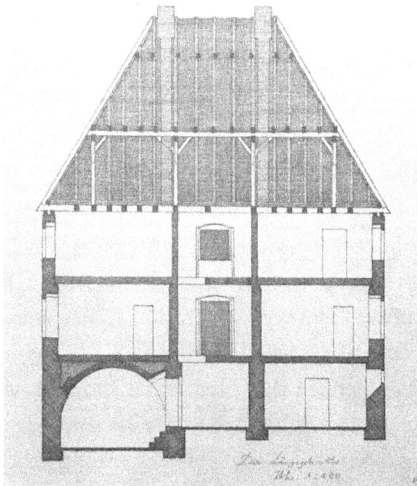

Figure 4: Elisabeth Prüss Schmitthenner, Der Längsschnitt, aus
Gebaute Form (longitudinal section, from Built Form) (1984). Source:
Archive Paul Schmitthenner, München/Johannes Schmitthenner.

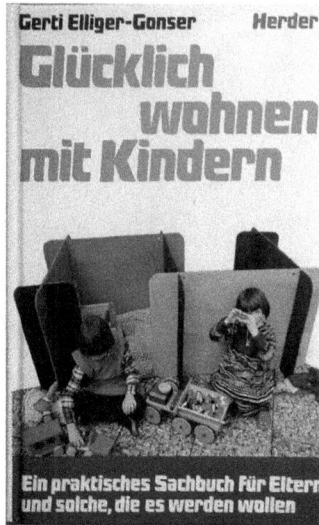

Figure 5: Gerti Elliger-Gonser, Glücklich Wohnen mit
Kindern (Living happily with children) (1983). Source:
Glücklich Wohnen mit Kindern/Ulrike Elliger.

She returned to her native city of Münster in Westphalia, married and, as Gerti Elliger-Gonser, had a successful career, establishing her own architectural office in 1949. Two of her brothers, who also studied in Stuttgart after 1945, became her employees—an atypical constellation in the 1950s.[35]

In the late 1970s and early 1980s she became known as the author of popular advice books about themes like "living happily with children." (Figure 5) As a mother and a wife, she was well qualified to write about these issues.[36] Like Margarete Schütte-Lihotzky a generation earlier, she found it necessary to perceive the spaces of everyday life through the eyes of children. Gerti Elliger-Gonser recommended that every child should have their own room and made proposals for furniture to suit the dimensions of children. While the standard living room planning at this time called for a seating area with a television and a dining table, she drew up proposals that, as a minimum,

---

35 Information cordially conveyed to the author and Mary Pepchinski by Stefan Rethfeld, Münster and the family of Gerti Elliger-Gonser.

36 Elliger-Gonser (1979); Elliger-Gonser (1979a); Elliger-Gonser (1981).

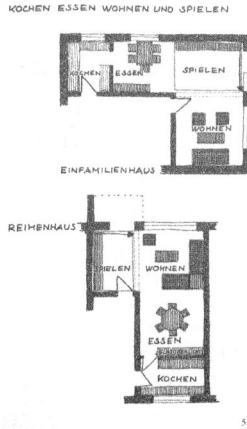

KOCHEN ESSEN WOHNEN UND SPIELEN

KOCHEN ESSEN SPIELEN WOHNEN

EINFAMILIENHAUS

REIHENHAUS SPIELEN WOHNEN ESSEN KOCHEN

53

Figure 6: Gerti Elliger-Gonser, Glücklich Wohnen mit Kindern (Living happily with children) (1983). Kochen Essen Wohnen und Spielen (cooking eating livng and playing); Einfamilienhaus (single family house), Reihenhaus (row house). Source: Glücklich Wohnen mit Kindern/Ulrike Elliger.

displayed a separate zone for children to play. Her drawings were intentionally simple and schematic to be accessible to everyone. (Figure 6)

It is noteworthy that two women, who emerged from this short, intense educational experience, later went on to engage in architectural theory. The work of Gerti Elliger-Gonser was directed towards laypersons, while Elisabeth Prüss Schmitthenner's book can be understood as a contribution to intellectual discourse, which presented a school of thought about architecture that had long been sidelined and was intended for architects working in local and non-globalized contexts.

Beyond details of individual biographies, glimpsed through the framework of gender analysis, Paul Schmitthenner's architecture class in Tübingen points to other relationships of power and pedagogy as well. During the final months of war, the sites of the two architecture faculties (Stuttgart and Tübingen) can be viewed as gendered, binary opposites. Stuttgart, albeit in ruin, remained "masculine": it was a large city, the location of the university where the remaining male students and teachers endured. Tübingen was "feminine": situated in the countryside, it was populated by those considered to be weak, that is, women, foreigners and wounded men, and instruction took place under the direction of a figure who was considered politically disposable and professionally antiquated.

Even if the class did have less status, Schmitthenner was committed to teaching this group in Tübingen. Why? On the one hand, he was a passionate educator. On the other, when his willingness to place his architectural vision in service of the Nazis in the early 1930s is considered, the heterogeneous class, comprised of students who were female, war injured or non-German, presents an unconscious foreshadowing of the make-up of post-war society. Imparting his kind of architectural knowledge to them can be seen as an attempt at absolution, like a washing away of sins through baptism, and an attempt to restart it with a different public for a post-war context.

When describing this class, Schmitthenner identified it as *Meisterklasse,* a form of teaching that implies a hierarchical relationship where an older male directs the intellectual and artistic development of a group of young acolytes.[37] With this in mind, the format of the *Meisterklasse* could be understood as a vehicle for Schmitthenner to regain lost status, if only briefly, and assert his control over a less authoritative group.

Nonetheless, despite Schmitthenner's fondness for it, the appellation *Meisterklasse* is perhaps somewhat misleading. As mentioned above, the notion of the master class is inherently gendered male, as there is no feminine equivalent (*Meisterinklasse?* mistress class?) and the students, like dutiful sons—but never dutiful daughters—are expected to perpetuate the master's tradition once they depart the class.[38] What happens to this appellation and the implicit gender dynamic when women replace the men? Although the class was clearly following Paul Schmitthenner's lead, the balance of power here was less explicit, and the Tübingen students should not merely be seen as a passive "herd." With the group's intimate scale and isolated location, toiling against the backdrop of deep anxiety, they should be considered as engaged participants in an intense, shared dialog. In this brief time, as war raged and no one dared contemplate the terrible aftermath, both sides,

37 Pollack (1988), 20–24.

38 Ibid.

infused with equal levels of passion for architectural education, contributed to the process and the results.[39]

Translated by Mary Pepchinski

Literature

Ardito, Vitangelo (2013) "Una conversazione con Elisabeth Schmitthenner," in: Ardito, Vitangelo (ed.), *Paul Schmitthenner 1884-1972*, Bari: Gangemi Editore Spa, 287–296.

Bauer, Corinne Isabel (2003), *Bauhaus und Tessenow-Schülerinnen. Genderaspekte im Spannungsverhältnis von Tradition und Moderne*. Diss. Kassel 2003, available online: https://kobra.uni-kassel.de/bitstream/hand le/123456789/2010090234467/DissertationCorinnaIsabelBauer.pdf;jses sionid=0E9CFB05A78315E406D13F9291476A81?sequence=7, accessed on October 2, 2020.

Droste, Magdalena (1991, orig. 1990), *Bauhaus 1919-1933*, Cologne: Taschen.

Elliger-Gonser, Gerti (1979), *Glücklich wohnen mit Kindern. Ein praktisches Sachbuch für Eltern und solche, die es werden wollen*, Freiburg/Basel/Vienna: Herder.

Elliger-Gonser, Gerti (1979a), *So wohnen unsere Kinder besser (Rund um die Familie) Lösungsvorschläge von A-Z*, Freiburg/Basel/Vienna: Herder.

Elliger-Gonser, Gerti (1981), *So wohnen unsere Kinder. Lösungsvorschläge von A-Z. Mit vielen Skizzen für Raumaufteilung und Einrichtung*, Freiburg/Basel/Wien: Herder.

Engler, Harald (2016), "Between state socialist emancipation and professional desire. Women architects in the German Democratic Republic, 1949-1990," in: Pepchinski, Mary/Simon, Mariann (eds.), *Ideological Equals. Women Architects in Socialist Europe 1945-1989*, London: Routledge, 7–19.

39 The author would like to thank Christina Budde for the encouragement to write this chapter; Mary Pepchinski for her pertinent comments and suggestions; Norbert Becker from the University Archive of the Technical University of Stuttgart for his help in researching this chapter; and Stefan Rethfeld for information about the biography of Gerti Elliger-Gonser.

Harlander, Tilman/Fehl, Gerhard (eds.) (1986), *Hitlers sozialer Wohnungsbau 1940-1945. Wohnungspolitik, Baugestaltung und Siedlungsplanung*, (Stadt Planung Geschichte 6) Hamburg: Christians.

Hüter, Karl-Heinz (1992), „Hoffnung, Illusion und Enttäuschung. Henry van der Veldes Kunstgewerbeschule und das frühe Bauhaus," in: Sembach, Klaus-Jürgen/Schulte, Birgit (eds.), *Henry van der Velde. Ein europäischer Künstler seiner Zeit*, Cologne: Weinand, 285–340.

May, Roland (2010), „Lehren und Bauen. Bonatz und die ‚Stuttgarter Schule‘," in: Voigt, Wolfgang/May, Roland (eds.), *Paul Bonatz 1877-1956*, Tübingen: Wasmuth, 69–78.

Philipp, Klaus Jan (2012), „Die Stuttgarter Schule. Eine Rezeptionsgeschichte," in: Philipp, Klaus Jan/Renz, Kerstin (eds.), *Architekturschulen. Programm, Pragmatik, Propaganda*, Tübingen: Wasmuth, 39–51.

Pollack, Griselda (1988), *Vision and Difference. Feminism, Femininity and Histories of Art*, London: Routledge.

Potočnik, Tina (2016), "Female students of Jože Plečnik between tradition and modernism," in: Pepchinski, Mary/Simon, Mariann (eds.), *Ideological Equals. Women Architects in Socialist Europe 1945-1989*, London: Routledge, 20–33.

Rössler, Patrick/Blümm, Anke (2019), "Soft Skills and Hard Facts: A Systematic Assessment of the Inclusion of Women at the Bauhaus," in: Otto, Elizabeth/Rössler, Patrick (eds.), *Bauhaus Bodies*, London: Bloomsbury, 3–24.

Scheffler, Tanja (2017), „Die großen Unbekannten—Architektinnen der DDR," in: *Bauwelt* 2, 2017, available online: https://www.bauwelt.de/themen/betrifft/Die-grossen-Unbekannten-Architektinnen-der-DDR-3045387.html?source=rss, accessed on December 1, 2020.

Schickele, René, „Die Arche über Stuttgart," in: *Die Dame*, vol. 55 (1927), no. 14, 9–10.

Schmitthenner, Elisabeth (ed.)(1984), Paul Schmitthenner. *Gebaute Form. Variationen über ein Thema*, Stuttgart: Alexander Koch.

Schmitthenner, Elisabeth/Frank, Hartmut (ed.)(1988), *La forma costruita. Variazioni su un tema*, Milano: Electa.

Schulte, Birgit (1992), „„Ich bin diese Frau, die um jeden Preis Ihr Glück will ...‘. Maria Séthe und Henry van der Velde—eine biographische Studie," in: Sembach, Klaus-Jürgen/Schulte, Birgit (eds.), *Henry van der Velde. Ein europäischer Künstler seiner Zeit*, Cologne: Weinand, 95–117.

Voigt, Johannes (1985), „Ein Architekt im Sog des Nationalsozialismus," in: Rieger, Klaus (ed.), *Paul Schmitthenner. Kolloquium zum 100. Geburtstag*, Stuttgart: Fakultät für Architektur und Stadtplanung der Universität, 18–19.

Voigt, Wolfgang (1999), „Vitruv der Moderne," in: Prigge, Walter (ed.), *Ernst Neufert. Normierte Baukultur*, Frankfurt: Edition Bauhaus Campus Verlag, 20–34.

Voigt, Wolfgang (2003), „Schmitthenners Werklehre und die Stuttgarter Schule," in: Voigt, Wolfgang/Frank, Hartmut (eds.), *Paul Schmitthenner 1884-1972*, Tübingen: Wasmuth, 27–46.

Voigt, Wolfgang (2003a), „Zwischen Weißenhof-Streit und Pour le mérite: Paul Schmitthenner im Architekturstreit der zwanziger bis fünfziger Jahre," in: Voigt, Wolfgang/Frank, Hartmut (eds.), *Paul Schmitthenner 1884-1972*, Tübingen: Wasmuth, 67–99.

Voigt, Wolfgang (2010), „Paul Bonatz: Kosmopolit in den Unwettern der Zeit," in: Voigt, Wolfgang/May, Roland (eds.), *Paul Bonatz 1877-1956*, Tübingen: Wasmuth, 11–37.

Voigt, Wolfgang (2018), „Elisabeth Schmitthenner (1921-2017)," in: *AIT*, vol. 128 (2018), no. 1/2, 19.

Archives

Architekturzentrum Wien, Archive, Vienna, Austria

Archive Paul Schmitthenner (APS), Munich, Germany

Heinrich-Heine-Institut Düsseldorf, Wilhelm Schäfer Papers, Düsseldorf, Germany

saai | Archiv für Architektur und Ingenieurbau am Karlsruher Institut für Technologie (KIT), Karlsruhe, Germany

University Archive, Technical University of Stuttgart (UaS), Stuttgart, Germany

Judith Stolzer-Segall
A cosmopolite between Europe and Mandatory Palestine/Israel

Edina Meyer-Maril

Let us begin with a suitcase. It was discovered in 1994 in the basement of a Jewish retirement home in Munich where its owner, Judith Stolzer-Segall (May 20, 1904-December 1, 1990), spent her last years.[1] Among the contents were several passports from different countries, address books, various records and a typewritten curriculum vitae. These personal belongings create a mosaic of the life of a remarkable person and serve as a 20th century case study of Jewish destiny, recalling the life of a woman, architect, Jewess, émigré and cosmopolite, who is listed as an "Architect and European" on her 1941 marriage contract. Like so many Jews, she spent much of her life looking for a new *Heimat*, or home. She had Lithuanian, Palestinian and ultimately German citizenship.

A small postcard[2] was also found in this suitcase. It contains an image of the owner's most significant accomplishment, the Hadera Synagogue, designed in 1935 and built between 1936 and 1940.[3] It is a magnificent reinforced concrete building, which, even today, is a unique structure in its surrounding region, displaying unexpected solutions for the fenestration as well as a sensitivity towards functional needs. The most surprising part is that its architect was female. (Figure 1)

---

1   The suitcase was discovered in the Saul-Eisenberg-Seniorenheim, Munich, Germany. The documents found inside belonged to Judith Stolzer-Segall and were given to the Khan Museum in Hadera, Israel. Unless otherwise noted, all references to Judith Stolzer-Segall are taken from the documents in this collection.

2   The photograph of the synagogue was made by Helene Bieberkraut (1896-1983), Tel Aviv.

3   For photos of the synagogue, see: https://commons.wikimedia.org/wiki/Category:Great_Synagogue_(Hadera), accessed on March 16, 2021.

Stations on a long and circuitous path

For the architect, the path leading to the construction of the synagogue was long and circuitous, as she resided in different places throughout Europe before her arrival in Mandatory Palestine in 1933. At the beginning, the education and employment of her father, Joseph Segall (1874-1943), determined the route. Judith Segall was born in 1904 in Prischib, Ukraine, a Protestant and Roman Catholic German settlement founded in 1804, situated 50 km north of Melitopol.[4] A few months after her birth, the family moved to Berlin, where her father first studied law, eventually earning a doctoral degree in this subject from the University of Giessen in 1914.[5] Judith Segall went to a kindergarten in Berlin and, from 1911 until the outbreak of the First World War in 1914, was enrolled at the *Cecilien-Lyzeum* along with many other Jewish girls.

Her father, who was born in the region around Tauragé in Lithuania, had attended a German school and tried to obtain German citizenship but the war thwarted his efforts. After living in Germany for eleven years, along with other Russians, the family was expelled, and they traveled first to Sweden and then to Russia. Their next home was in Kharkov (Kharkiv), which became the capital of Ukraine after 1919, where Judith Segall attended the German *Gymnasium*.[6] When her father opted for a position as the director of the Jewish Public Bank in Kovno (Kaunas), the family located to Lithuania. There she went to the Hebrew *Gymnasium*[7] in Kovno, which she later referred to in her curriculum vitae as a humanistic *Gymnasium* to conceal her Jewish roots. She graduated with an academic high school diploma in 1924. This bilingual document, written in Hebrew and Lithuanian, shows Judith Segall's impressive breadth of knowledge and various talents. She mastered Russian, Lithuanian, German, French as well as Latin, crucial for the European humanistic tradition. Her grades in history, religion, physics and mathematics

---

4 On some documents Melitopol is given as Judith Stolzer-Segall's birthplace.

5 This information was cordially conveyed by Dr. Felschow, Archive of the Justus Liebig University Giessen. Email correspondence from August 28, 2017 to the author.

6 The German *Gymnasium* (secondary academic high school) offered German as the main language of instruction.

7 The Hebrew *Gymnasium* (secondary academic high school) offered Hebrew as the main language of instruction.

Figure 1: Synagogue in Hadera, model, 1935; photographer: Helene Bieberkraut
(1896-1983). Source: Legacy of J. Stolzer-Segall, Khan-Museum, Hadera, Israel.

were excellent, and her drawing and artistic abilities were also above average. A group photo with her teachers and her classmates reveals that her appearance was appealing too.

The next stop was Free City of Danzig (Gdańsk), because her father became the director of the local Jewish Public Bank. Although architecture was well suited to Judith Segall's abilities, technical studies were highly unusual for a woman at that time. Nonetheless she enrolled at the architecture department of the local technical university, where she studied from 1924 to 1929. Founded in 1904 as the Royal Prussian Technical University of Danzig,[8] one of Judith's professors, Albert Carsten (1859 Berlin–1943 Terezín), who used the name Cohn until 1899,[9] designed the monumental eclectic building. Classes were in German, and the curriculum followed the Prussian model.

During her studies, Judith Segall apprenticed in the office of Dr.-Ing. Abraham in 1927. He was an engineer who was involved in the planning of a new synagogue in Danzig-Langfuhr,[10] a project which provided her with

---

8 https://de.wikipedia.org/wiki/Technische_Universität_Danzig, accessed on March 16, 2021.

9 https://pl.wikipedia.org/wiki/Albert_Carsten, accessed on March 16, 2021.

10 Schaefer (1928).

invaluable experience for her future career. In the summer of 1928, she took a job as a draftsperson in the carpentry workshop of H. Scheffler. Summing up her activities, his letter of reference recounted her great enthusiasm for the work at hand, and that she took the opportunity to become acquainted with diverse aspects of joinery and furniture construction.

Judith Segall received her degree in 1929 after nine semesters with the final grade *ziemlich gut* (quite good). Her final examination project was a health resort, which displayed a hipped roof in a "moderately modern" style in the manner of Heinrich Tessenow (1876-1950). She subsequently worked from mid-April to mid-October 1929 for the architect Arthur Megies, with whom she later shared an office in Berlin. In his letter of recommendation, Megies noted that she quickly learned the functional requirements and financial aspects of residential design, and was versatile, as she easily worked out structural problems, in addition to construction, detailing and furniture. He praised her professional skills and engagement in his office, while acknowledging that she had decided to seek other work of her own volitation.

At the end of 1929, Judith Segall went to Berlin, at the time one of the most important centers of modern architecture in Europe. The well-known Jewish architect, Leo Nachtlicht (1872-1942), hired her, but she only stayed in his office for two and a half months due to the onset of the Great Depression. Nachtlicht observed in his referral that she was extremely hard-working and competent, and while on his staff had worked out details for wood and steel constructions along with other architectural elements. Later Judith Segall found employment at the building department of the Jewish community in Berlin under the chief architect Alexander Beer (1873-1944).

Compared to her earlier places of employment, she was finally able to work for an extended period on large-scale public projects that engaged her sizeable talents and provided her with valuable training. Beer's testimonial for the period of December 1, 1929 to September 30, 1931 reports that she developed the design and prepared details for a synagogue in Herborn and a mortuary hall in Forst, and planned a hall for sporting activities with an adjacent athletic grounds in Berlin-Grünewald. She was assigned smaller tasks too, such as the design of tombstones or the supervision of the interior painting of a synagogue in Stendal. Like her previous employers, Beer was completely satisfied with her professional skills, and complemented her artistic talent and practical knowledge.

Once again, due to a lack of commissions, Judith Segall was forced to seek other work. There was a general public building freeze in 1931, and in January 1932, she opened an office together with Arthur Megies and the engineer Max Heinrich Sinjen. Two private projects are known from this collaboration, a shopping passage and a large coffee house.

Segall and Sinjen were arrested in 1933 for political reasons. We know from an interview conducted by Myra Warhaftig with Judith Segall, which took place four years before her death, that she was a staunch communist. After her second arrest, possibly in connection with communist political activity, Arthur Megies was able to have her released from jail and brought her to Danzig. Apparently, it was Judith's father who convinced her to emigrate to Mandatory Palestine. In contrast to his daughter, he was a committed Zionist who had purchased a tract of land in Afula, the city known as the "Capital of the Valley" and planned by the architect Richard Kauffmann in 1926.

Immigration to Mandate Palestine

Thanks to the various documents Judith Segall needed for her immigration, we know about her physical condition and some other details about her life. Her Health Identity Card stated: "structure of the body: middle robust, musculature well developed, nutritional condition good, sight: mildly short-sighted, hearing: good, lung and heart normal healthy." The Palestine Immigrant Certificate, issued in Berlin by the Jewish Agency for Palestine (*Palästina-Amt*), confirmed that she knew Hebrew, German, Russian and Lithuanian and that she was a member of Maccabi trade union. Judith Segall received her immigration certificate and left Europe from Triest on August 16, 1933, on the ship "Tel Aviv," later named the "USS Martha Washington."

Upon arriving in Mandatory Palestine, Judith Segall settled in Tel Aviv, commencing a period of residence that lasted twenty-four years. (Figure 2) In her curriculum vitae from 1968, only one event, her marriage in 1941 to the architect Dr. Eugen (Jenö) Stolzer (1886-1956), was recorded! Nonetheless, her career began auspiciously. She joined the office of the recognized architect Lotte Cohn (1893-1983),[11] where she won an internal competition for a

---

11 Information cordially relayed by Dr. Ines Sonder, Moses Mendelssohn Zentrum, Potsdam, Germany.

*Figure 2: Judith Segall in 1940. Source: Legacy of
J. Stolzer-Segall, Khan-Museum, Hadera, Israel.*

single-family house. In 1935 she was awarded the first prize in a limited competition for a housing development in Talpiot, Jerusalem, which included a
restaurant, shops and community recreational areas. Although this scheme
never materialized due to a lack of funds, other projects came to fruition.
She entered a public competition for cooperative housing requiring 300
apartments with large garden patios in Tel Aviv (1935-36) and, of the twen-
ty-one submissions, her scheme received the fourth prize along with a special commendation. Shortly thereafter, in 1936, Segall won a limited competition with twelve participants for the design of a neighborhood in northern
Tel Aviv, which was realized.[12] Known as the "Kiryat Meir Neighborhood,"
the quarter contains 200 freehold apartments, a kindergarten, shops, community rooms and extensive gardens, having been erected at the behest of
the Jewish Public Bank. Professionals and the residents praised the layout of
the apartments and the functional kitchens, and the neighborhood remains
one of the most remarkable examples of public housing in the White City of
Tel Aviv.

---

12 Judith Segal [sic!], Kirjat Meir Quarter, multi-family residential blocks in Kuppat-Am
   Bank, Tel Aviv, in: *Habinjam Bamisrach Hakarov* 1 (1937).

The Great Synagogue in Hadera

The highlight of Judith Segall's professional life in Mandatory Palestine (and later the State of Israel) was undoubtedly the building of the Great Synagogue in Hadera. The competition was open to all Jewish architects in Mandatory Palestine and attracted 41 submissions. After the judging, the jury was caught off guard when the envelope containing the name of the winner of the first prize was unsealed and it was revealed that a woman made the design. Not only the rabbis but also those who were devoutly religious were confounded because there was no historical precedent for a woman architect in the history of synagogue architecture. However, they could not find any reference in the scriptures to prohibit women from designing a house of worship. Who could predict that someday women would be architects? At this time in Mandatory Palestine, women could win competitions only when they were anonymous proceedings, as in this case. Prejudice against women professionals was real and, to conceal their gender, they often used only their family name and their first initial when listing their services in the telephone directory.[13]

Back to the inception of the Great Synagogue in Hadera. The competition program was published on December 18, 1934, and the submission date was February 1, 1935, a short amount of time for such a large project. The construction site had an area of 6239 square meters and was the so-called *Khan*, a farmstead that had accommodated the first Jewish settlers in Hadera in 1891. A wall was needed to enclose the complex, and the forecourt required space for 4000 to 5000 people to gather in public assemblies. At this time Hadera had a population of around 3000 Jewish citizens. By 1941 their numbers had grown to 6,500 and today there are more than 90,000 inhabitants.

The synagogue's program called for a main prayer hall for 850 men, a study hall (*Beit Midrash*) for approximately 160 men and 50 women; an upper floor with a women's section containing 500 seats; and other facilities. The requirement to build a tower was unique. It was to house a water reservoir, a guard room and steps leading to the roof. In addition, it had to be at least eight meters higher than the main prayer hall. When completed, thanks to the elevated site, the tower offered a broad panoramic view of the region. The budget was limited to 8000 Palestine Pounds, and a further request was a

---

13 Meyer-Maril (2019); Davidi (2017).

desire for simplicity. The choice between reinforced concrete or stone, to be faced in stucco, was left to the architect.

The jury was made up of two professionals. Dr. Ezra Rootmann (1907-1979) studied architecture in Italy and built many International Style buildings in his hometown of Hadera. Dov (Bernhard) Kuczynski (1891-1980), formerly from Berlin, was also an advocate of this type of architecture. It is therefore not surprising that the top prize winners among the 41 submissions were modernists. The protocol of the competition documents the selection process. It was completely anonymous and the envelopes with the winners' names were only opened after the final decision was reached. After the third round of judging, project no. 24, by Dipl.-Ing. Segall of Ha'Ari St. 32, Tel Aviv, won the first prize and received a sum of 80 Palestine Pounds.

The minutes of the jury's proceedings, written in Hebrew, mentioned that project no. 24 provided the best architectural solution regarding the topography and the use of the site to serve the exterior functions of a synagogue. It stated that the interior of the main prayer hall shows pleasing and elegant proportions; the quality of the lighting is satisfying; and the means of construction is good. Several details were criticized, such as the placement of the study hall, which was accessed via 20 steps and might be difficult for the elderly when they attended daily prayers, and that the delineator forgot to draw entrances to the galleries.

A comparison of the published designs of the top winners shows that Judith Segall's Hadera synagogue is a most impressive building.[14] The symmetry of the prayer hall and the tower intensifies the monumentality of this simple structure, especially when seen from street level. The numerous, nearly semicircular openings on the tower and walls of the building echo the form of the main entrance and the arcades. They are simultaneously functional and decorative and can be found in contemporary houses of worship like St. Kamillus Church (1928-31) in Mönchengladbach by Dominikus Böhm (1880-1955).[15] These openings have often been incorrectly interpreted as embrasures. In doing so, they connect the Hadera synagogue to the prominent Polish *Wehrsynagogen* (defense synagogues), like those found in Brody and other places. However, a closer look at these parabolic openings refutes this absurd statement.

---

14 *Habinyan Bamisrach Hakarov* (1935), 9.

15 Voigt (2005) and the photograph on page 14.

Figure 3: Judith Stolzer-Segall and Dr. Eugen
Stolzer, Jerusalem, October 1945. Source: Legacy of
J. Stolzer-Segall, Khan-Museum, Hadera, Israel.

Marriage and partnership with Eugen Stolzer

With the money that Judith Segall earned for the synagogue, she opened an office in Tel Aviv in association with Dr. Eugen Stolzer,[16] with whom she had signed the contract to construct the Hadera synagogue. Stolzer, an accomplished architect, was of Hungarian origin. After studying in Munich, he moved to Berlin, becoming the partner of the famous theater architect, Oskar Kaufmann (1873-1956). In 1934, together with the architects Meir Rubin (1893-1967) and Alexander Friedman (1905-1987), Stolzer won the competition for the Yeshurun Synagogue in Jerusalem, known as one of the first modern synagogues in Mandatory Palestine and completed in 1936.[17]

---

16 Warhaftig (1996), 180–183.
17 Solomon (2015); Ormandag (ed.)(1934-35), 124. "Stolzer, Eugen, architect..., won the first prize for the plan of the new Jeshurun Synagogue, Jerusalem, also for the Hedera Synagogue, ...".

The construction of the Hadera synagogue was completed in 1940 and the building was inaugurated in the following year. In February 1940, Judith Segall received Palestinian citizenship. She had hoped to emigrate to the United States, but the apparent reason for the rejection of her July 1940 visa application was that her birthplace was in the Soviet Union and that she could not produce certificates issued by the police attesting to her character from all the places in which she had resided prior to her arrival in Mandatory Palestine.

Due to the outbreak of World War II, there was a general halt to all public construction in 1940. Together with many other Jewish architects, Judith Segall found employment as a "civilian draughtsman" (sic!) in the War Department of the Chief Engineer of Palestine. She moved to Jerusalem where she married Dr. Stolzer on August 13, 1941. They henceforth worked together in their own office. (Figure 3)

After the founding of the State of Israel in 1948, their most important project was the representative building of the *Histadrut* (trade union) in Jerusalem, erected between 1950-58, near to the border of the divided city.[18] The six-story building follows the curved street, which gives the imposing structure a unique form. Groups of different-sized windows rhythmically pattern the main facade. Panels made of massive, cream-toned Jerusalem limestone cover much of the structure, creating a contrast to the glazed horizontal, two-story entrance zone, which is articulated with two rows of columns. The motive of the columns appears again in the pergola, which articulates the top of the building and lends the composition a sense of lightness. Such elements and materials taken from the vocabulary of modernism create an impression of compactness. Local newspapers and professional publications praised the large complex with its different facilities, including a library, an auditorium and areas for sport.

Return to Europe

For the Stolzer-Segall couple, the money that they earned after a long period of financial hardship enabled them to travel to Europe and enjoy the continent's sophisticated cultural milieu, which they so sorely missed. They first stayed in Berlin where Eugen Stolzer was again able to see the theater buildings which he had built together with Oskar Kaufmann three decades earlier. He also tried to

---

18 Warhaftig (1996), 183.

receive restitution payments. Their next station was Rome, where he died unexpectedly on December 22, 1958. He is buried in the Jewish cemetery of the city.

Judith Stolzer-Segall settled in Munich and also applied for restitution payments. Due to her affiliation with the *Deutscher Kulturkreis* (German Cultural Circle) and her professional work as an architect in Germany before the war, she eventually succeeded. She pursued cultural, political and intellectual interests, and her address book lists her contacts to pacifist organizations, progressive circles and Jewish groups. She was also interested in psychological and scientific issues but never again dealt with architecture. As a result of a car accident, she was declared profoundly handicapped. She spent her final years in a Jewish retirement home, largely forgotten, and died on December 1, 1990. She is buried in the Jewish Cemetery in Munich.[19]

Thus, the story of the suitcase ends.

Literature

Davidi, Sigal (2017), "German and Austrian Women Architects in Mandatory Palestine, 1920-1948," in: Pepchinski, Mary/Budde, Christina/Voigt, Wolfgang/Schmal, Peter C. (eds.), *Frau Architekt. Seit mehr als 100 Jahren: Frauen im Architekturberuf/Frau Architekt. Over 100 Years of Women in Architecture*, Ausstellungskatalog/Exhibition Catalogue, Deutsches Architekturmuseum (DAM), Frankfurt-am-Main (30.09.2017-08.03.2018), Tübingen/Berlin: Wasmuth, 49–57.

Habinyan Bamisrach Hakarov, 3, Tel Aviv, August 1935, 9.

Habinjam Bamisrach Hakarov, 1, Tel Aviv, August 1937, 18–19.

Meyer-Maril, Edina (2019), „Drei Frauen, drei Wege, eine Moderne: Genia Averbuch, Judith Segall-Stolzer und Elsa Gidoni-Mandelstamm planen und bauen in Eretz Israel," in: Stabenow, Jörg/ Schüler, Ronny (eds.), *Vermittlungswege der Moderne—Neues Bauen in Palästina (1923–1948)*, Berlin: Gebr. Mann, 69–82.

Ormandag, M. Z. (ed.) (1934-35), *Who is Who in the Balkans and the Orient*, vol. IV, Jerusalem: Syrian Orphanage Press.

---

19 Letter from the Saul-Eisenberg-Seniorenheim, Munich, Germany to Edina Meyer-Maril, Tel Aviv, Israel, December 21, 1992.

Schaefer, Paul (1928), „Die neue Synagoge in Danzig-Langfuhr. Arch.: Paul Imberg und Leopold Friedmann, Berlin-Dahlem," in: *Bauwelt*, 1928, no. 18, 425–6.

Solomon, Jacob (2015), „Bauhaus in Jerusalem: The Yeshurun Synagogue," *Haaretz*, March 16, 2015, https://www.haaretz.com/israel-news/travel/bauhaus-in-jerusalem-the-yeshurun-synagogue-1.5337687, accessed on February 20, 2021.

Voigt, Wolfgang (2005), „,Neue Formen mit dem Urgehalte der Tradition'. Dominikus Böhm zwischen den Strömungen und Brüchen seiner Zeit," in: Voigt, Wolfgang/Flagge, Ingeborg (eds.), *Dominikus Böhm 1880-1955*. Ausstellungskatalog, Deutsches Architekturmuseum (DAM), Frankfurt-am-Main (16.04.-19.06.2005), Tübingen/Berlin: Wasmuth, 9–27.

Warhaftig, Myra (1996), *Sie legten den Grundstein. Leben und Wirken deutschsprachiger jüdischer Architekten in Palästina, 1918-1948*, Tübingen/Berlin: Wasmuth.

Internet Sources

Albert Carsten https://pl.wikipedia.org/wiki/Albert_Carsten, accessed on June 28, 2022.

Great Synagogue Hadera https://commons.wikimedia.org/wiki/Category:Great_Synagogue_(Hadera), accessed on June 28, 2022.

Technical University of Danzig https://de.wikipedia.org/wiki/Technische_Universität_Danzig, accessed on June 28, 2022.

Yeshurun Synagogue https://jerusalempedia.com/Yeshurun-Synagogue.html, accessed on June 28, 2022.

Archives

Justus Liebig University Giessen, Archive, Giessen, Germany
Legacy of J. Stolzer-Segall, Khan-Museum, Hadera, Israel

Politics, Privilege and Architecture
Victoria zu Bentheim und Steinfurt (1887-1961), a pioneering woman architect in the tradition of the European high nobility during the 1930s and the 1940s

Karl Kiem

For the most part, the recent interest in women architects has turned to historical figures who correspond to the present-day notion of an architect, that is, a person directing or laboring in a private or public office for remuneration. Assumptions regarding class and power are inscribed in this figure, considered to be a someone with sufficient resources and status to acquire an education; gain the trust of clients to carry out their commissions; and engage with the public sphere to disseminate their ideas. How gender complicates this claim to knowledge, practice and representation is at the heart of many investigations. Yet there are—and have been—other modes of engaging with architecture production that are intimately bound to one's status in a given society. When considered from the perspective of a gender analysis, these overlooked approaches shed light on the opportunities that women have found in other contexts. This chapter examines this topic from the perspective of Princess Victoria zu Bentheim und Steinfurt (1887-1961), a woman architect who practiced from a uniquely privileged stance. During the first half of the 20th century in Germany, she labored largely outside the parameters that defined traditional architectural practice and—one can argue—the political currents that violently upended everyday life and professional activity in Germany.

A pioneering woman architect: Victoria zu Bentheim und Steinfurt

Until the end of the millennium, Victoria zu Bentheim und Steinfurt belonged to the ranks of those women architects who had been lost to history. In connection with her 1999 dissertation, Despina Stratigakos discovered her name in the files of the Technical University of Berlin and then located her surviving drawings and the photographs of her buildings that were preserved in the archives of the Counts zu Bentheim und Steinfurt in the castle of Burgsteinfurt in northwestern Germany. She also produced the first scientific assessment of this architect's work, focusing on her activities prior to 1920.[1] For the catalogue of the exhibition *Frau Architekt*, I authored the first survey of the entire life and architecture of Victoria zu Bentheim und Steinfurt,[2] relying upon the materials in the aforementioned archive. This chapter builds upon my catalogue entry to focus on Victoria zu Bentheim und Steinfurt's life and architecture during the 1930s and 1940s and her engagement with politics during these years.

First, I would like to explain how I understand the word "politics." As the feminist writer, Kate Millett, noted in the introduction to her 1969 book, *Sexual Politics*, politics is not "that relatively narrow and exclusive world of meetings, chairmen, and parties. The term 'politics' shall refer to power-structured relationships, arrangements whereby one group of persons is controlled by another."[3] Or, one might add, as in the case of Victoria zu Bentheim und Steinfurt, how one group either has control over another or can exist outside the rules and structures of the normative "power-structured relationships, arrangements" and other methods of social control. In other words, politics is not only the result of being subordinated, but also the ability to control others or to exist independently of "power-structured" relationships.

This definition helps us to understand the life and professional accomplishments of Victoria zu Bentheim und Steinfurt, who was a woman architect *and* an aristocrat. As a member of the European high nobility, she had

---

1   Stratigakos (1999), especially 354–380 and Appendix 1, 389–390.

2   Kiem (2017), 95–104. Unless otherwise noted, the biographical information about Victoria zu Bentheim und Steinfurt is taken from this publication and the sources cited there.

3   Millett (orig. 196; 1980), 31–32.

Figure 1: Princess Victoria zu Bentheim und Steinfurt, late 1930s.
Source: Fürstliches Archiv, Burgsteinfurt.

power over people and was not required to conform exclusively to the prevailing mores of modern bourgeois society. Her class status also shielded her from the usual prejudices about gender roles, which limited the opportunities that were available to her bourgeois sisters. (Figure 1)

Architects of the European aristocracy

The modern architect emerged in the 19th century. He was a middle-class man, who studied at a technical university, underwent an apprenticeship in an architectural office and then either worked as an employee, ran his own practice or labored in a public bureaucracy.[4] Needless to say, women were excluded from this professional ideal. But as a member of the high nobility, Victoria could look to another, much longer, tradition to affirm her desire to become an architect. And this tradition included both women and men.

---

4 See Pfammatter (1997).

The ability on the part of the European high nobility to wield influence, exert power and control vast amounts of wealth has its roots in the Middle Ages. During this period, their ancestors constructed castles, defended themselves from attack, ruled the surrounding countryside and lived off the tributes that were paid to them by their subjects. Victoria's ancestors, the Counts zu Bentheim und Steinfurt, for example, occupied the two basic types of medieval castles, one built on a mountain, a hill castle, in the village of Bad Bentheim, and the other surrounded by a moat, a water castle, next to the town of Burgsteinfurt. In return for their privileges, the nobles were obliged to go to war as knights when the emperor demanded their support. As the techniques of war evolved, notably with the introduction of firearms, the nobles were no longer required to serve as warrior knights to protect their subjects. For this reason, during the Baroque period, their political influence decreased. At the same time, their administrative and representative obligations became more important, and it was necessary for their children to master a range of skills including foreign languages, poetry, drawing, painting and music, as well as to have a basic understanding of architectural and engineering concepts. Depending on the status and wealth of the noble family, tutors could be renowned scientists or famous artists. As women of the nobility could also become rulers, some received excellent educations. And these powerful women could act as role models for younger women as well.[5]

During the Baroque period, many nobles were engaged in building activities. On the one hand, their palace architecture and grounds had to adequately reflect their wealth and status. On the other, their income increased when their subjects resided in decent houses, built by using cost-saving methods. Thus, they were very concerned about architecture because it enabled them to affirm their status and to exert control over other people.

The nobility was educated to become well-informed clients, who were able to communicate what a proposed building should look like and how it should function. They hired architects to develop their ideas, produce construction drawings and manage a building site. And if the completed edifice did not meet the expectations of their aristocratic clients, it could be a disaster for the architect! In this manner, several noble women undertook the role of the client-architect. Sophie von Hannover, born Sophie von der

---

5 Malinowski (orig. 2003; 2004), passim.

Pfalz (1630-1714), spent three decades overseeing the planning of the *Große Garten* of Herrenhausen in Hannover[6] and Wilhelmina of Prussia (1709-1758), as the Markgravine of Brandenburg-Bayreuth, directed a building program that included gardens and monuments in Bayreuth.[7] In the 19th century, the Empress Friedrich, born Victoria of Great Britain and Ireland (1840-1901), had "English type" sanitary rooms installed in her palaces and castles in Germany and introduced British horticultural practices to the Sanssouci Park in Potsdam. As a widow, she supervised the building of Castle Friedrichshof and its gardens in Kronberg.[8]

Sometimes wealthy nobles became obsessed with architecture. One such figure was an ancestor of Victoria zu Bentheim und Steinfurt, namely Count Karl Paul Ernst von Bentheim-Steinfurt. In 1765, he created a French park on land adjacent to the Steinfurt castle and populated it with pavilions and monuments. His son, Ludwig Wilhelm Geldricus, inherited this obsession. In 1791 he documented this architecture which included a Chinese palace; Greek, Roman and Moorish temples; pyramidal towers; ruins; waterworks and farmhouses. At its high point the park had 93 structures. During the winter months, the count often traveled anonymously with his architect to foreign countries to study new buildings. After the Napoleonic Wars the park went into decline. A local researcher documented the history of this park[9] and published his findings in 1907 and 1909, which may have also inspired Victoria zu Bentheim und Steinfurt to study architecture. Along with her older sister Elisabeth, who became an accomplished painter, she received an excellent education from private tutors.

Although Victoria initially encountered resistance among the nobility when she expressed an interest in acquiring a university education, she received support from her aunt, Queen Sofia of Sweden, who quashed the objections of her relatives and championed her cause.[10] Combined with her

6 https://www.hannover.de/Herrenhausen/Museum-Schloss-Herrenhausen/Historische-Persönlichkeiten/Sophie-von-Hannover, accessed on October 7, 2020.

7 https://de.wikipedia.org/wiki/Wilhelmine_von_Preußen_(1709–1758), accessed on October 7, 2020.

8 Siemer (1997), 131–133; 137–139.

9 Döhmann (1907, 1909).

10 Schock (1961).

intelligence and self-confidence, Victoria zu Bentheim und Steinfurt was well equipped to become a successful architect.

The Royal Bentheim Building Authority

As previously mentioned, the nobility descended from medieval warriors, and in the modern period they adapted this role to assume positions of leadership in the military. For example, Victoria zu Bentheim und Steinfurt's grandfather, Ludwig, was a major general in the Prussian army and her father, Alexis, was also a major general and had fought in the 1870–71 Franco-Prussian War.[11] Educated by private tutors, she took her *Abitur* (academic high school completion examination) at the *Gymnasium* in Osnabrück and enrolled at the Technical University of Berlin-Charlottenburg in 1913. This institution had developed out of the Prussian *Bauakademie* (Building Academy) where architects had been trained to serve in the construction authorities of the Prussian king, and later, the emperor.[12] During the First World War, her close friend, Elisabeth von Knobelsdorff, the first woman in Germany to receive the Diploma Engineer degree in architecture and also the daughter of a Prussian general, worked as an architect for the Prussian military. On two occasions, Victoria zu Bentheim und Steinfurt interrupted her studies to join her friend as an architectural apprentice, first at the military headquarters in Döberitz near Berlin and later in occupied northern France, where she produced measured drawings of historic monuments.[13] Victoria graduated in 1919 and, following in the footsteps of Elisabeth von Knobelsdorff, applied to and was accepted as a member of the prestigious Architects and Engineers Society (AIV) in Berlin.

She then returned to Burgsteinfurt and, for roughly a decade and a half, took up the building practices associated with past generations of the nobility. Having heavily invested in war bonds, her family endured large financial

---

11 https://de.wikipedia.org/wiki/Ludwig_zu_Bentheim_und_Steinfurt, accessed on October 8, 2020; https://de.wikipedia.org/wiki/Alexis_zu_Bentheim_und_Steinfurt, accessed on October 8, 2020.

12 Strecke/Geheimes Staatsarchiv Preußischer Kulturbesitz/Kunstbibliothek Berlin (eds.) (2000), 161–66.

13 Stratigakos (2007).

losses and was intent on improving conditions on their estates to make them more productive. The newly established Royal Bentheim Building Authority was created for this purpose. As its sole architect, Victoria designed agricultural structures; additional buildings for the castle; furniture; housing; monuments to the fallen in the First World War; and planned pastures for grazing cattle. Her family had inherited estates in Gaildorf in Bavaria, and her activities extended to this location as well. (Figure 2) Within a few years she had produced an impressive oeuvre; upon at least two occasions, she exhibited drawings and photographs documenting the work of the Royal Bentheim Building Authority at meetings of the German Agricultural Society.[14] (Figure 3)

Although Victoria zu Bentheim und Steinfurt was active as an architect into the early 1940s, starting in the mid 1930s her productivity declined. Her brother, Count Victor Adolf, who had become head of the family in 1919, had been widowed in 1925. He remarried in 1931, and this new arrangement may have given her cause to leave Burgsteinfurt. For whatever reason, in 1935, she relocated to Mittenwald, a small town in the Bavarian Alps on the border to Austria. In 1937, she purchased a large house there which she sometimes ran as a pension. Her professional activity now resembled that of an architect in private practice. Drawings for residential work and a few public buildings from this time exist, but it is not known to what extent these projects were realized.

Victoria zu Bentheim und Steinfurt in the 1930s and 1940s

In 1933 Victoria zu Bentheim und Steinfurt joined the Nazi party, yet there is no evidence that she built for them. Stephan Malinowski notes that many of Germany's high nobility were attracted to the Nazi party because they were encouraged to believe that this organization would restore their status and rule. They turned a blind eye to this party's extreme programmatic intentions.[15] Victoria does not appear to have been an enthusiastic follower.

---

14 Photographs and sketches documenting exhibitions in 1925 and 1930 at the *DLG – Deutsche Landwirtschafts-Gesellschaft* (German Agricultural Society) are found in the Victoria zu Bentheim Papers, Burg Steinfurt.

15 Malinowski (orig. 2003; 2004), 583.

Figure 2: Guardhouse. Schloss Gaildorf, Victoria zu Bentheim und Steinfurt, 1920. Source: Mary Pepchinski.

Figure 3: Exhibition of the Royal Bentheim Building Authority at the German Agricultural Society or DLG (Deutsche Landwirtschafts-Gesellschaft), Exhibition, Stuttgart 1925. Source: Fürstliches Archiv, Burgsteinfurt.

In 1941, due to her inactivity, she was given a formal warning and her membership in the *Reichskulturkammer* (German Chamber of Culture), which also licensed the work of professional architects, was revoked in 1941.[16]

It is also possible that Victoria zu Bentheim und Steinfurt was not concerned about or aware of the potential repercussions that political engagement might entail, and she never renounced her membership in the Nazi party. According to Stefan Malinowski, this stance may also have reflected a "double misunderstanding": whereas the Nazis never intended the nobility to regain the power that it had previously wielded, the nobility, who had been accustomed to asserting their authority on their ancestral lands, often failed to conform to the dictates set down by this political organization.[17] With this disparity in mind, it is worth noting that during the war she did not care much about Nazi politics. Testimonials written after 1945 state that she hid ritual artifacts and books used by the anthroposophically-oriented Christian congregation in Mittenwald, which the Nazis had banned, and aided Jewish families on two occasions.[18]

Having been a member of the Nazi party, Victoria zu Bentheim und Steinfurt worked hard to clear her name after World War Two. In her denazification process, her first petition resulted in a judgement against her, declaring that she was a *Mitläufer* (nominal party member). Although the case would have been closed if she had accepted the judgement and paid a fine and the court fees, it was important for her to have this decision rescinded. She hired a lawyer who was able to have her exonerated in 1949. Her appeal included sworn statements from those she had actively helped in addition to her mention of powerful persons in British diplomacy who would testify to her innocence.[19] Due to her extremely well-connected, extended noble family, she could rely on the aid of influential persons to support her cause if need be.

16 Garmisch-Partenkirchen Tribunal, file number A8-127/1285/47, carton 4234, SpkA K 4234 Bentheim & Steinfurt, Meldebogen, State Archive Munich.

17 See Kiem (2017) footnote 2, especially 102–103 and footnote 55.

18 Grossmann (orig. 1959; 1961), 103–7, especially 106–7.

19 Garmisch-Partenkirchen Tribunal, file number A8-127/1285/47, carton 4234, SpkA K 4234 Bentheim & Steinfurt, State Archive Munich.

Gender and architecture, power and privilege

Viewed with the framework of this publication—namely gender, architecture and politics—Victoria zu Bentheim und Steinfurt should be understood as a cross-over figure. She bridged the spheres inhabited by two distinct classes, the nobility and the bourgeois. Her practice of architecture was very much rooted in the tradition of the noble-architect who built on her family's estate to uphold their status, enrich their wealth and control those who were her subjects or employees. In choosing to study, earn the Diploma Engineer degree and even to participate in what we today call *Baukultur* (architecture culture), like organizing exhibitions of her work for the Royal Bentheim Building Authority or joining a professional organization, she affiliated herself with that handful of pioneering women, largely from the middle class, who sought a role for themselves in public life. Despite these activities, she remained free of the typical day-to-day struggles that architects endure to maintain and please clients as well as to earn a living from their work. Being a member of the nobility also shielded her, to a large degree, from the prevailing bourgeois gender prejudices that a non-noble woman architect would have encountered during her lifetime.

Unlike middle class women, when her actions in modern society were chastised or when she ran the risk of losing status, she could rely on her membership in the nobility to restore her position. Following Kate Millett at the start of this chapter, by the fact of her noble birth, she exerted authority or controlled people through her architecture and also enjoyed exceptional privileges outside of the system of normative bourgeois "power-structured relationships and arrangements."

Translated by Mary Pepchinski

Literature

Döhmann, Karl Georg (1907, 1909), *Das Bagno, Geschichte des Fürstlich Bentheimschen Parks Bagno bei Burgsteinfurt.* 2 parts, Burgsteinfurt.
Grossmann, Kurt R. (orig. 1959; 1961), *Die unbesungenen Helden. Menschen in Deutschland dunklen Tagen*, Berlin: Ullstein.

Kiem, Karl (2017), "The Liberated Territory: Victoria zu Bentheim and the Royal Bentheim Building Authority," in: Pepchinski, Mary/Budde, Christina/Voigt, Wolfgang/Schmal, Peter C. (eds.), *Frau Architekt. Seit mehr als 100 Jahren: Frauen im Architekturberuf/Frau Architekt. Over 100 Years of Women in Architecture*, Ausstellungskatalog/Exhibition Catalogue, Deutsches Architekturmuseum (DAM), Frankfurt-am-Main (30.09.2017-08.03.2018), Tübingen/Berlin: Wasmuth, 95–104.

Malinowski, Stefan (orig. 2003; 2004), *Vom König zum Führer: Deutscher Adel und Nationalsozialismus*, Frankfurt/Main: FTB, 2004.

Millett, Kate (orig. 1969; 1980), *Sexual Politics*, New York: Ballantine Books.

Pfammatter, Ulrich (1997), *Die Erfindung des modernen Architekten*, Basel/Boston/Berlin: Birkhäuser.

Schock, Elsbeth (1961), „Eine bescheidene und beliebte Frau. Erinnerungen an Prinzessin Victoria," *Der Kocherbote. Rundschau für den Schwäbischen Wald*, August 2, 1961.

Siemer, Meinolf (1997), „Kaiserin Friedrich als Bauherrin, Kunstsammlerin und Mäzenin—»Das schönste Ziel wäre wohl ein ganz neues Gebäude ...«," in: Wilfried Rogasch (ed.): *Victoria &Albert, Vicky & The Kaiser*, Ausstellungskatalog, Deutsches Historisches Museum, Berlin (10.01.-25.03.1997), Ostfildern-Ruit: Verlag Gerd Hatje, 131–133; 137–139.

Stratigakos, Despina Maria (1999), *Skirts and Scaffolding. Architects, gender, and design in Wilhelmine Germany*, Dissertation Bryn Mawr College, Bryn Mawr, Pa. USA; Ann Arbor [Mich.]: University Microfilms.

Stratigakos, Despina (2007), "The Professional Spoils of War: German Women Architects and World War 1," *Journal of the Society of Architectural Historians*, vol. 66, 2007, 467–75.

Strecke, Reinhard/Geheimes Staatsarchiv Preußischer Kulturbesitz/Kunstbibliothek Berlin (ed.)(2000): *Calcul und Sinn für Ästhetik; Die preußische Bauverwaltung 1770-1848*, Ausstellungskatalog/Exhibition Catalogue, Geheimes Staatsarchiv Preußischer Kulturbesitz in Zusammenarbeit mit der Kunstbibliothek der Staatlichen Museen zu Berlin, Preußischer Kulturbesitz, 16.02.-26.03.2000, Berlin: Duncker & Humblodt.

Internet Sources

Alexis zu Bentheim und Steinfurt https://de.wikipedia.org/wiki/Alexis_zu_ Bentheim_und_Steinfurt, accessed on October 8, 2020.

Ludwig zu Bentheim und Steinfurt https://de.wikipedia.org/wiki/Ludwig_ zu_Bentheim_und_Steinfurt, accessed on October 8, 2020.

Schloss Herrenhausen https://www.hannover.de/Herrenhausen/Museum-Schloss-Herrenhausen/Historische-Persönlichkeiten/Sophie-von-Han nover, accessed on October 7, 2020.

Wilhelmine von Preußen https://de.wikipedia.org/wiki/Wilhelmine_von_ Preußen_(1709–1758), accessed on October 7, 2020.

Archives

Munich State Archives, Munich, Germany

Victoria zu Bentheim und Steinfurt Papers, Fürstliches Archiv, Burgstein-furt, Germany

"Ideas that may be of benefit to your own country." Two German women architects and the American Cultural Exchange Program during the early post-war years

Kerstin Renz

This chapter recounts the history of two female architects who, together with a group of women from the American occupied zone of West Germany, visited the United States within the framework of the US Cultural Exchange Program in 1951-52.[1]

What was this trip about? After 1945, following a resolution handed down by the allied forces, Germany was subjected to comprehensive re-education policies that were built upon three pillars: Democracy, Demilitarization and Denazification. In the eastern zone of occupation, professionals in the building industry became involved in an intensive exchange with Moscow.[2] In the western zones of occupation, different exchange programs that were organized by the High Commissioner of Germany (HICOG) and financed by the United States Department of State became effective tools to steer the re-education efforts.[3] The study trips took place between 1949 and 1955 and were to give participants an authentic impression of society and culture

---

1 This chapter is based on interviews carried out by the author with Dorothee Keuerleber (January 2012) and Maria-Verena Gieselmann-Fischer (October 2010) in addition to Renz (2017), 229–241 and Renz (2015). If not otherwise stated, information is taken from the diary entries of Keuerleber (private archive) and the written memoirs of Gieselmann-Fischer (saai | Archiv für Architektur und Ingenieurbau am Karlsruher Institut für Technologie (KIT), Collection Maria-Verena Gieselmann; hereafter cited as Gieselmann-Fischer (2013)). The author would like to thank Dorothee Keuerleber for her attentive critique of this text (August 2020).

2 Castillo (2004), 10, 17 with additional literature from the 1990s.

3 Concerning the basic literature about this program: Latzin (2005), Renz (2015).

in the United States. In addition to the three "Ds," long term foreign policy goals, specifically the alignment of the Federal Republic of Germany with the West, lent impetus to the program. Upon their return home, the recipients of these scholarships and travel grants were to assume a leading role as *experts* in the democratic rebuilding of West Germany. In addition to university professors, civil servants or union members, architects and urban planners also took part in the exchange program.[4] The American occupation authorities considered them to be ideal participants because their work presented opportunities to implement democratic procedures such as the introduction of public participation in federal and communal development projects.[5]

Notable participants included: the Stuttgart architect and university professor Günter Wilhelm, who played an important role in the reform of educational facilities in the Federal Republic of Germany and was a member of the committee on school buildings of the UIA (Union International des Architectes) and the UNESCO; Otto Apel who, as an employed architect of the American occupation authorities, designed housing estates and built US consulates in West Germany in partnership with the American firm Skidmore, Owings and Merrill (SOM); and Sep Ruf, the designer of the elegant *Kanzlerbungalow* (chancellor's bungalow), the residence and reception building of the West German federal chancellor in Bonn. Among this group of professionals, there were also female participants.[6] From the *Technical Hochschule* (TH or technical university) in Stuttgart, the architecture student Dorothee Keuerleber (1924-) came forward, and from Karlsruhe, the architect Maria-Verena Fischer (1925-2013) who had just received her degree from the *Technical Hochschule* there.[7]

---

4 In 1950, in collaboration with the US occupation authorities (HICOG), the Department of City and Regional Planning of the University of North Carolina at Chapel Hill, North Carolina, USA offered an apprenticeship program for young architects. Students from universities in Munich, Stuttgart and Karlsruhe participated. See: Castillo (2004).

5 Castillo (2004), 13.

6 A few women architects took part in these and similar exchanges, notably Nina Kessler, Berlin (late 1950s); Wera Meyer-Waldeck, Bonn (1953); Brigitte D'Ortschy and Brigitte Feyerabendt (married Eiermann), Munich (1950). The professional travels of women architects collectively have not been investigated in depth. For D'Ortschy and Feyerabendt see: Castillo (2004).

7 Maria-Verena Fischer's photo album, diverse documents pertaining to the trip to the United States and the memories of Maria-Verena Fischer-Gieselmann (Typescript 2013) are

Concerning the transatlantic exchange of information about architecture, recent German scholarship has concentrated on the period from the late 1950s to the end of the 1960s and has focused almost exclusively on masculine protagonists.[8] Against the backdrop of the post-war construction boom, West German architects like Egon Eiermann, Friedrich Wilhelm Kraemer, Walter Henn or Paul Schneider-Esleben could afford to make privately financed study trips to the USA or were courted and invited by American companies as future partners of the building industry. Frequently the context was that of an exclusive "men's tour group"[9] within a business trip. So far, so much is known. In the case of Fischer and Keuerleber, the initial situation was different. Both understood the offer of a travel stipend to visit the United States as an opportunity to become acquainted with the renowned architecture of North America, which previously they had only encountered in publications and, at least temporarily, to escape from the atmosphere of narrowness and confinement permeating everyday life in the post-war years. Particularly for educated, professional women, there were few substantial career opportunities. At the time when they applied to the program, Keuerleber was preparing to make her final diploma examination and Fischer, whose academic title was a Diploma Engineer in architecture, was working at her first job as an employee in an architect's office and—totally in keeping with a traditional understanding of gender roles—was designing the interior furnishings for the *Amerika Haus* in Heidelberg.[10] In their applications, both women indicated that they were interested in urban planning and educational facilities, of which there was an immense need in post-war Germany. In doing so, they were predestined for the travel program. Like all recipients of the stipendium, they signed a document which obligated them to return to Germany after the trip. In the fall of 1951, they boarded an airplane in Frankfurt-am-Main that was headed to New York, the starting point of a three-month long excursion through the United States. According to documentation at the

---

contained in the architect's papers at the saai (see note 1). The diary kept by Dorothee Keuerleber during her trip through the USA is in private possession.

8 Wilhelm (2008).

9 Ibid, 125.

10 After completing her diploma project under Egon Eiermann, she was employed in the office of Lange & Mitzlaff in Mannheim. Gieselmann-Fischer (2013), 51 (see footnote 1).

United States Consulate, they did not travel in a special program for architects, but as "Experts for Women's Affairs." [11] (Figure 1)

Fischer, a quiet, reserved person, recalled the first meeting with her
travel companion, Dorothee Keuerleber, who she described as the self-confident and extroverted daughter of an architecture professor from Stuttgart.[12]
Despite their differences they became a good team. Although they traveled
with a group of women experts, early on they more or less opted out of the
official program, which made a priority of visiting local women's organizations. In her diary, Fischer noted that their chaperone from the US Department of State requested they make suggestions about what they would like
to visit. The two young women went to the Musuem of Modern Art in New
York, obtained a list of modern American architecture and showed it to the
chaperone. While the latter was delighted to see their initiative and origi-
nality, the two women were satisfied that they would not be spending their
time with "Women's Affairs" issues.[13] The destinations of the women's group
included New York, Washington, Madison, Philadelphia, Boston, Detroit
and Chicago, and then on to Salt Lake City, San Francisco and Los Angeles in
the west, with New Orleans on the way back as the last city. The route resembled those completed by numerous German experts under the aegis of the
Cultural Exchange Program.[14] Yet as their interests differed from the main
women's group, Keuerleber and Fischer were frequently on their own.

Both women faithfully documented their trip. Keuerleber was a passionate writer and kept a detailed diary, Fischer wrote less but photographed a
good deal and made two photo albums with the material that she collected.
These albums give an insight into her view of the United States. Fischer
pasted pictures of a slum and a new housing estate by Walter Gropius/TAC
(The Architects Collaborative) on the same page: the optimistic project by
her professional colleagues next to an urban district with profound social
problems like poverty and racism. The massive disparities between urban,
suburban and rural areas certainly made a deep impression upon the young
architects.

---

11 Herein lies the difference between these two young women and the scholarship recipients who Castillo documents.

12 Gieselmann-Fischer (2013), 57 (See footnote 1).

13 Ibid.

14 Compare Meier (1953). This booklet recounts a trip with the identical itinerary.

Figure 1: "First snapshot in Washington." From the USA photo album of Maria-Verena Fischer. Dorothee Keuerleber (left) and Maria-Verena Fischer (right). Source: Collection Maria-Verena Gieselmann/saai | Archiv für Architektur und Ingenieurbau am Karlsruher Institut für Technologie (KIT).

Like all the recipients of travel grants, the women first took part in a so-called "Training Course in Democracy"[15] in Washington before they embarked on their trip. They had great expectations for the new architecture in the United States. Both knew about the legendary avant-garde architects, many of whom now were living there, but they had little knowledge of vernacular buildings. Keuerleber was enthusiastic about Mies van der Rohe, Fischer had a penchant for the architecture of Frank Lloyd Wright. She later described her encounter with Wright's buildings, among others the Unitarian Church in Salt Lake City, Utah, the Taliesin Ateliers in Scottsdale, Arizona and the Johnson Wax Company in Racine, Wisconsin, as an inspirational

---

15 Castillo (2004), 12.

experience.[16] While in California, Keuerleber enthusiastically discovered the work of Charles and Ray Eames. They made visits to architects' offices and faculties of architecture, including Walter Gropius at Harvard and TAC in Cambridge, Massachusetts; the famous skyscraper architect Pietro Belluschi at MIT, also in Cambridge; Mies van der Rohe at IIT in Chicago; and, finally, Erich Mendelsohn in San Francisco and Richard Neutra in Los Angeles. The framework of the Women's Affairs Program notwithstanding, Keuerleber and Fischer never mentioned being introduced to practicing women architects in the United States who could have served as role models.[17] Meanwhile, when in contact with their contemporaries, American architecture students repeatedly asked them about the Bauhaus and their personal opinion of it. For both women, this was a surprise and they reacted to the queries with helplessness.[18] Educated in the 1940s at two highly respected, academically rigorous and tradition-oriented institutions, they did not value the influence of the Bauhaus to the same degree as their contemporaries in the USA, who had been introduced to the second generation of Bauhaus pedagogy at Black Mountain College in North Carolina and the Harvard Graduate School of Design in Cambridge.

With the destroyed cities at home in mind, both women joined local excursions for selected participants to inspect new urban planning projects.[19] Their visits to residential complexes by local housing authorities in large cities like Chicago, Detroit or New York made them aware of the goals of "low-cost housing" and radical "slum clearance" in addition to the dilemma of real estate speculation. Nevertheless, neither woman mentioned the overt racism in American society and the gentrification resulting from such radical urban planning projects when they made notes about these experiences. Trained as architects, they only discerned the absence of the precepts of modern build-

---

16 Gieselmann-Fischer (2013), 58 (see footnote 1).

17 Women architects received widespread attention for the first time in the USA in two issues of *Architectural Record* in 1948. Only two practitioners in this publication—Marie Frommer and Elsa Gidoni, both of whom had trained and practiced in Germany and went into exile in the late 1930s—had realized public or commercial architecture. In contrast, most women who were featured in this publication had trained in the USA and designed residential buildings.

18 Renz (2017), 238.

19 Castillo describes similar excursions in connection with the Chapel Hill Program for West German architecture students. See, Castillo (2004), 14–15.

ing, namely "light, air and sun," when considering the height and density of these structures. Fisher noted in her diary that a concern for solar orientation was ignored when the Farragut Houses, a sprawling public housing project in the New York Borough of Brooklyn, was conceived.[20] Nevertheless, she observed that the public outdoor areas provided occupants with a modestly welcoming environment. (Figure 2) Keuerleber felt the design of the residential towers with cruciform plans was typical for social housing yet was well executed in materials such as brick and steel crossbar fenestration.

At their request, visits to schools and sports facilities were a key component of the travel program. The architects were more impressed with the atmosphere in the schools than the architecture, and both enjoyed observing the relaxed and unencumbered social interactions among the students. They were amazed at the size and layout of the schools that included: classrooms with natural illumination on two sides and moveable furniture; halls for sport and public events that were furnished with up-to-date equipment; libraries; and generously dimensioned entrance lobbies where the students could gather. Such spaces and amenities were extremely rare in Germany at that time. When inspecting some progressive schools, they were surprised to encounter the widespread use of lightweight, easily assembled construction just as much as the preference of American municipalities for the pavilion school type, which relied on exterior circulation to access some rooms in the southern states. Over the course of their trip, both women developed a more critical opinion of the typical American school, and the commentary in their diaries became more caustic. Even when confronted with modern icons, their sharp appraisals did not cease. Fischer's own photographs of the Bell Experimental School designed by Richard Neutra in California are sober commentaries, and the contrast to the elaborately staged images by the acclaimed architectural photographer, Julius Shulman, of the same building could not be greater. (Figure 3)

---

20 The Farragut Houses, some buildings rising to a height of 14 stories, was a model residential complex built by the New York City Housing Authority (NYCHA). During the construction phase, visitors, especially city planners and architects, toured the site. In 1952 the new inhabitants moved into the first blocks.

Figure 2: Farragut Houses in Brooklyn, New York, photograph by Maria-Verena Fischer, 1951. Source: Collection Maria-Verena Gieselmann/saai | Archiv für Architektur und Ingenieurbau am Karlsruher Institut für Technologie (KIT).

An interview conducted by a journalist from the *Wisconsin State Journal*, a local newspaper in Madison, Wisconsin, with the two women shows the extent to which the exchange program was dictated by the prevailing political conditions of the Cold War. The journalist coaxed Fischer to comment on the political situation in West Germany. Later, she noted with some indignation that certain statements were not authorized by her. The interview stated, that according to Fischer, West Germans lived with the fear that the "Russians" could invade upon short notice, and that refugees from Soviet-occupied East Germany were causing disruption, competition for jobs and widespread anxiety, conditions which could bring about an embrace of communism.[21] (Figure 4) Here, not simply the intended re-education, but more

---

21 Collection Maria-Verena Gieselmann, saai |KIT. The newspaper article is undated. Gieselmann-Fischer (2013), 58 (see footnote 1).

importantly the instrumentalization of the participants in support of the
political propaganda of the USA, was blatantly obvious.

Keuerleber was the first to return to Germany in order to complete her
final project and receive her diploma from the TH Stuttgart.[22] Fischer trav-
elled the final stretch alone. In the State of Tennessee, a highly charged stop
on the study tour awaited her: Together with a women's group, she visited
the city of Oak Ridge, also known as the Atomic City or the Secret City.[23]
Oak Ridge was presented to the group as the vanguard of cost efficient and
quickly constructed educational and residential architecture. During the
Second World War, as part of the secret armament program, the Manhat-
tan Project, the city was a restricted military area. The residents worked
on developing the atom bomb which was dropped on Hiroshima in August
1945. On behalf of the American government, the Chicago-based architectural firm Skidmore, Owings and Merrill (SOM) acted as the general contractor for the urban and landscape design and also planned the residential and public buildings. John O. Merrill (1896-1975), a partner in the firm,
directed the project on site. Here Fischer observed a city that, between 1942
and 1945, was erected for approximately 75,000 inhabitants and seemingly
arose from the ground overnight. Numerous temporary barracks that were
used for housing were in evidence, indicating the haste of this endeavor. The
enclosed "secret" city contained ten schools, seven cinemas and theaters, 17
restaurants and cafés, 13 supermarkets and one library.[24] In the residential
areas, Merrill organized the planning around "Neighborhood Units" where
traffic-reduced, residential estates are clustered around schools and day
care centers. Fischer photographed the prefabricated, lightweight houses
for workers as well as the homes for the executive staff that were built using
masonry. Although social segregation and racial separation were the unspoken tenets that informed the design of the city, she did not comment upon
them. The architecture of the high school, designed by Merrill and for use
by white students exclusively, deeply impressed her; upon her return to
Germany she published an image of it in an exhibition catalogue about new

22 Chief examiner was Rolf Gutbrod (1910-1999), one of the prominent architects in West
    Germany.
23 For further reading, see Olwell (2004).
24 https://en.wikipedia.org/wiki/Oak_Ridge,_Tennessee, accessed on September 25, 2020.

Figure 3: An icon of modern school architecture? Bell Experimental School by Richard Neutra, 1935. Photograph by Maria-Verena Fischer, 1951. Source: Collection Maria-Verena Gieselmann/saai | Archiv für Architektur und Ingenieurbau am Karlsruher Institut für Technologie (KIT).

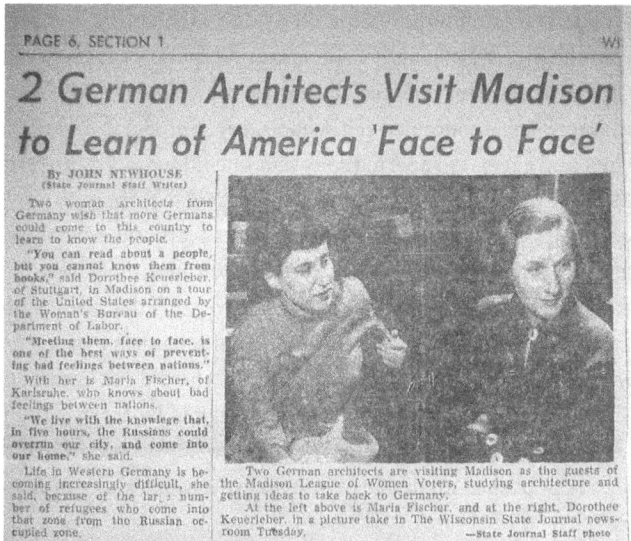

Figure 4: "Two German Architects visit Madison to learn of America 'Face to Face'," Wisconsin State Journal, 1951; Maria-Verena Fischer (left), Dorothee Keuerleber (right). Source: Collection Maria-Verena Gieselmann/saai | Archiv für Architektur und Ingenieurbau am Karlsruher Institut für Technologie (KIT).

school buildings.[25] Furthermore, Oak Ridge permitted unions to organize, and they called for improved working conditions and healthcare while women's organizations lobbied for pay equity (equal pay for equal work) and—as a special demand—social housing.[26] Like the City of Greenbelt, Maryland, Oak Ridge was presented to visiting groups from West Germany as an ideal example of comprehensive new town planning employing prefabricated housing and financed by public-private partnerships. Fischer's time at Oak Ridge clearly demonstrates that only five years after the end of the Second World War, a young German woman architect was able to visit the city which originally had been constructed to destroy her home country. The Cold War had shifted the positions of the adversaries.

Upon her return to Germany, the US Consulate in Stuttgart politely but emphatically requested Fischer to write a report and evaluate the trip. The form letter from the consulate reminded her that: "You were chosen as one of the persons who would not only personally benefit from a visit to a foreign land, but who would also do his or her share in contributing work and ideas that may be of benefit to your own country."[27]

The last part of this statement, "of benefit to your own country," is worth noting. From the perspective of a US authority and in light of the demographic situation post-war Germany, this expectation regarding the future professional and political situation of a woman and an architect may have seemed obvious, but prevailing attitudes about gender only complicated this imperative. In the postwar years, although women made up the majority of the adult population in East and West Germany, the extent to which they could realize their career ambitions relied to a certain degree upon where they resided. In the Soviet Zone of Occupation (SBZ), which became the German Democratic Republic (GDR) in 1949, the integration of women into professional life was systematically promoted and architects typically worked in collective, state-run offices. In a few instances, those who were acceptable to the Communist Party could rise to leading positions in these offices or at

---

25 Fischer (1953), 57. Fischer organized the publication and accompanying exhibition with her father, the architect Alfred Fischer. The catalogue appeared only under his name (!). See also footnote 31 in this chapter.

26 Olwell (2004), 83.

27 saai | KIT, Collection of Maria-Verena Gieselmann.

a university.[28] In the Federal Republic of Germany, women architects often worked as employees in the civil service or were self-employed; they rarely rose to positions of power. Due to the more difficult working conditions and the economic and personal risks associated with becoming an architect, the professional challenges were much greater for women in the west. This was the experience of Maria-Verena Fischer. Looking back upon her USA trip, she recalled it as a time of great personal autonomy and lacking in restraints, an experience that shaped her future life.[29]

Around 1952, she applied for immigration to the United States and the American authorities granted her request.[30] Fischer, however, abandoned this plan and directed a "one-woman" architecture office in Karlsruhe from 1952 to 1957. In compliance with the stipulations of her American study trip, she made an effort to publicize what she had learned, especially regarding educational facilities. In 1953, together with her father Alfred Fischer, an architect and member of the municipal building authority, she produced the catalogue Neue Wege im Schulbau (New paths in school architecture) which supplemented the 1951 exhibition Das neue Schulhaus (The new school).[31] (Figure 5) It contained a cross-section of exemplary educational facilities from Scandinavia, Switzerland and the USA.

The Americanization of the West German Building industry during the post-war years and the economic miracle did come into being, as the Cold War re-education nurtured close political and economic partnerships. But what happened to the two women who received travel grants to the USA? For Maria-Verena Fischer, the most direct benefit was the design of the primary school in the rural village of Pfinztal-Berghausen, completed in 1953. (Figure 6) Here she applied the knowledge that she acquired during her USA sojourn, designing a school with three wings on a large site. It has a spacious lobby with niches for reading and classrooms that were lit from two sides and have direct access to the outdoors. Like an American community center, the building can be used for diverse public activities when school is not in session. Fischer subsequently received commissions for schools, residential buildings, and

---

28 Droste/Huning (2017).

29 Gieselmann-Fischer (2013), 59.

30 Ibid. 60.

31 The eponymous exhibition opened in 1951 at the Orangerie in Karlsruhe.

remodeling projects.[32] She was a successful, independent practitioner until 1957 when she married the aspiring architect and future university professor, Reinhard Gieselmann (1925-2013). Henceforth she subordinated her own interests to the success of her husband.[33] Although the pair officially worked collaboratively, she assumed a traditional role for this time and cared for their two children. Maria-Verena Gieselmann, or Verena Gieselmann-Fischer, as she called herself shortly before her death, passed away in Karlsruhe in 2013.[34]

After the USA trip, Dorothee Keuerleber worked in different architectural offices, specializing in schools and sports facilities. She remained an independent, professional woman who lived alone with her son and never revealed the name of her offspring's father—in the 1950s and the 1960s, this was a small scandal.[35] From 1969 to 1974 she directed the school architecture information center of South Württemberg and, until her retirement, was employed in the Baden-Württemberg Ministry of Culture and Sport. Together with her colleagues (the overwhelming majority of whom were men), she undertook further study excursions to the USA. For Keuerleber, the American educational facilities were not models to be imitated, but rather examples to lend orientation. An American-inspired appreciation for grass-roots processes and a fierce support for women's equality has accompanied Dorothee Keuerleber throughout her long life and up to the present day. In 1981 she was the co-founder of the task force for women architects at the Chamber of Architects in Baden-Württemberg and, most recently, took part in the protests against the partial demolition of the Stuttgart Main Train Station to accommodate the vast transportation project Stuttgart [20]21.[36]

---

32 Her architecture office in Karlsruhe was located at the Stephanienstrasse 31. Other projects include: single family house in Grötzingen; workshop in Bulach; bicycle store in the Kaiserstrasse, Karlsruhe; primary school in Bammental (1954-1955); and the Wüstenrot housing estate und dormitory tower in Karlsruhe-Weststadt (together with Alfred Fischer und Reinhard Gieselmann)(1957).

33 Gieselmann-Fischer (2013), 63 (see footnote 1).

34 For further information about Gieselmann, see, Kabierske (ed.) (2006); saai | KIT, Collection Reinhard Gieselmann.

35 Interview with D. Keuerleber in January 2012.

36 Widespread protests against the destruction of a section of the monumental Stuttgart Main Train station, constructed between 1914 and 1928 by the architect Paul Bonatz, have taken place. Part of the station was demolished to create an underground train station.

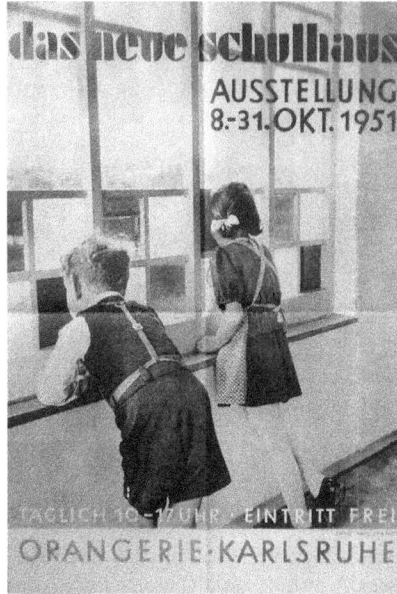

Figure 5: New perspectives: Das neue Schulhaus (The new school),
1951. Source: Fotostiftung Schweiz, Bernhard Moosbrugger Papers.

Figure 6: A large garden and light-filled interiors: Primary school
by Maria-Verena Fischer in Pfinztal-Berghausen, 1954. Source:
Collection Maria-Verena Gieselmann/saai | Archiv für Architektur
und Ingenieurbau am Karlsruher Institut für Technologie (KIT).

The post-war trip of the two young women architects within the framework of the Cultural Affairs Program reveals a chapter of German-American cultural and economic transfer during the Cold War years. After 1945, the USA was intent on influencing the planning and construction methods of the West German building industry, and the Cultural Exchange Program was part of these efforts. Yet their trip was related to other concerns of the time, notably the growing fears of excessive communist influence during the McCarthy Era. In reaction to Soviet pressure on German women's organizations in the SBZ, in 1948 the Americans created the Women's Affairs Section within their military administration (OMGUS or Office of Military Government of the United States) to foster civic education, equal rights and the political engagement of women in the western part of Germany.[37] However, the American administrators did not focus on women in architecture. In the United States, woman architects in the 1950s were not well known, were few in number and faced rampant misogyny in the workforce.[38]

Dorothee Keuerleber and Maria-Verena Fischer were exceptional personalities in the post-war years in West Germany. Both enjoyed favorable starting conditions. After the Second World War, Keuerleber's father, Hugo Keuerleber, an advocate of modern architecture, reformed the architectural curriculum at the *Technische Hochschule* in Stuttgart and, as dean, was a unifying figure at this extremely polarized faculty.[39] A representative of *Neues Bauen*, Alfred Fischer supervised the construction of the seminal Dammerstock Housing Estate in Karlsruhe in 1928/29. In the post-war years, he was an influential civil servant and later became a university professor at the *Technische Hochschule* in Karlsruhe. These two daughters of architects could thank their liberal and progressive families who enabled them to receive a

---

37 Schissler (2001), 849.

38 In the USA, women were only admitted to most leading architecture schools, such as Columbia, Yale and Harvard, in the 1940s. Nonetheless it is worth noting that the well-known American office TAC (The Architects Collaborative), founded by Walter Gropius and seven recent graduates of leading American architecture schools, did have two women partners (Sarah P. Harkness and Jean B. Fletcher). For the situation at Yale: https://www.architecture.yale.edu/about-the-school/yale-architecture-women, accessed on Sept. 27, 2020; For the situation of women architects in corporate practice: https://www.nytimes.com/2013/08/01/nyregion/an-architect-whose-work-stood-out-even-if-she-didnt.html?hp=&_r=2&, accessed on Sept. 27, 2020.

39 See, Schmidt (2004).

university education and supported their professional interests. Yet the main reason for their American journey as stated by their host nation, namely "to be of benefit to one's own country," was not a primary concern to them. They belonged to a generation shaped by armed conflict and the immediate post-war years, experiences which had thoroughly eviscerated such national sentiments. Nevertheless, the journey to the United States was revelatory for both Keuerleber and Fischer. Afterwards they were emboldened to pursue careers in the masculine-dominated profession of architecture. During a period that offered women mostly reactionary notions for how they should lead their lives, the story of their trip and its aftermath is a powerful one.

Translated by Mary Pepchinski

Literature

Architectural Record (1948), "A Thousand Women in Architecture," *Architectural Record* 103, March 1948, 105–113; part 2, June 1948, 108–115.

Castillo, Greg (2004), "Design Pedagogy Enters the Cold War: The Reeducation of Eleven West German Architects," *Journal of Architectural Education* 57/4 (May 2004), 10–18.

Droste, Christiane/Huning, Sandra (2017), "Ms. Woman Architect and Ms. Architect. Social Frameworks for the Careers of Women Architects in West and East Germany," in: Pepchinski, Mary/Budde, Christina/Voigt, Wolfgang/Schmal, Peter C. (eds.), *Frau Architekt. Seit mehr als 100 Jahren: Frauen im Architekturberuf/Frau Architekt. Over 100 Years of Women in Architecture*, Ausstellungskatalog/Exhibition Catalogue, Deutsches Architekturmuseum (DAM), Frankfurt-am-Main (30.09.2017-08.03.2018), Tübingen/Berlin: Wasmuth, 59–67.

Fischer, Alfred (1953), *Neue Wege im Schulbau. Sonderheft Badische Werkkunst*, Karlsruhe/Baden: Braun.

Kabierske, Gerhard (ed.)(2006), *Reinhard Gieselmann—In search of style/Auf der Suche nach Stil*, Stuttgart: Edition Axel Menges.

Latzin, Ellen (2005), *Lernen von Amerika? Das US-Kulturaustauschprogramm für Bayern und seine Absolventen*, Reihe Transatlantische Historische Studien, vol. 23, Stuttgart: Franz Steiner Verlag.

Mikkonen, Simo/Scott-Smith, Giles/Parkkinen, Jari (eds.) (2019), *Entangled East and West. Cultural diplomacy and artistic interaction during the Cold War*, Berlin/Boston: De Gruyter Oldenbourg.

Olwell, Russell B. (2004), *At Work in the Atomic City. A Labor and Social History of Oak Ridge, Tennessee*, Knoxville: University of Tennessee Press.

Platzer, Monika (2019), *Kalter Krieg und Architektur/Cold War and Architecture*, Ausstellungskatalog/Exhibition Catalogue, Architekturzentrum Wien, 17.10.2019-24.02.2020, Zürich: Park Books.

Renz, Kerstin (2017), *Testfall der Moderne. Diskurs und Transfer im Schulbau der 1950er Jahre*, Tübingen/Berlin: Wasmuth.

Renz, Kerstin (2015), „Reisen für den Wiederaufbau. Das Cultural Exchange Programm und seine Bedeutung für das deutsche Nachkriegsbauwesen," in: Panzer, Gerhard/Völz, Franziska/Rehberg, Karl-Siegbert (eds.): *Beziehungsanalysen. Bildende Künste in Westdeutschland nach 1945. Akteure, Institutionen, Ausstellungen und Kontexte*, Berlin: VS Verlag für Sozialwissenschaften, 271–285.

Schmidt, Dietrich W. (2004), „Verantwortung für technischen Fortschritt, Brauchbarkeit und Machbarkeit: Hugo Keuerleber," in: Becker, Norbert/ Quarthal, Franz (eds.), *Die Universität Stuttgart nach 1945. Geschichte, Entwicklungen, Persönlichkeiten*, Stuttgart: Jan Thorbecke Verlag, 106–111.

Hanna Schissler (2001), „Zwischen Häuslichkeit und Erwerbstätigkeit. Frauen in den USA und Deutschland," in: Junker, Detlef (ed.): *Die USA und Deutschland im Zeitalter des Kalten Krieges 1945-1990. Ein Handbuch*, vol. I, 1946-1968, Stuttgart/München: Deutsche Verlags-Anstalt, 847–857.

Wilhelm, Karin (2008), „Deutsche Architekten reisen nach Amerika. Aufbauarbeit in der BRD nach 1945. Amerika in Bildern," in: Köth, Anke/ Krauskopf, Kai/ Schwarting, Andreas (eds.), *Building America. Eine große Erzählung*, vol. 3, Dresden: Thelem, 115–137.

Internet Sources

Oak Ridge, Tennessee, USA https://en.wikipedia.org/wiki/Oak_Ridge,_Tennessee, accessed on September 25, 2020.

Women Architects in the United States; corporate practice https://www.nytimes.com/2013/08/01/nyregion/an-architect-whose-work-stood-out-even-if-she-didnt.html?hp=&_r=2&, accessed on Sept. 27, 2020.

Yale University, Faculty of Architecture https://www.architecture.yale.edu/ about-the-school/yale-architecture-women, accessed on Sept. 27, 2020.

Archives

Dorothee Keuerleber, private archive, Stuttgart, Germany
saai | Archiv für Architektur und Ingenieurbau am Karlsruher Institut für Technologie (KIT), Collection Maria-Verena Gieselmann, Karlsruhe, Germany

Conservative Ideology, Progressive Design
Planning SAFFA 1958[1]

Katia Frey, Eliana Perotti

SAFFA 1958 is the acronym for the *Schweizerische Ausstellung für Frauenarbeit* (Exhibition of Swiss Women's Work), that was held from July 17th to September 15th, 1958 in Zürich. The *SAFFA*'s displays explored the lives and activities of Swiss women, and its pavilions, gardens and landscaping presented an impressive showcase of contemporary design by female professionals in Switzerland.[2] Because the exhibition was to have significance for all of Switzerland, the organizers selected the Landiwiese, the site of the 1939 *Landesausstellung* (national exhibition or *Landi 39*), along the western shore of Lake Zürich. In addition to the Landiwiese, the *SAFFA 1958* occupied the nearby Schneeligut Park and the shoreline along the Mythenquai. The total area occupied a vast, ca 100,000 square meter site. (Figure 1)

The publicity surrounding the exhibition was impressive. A variety of women's associations, in addition to the voluntary assistance of women from all over the nation and official support on many levels (municipalities, cantons, confederation and many sectors of public services), contributed to the propaganda about and the marketing of the event, achieving a high degree of visibility. There was a *SAFFA 1958* stamp, a *SAFFA 1958* stamp page, *SAFFA 1958* pins, *SAFFA 1958* bowls and all sorts of gadgets. All were

---

1 The first research work on *SAFFA 1958*, conducted by the research group dedra (http://www.dedra.ch, accessed on March 2, 2021), resulted in a small exhibition in 2018 at the *Museum für Gestaltung* in Zürich. Since January 2020, the project is funded by the Swiss National Science Foundation and located at the Zürich University of Applied Sciences. The research team, under the direction of Eliana Perotti, comprises the dedra group members, a doctoral researcher and associated experts (http://www.saffa1958-snf.ch, accessed on March 2, 2021).

2 Saffa 1958 (1958a), 2.

adorned with a logo representing the symbol of women—a bold, abstract motif designed by the graphic artist Heidi Soland, who had won a competition for the image.[3] Like the national exhibition in 1939, the organizers constructed and operated a temporary cable car, and there were several boat lines from different parts of the city in addition to a direct bus from the main train station to the site. Once inside, a railway transported visitors around the grounds. A major adjacent thoroughfare was closed to traffic during the exhibition time to avoid congestion and regulate the access to the exhibition.

On the one hand, the *SAFFA 1958* was arranged in thematic sections which explored the domestic and professional activities of women. These reflected the conservative, three-phase model promoted by the organizers as the ideal trajectory for a woman's life: education and professional activity before marriage; motherhood; and an eventual return to the labour market.[4] Several sections, "Housing," "Fashion," "Education," and "Nutrition" were concerned with domestic life. Others, such as "Women at the Service of Community," "Women and Money" and "Recreation and Recollection," dealt with women's activities outside the family. Women's professional activities were summed up in the section "[In] Praise of Work."[5] On the other hand, beyond this restrictive and antiquated framing, the professional Swiss women who designed and realized the event created highly sophisticated modern exhibition architecture. In doing so, they imparted a progressive, emancipated and technically refined image of *SAFFA 1958*—and, by extension, of contemporary Swiss women—to the nation. Although this impression was profoundly misleading, it silenced sceptics and detractors who had bet against the success of a women's fair since the beginning of the venture.

---

3 Cf. „Was bedeutet das SAFFA-Zeichen?" (1958).

4 Cf. Joris (2018), 95–106, especially 95.

5 Cf. Saffa 1958 (1958b).

Figure 1: Aerial view, SAFFA 1958 on the Landiwiese along Lake Zürich, showing the pavilions, the SAFFA Tower and the SAFFA Island. Source: ETH-BIB-Zürich, Saffa-LBS_H1-021321.tif (Open access).

Figure 2: Women architects visiting the SAFFA Tower construction site, 1958. Source: Bequest Annemarie und Hans Hubacher (gta Archives, ETH Zürich).

"The world as a living room"

Largely due to the contributions of women during wartime, between 1918 and 1945, the majority of European countries had granted women suffrage. Switzerland was not among them and became one of the last European nations to give women the vote in 1971. The fact that Switzerland had not been involved in armed conflict during the Second World War had a substantial impact on the division of labour in Swiss society. In contrast to other European countries, the employment of women declined while the number of births rose during the war years. The only new jobs emerging for women were a consequence of the innovative measures introduced by industrial manufacturing.

After the Second World War, organisations such as Pro Familia and the Union of the Women's Army Auxiliary Corps propagated a feminine ideal that reinforced traditional gender hierarchy. In 1945, a constitutional amendment on family policy further strengthened this lopsided dualism,[6] affirming as normative the model of a male breadwinner and an unemployed female, that is, an economic appendage of the husband, and blatantly discriminating against unmarried women. Regulations governing retirement and pensions that were supported not only by conservative politicians but also by the trade unions bolstered this paradigm.

A kind of anthropological argument was constructed to insert women into the labor market and to conform to the prevailing social premises and political arrangements. Within this narrow framework, contemporaneous discourses confined women's contributions to the world of remunerative work to auxiliary, caring and nurturing activities.[7]

SAFFA 1958 was a product of the conservative ideological context of the 1950s. Originally, the *Bund Schweizerischer Frauenvereine* (Union of Swiss Women's Associations or BSF) intended to organize an exhibition about housing. During the planning, they decided to extend the concept to present a more comprehensive exhibition that would include displays not only about the home and domestic activities, but also those illustrating the professional accomplishments of women in public life. This enlargement of the female sphere reflected the middle-class women's movement idea of "the world as a living room," where women were assigned the reciprocal duties of

---

6 Cf. Joris (2011), especially 247, 250; Mesmer (2007), 292–298.

7 Cf. Lustig (1958); Morell-Vögtli (1958); Oettli (1958).

caring, nursing and community building in private and in the world at large to render both more humane and accommodating.[8] The BSF invited all Swiss women's organizations to participate in the exhibition, excluding only the Communist League due to ideological incompatibility. During the preparations, however, the middle-class women's fraction of the BSF, comprised of the Swiss League of Catholic Women, the Swiss Federation of Protestant Women and the Swiss Women's Charitable Association, took charge and subsequently directed the enterprise.[9]

Displaying women's work and creative endeavors

SAFFA 1958 was in fact one of the few opportunities for Swiss women to collectively present their skills and abilities to the public sphere. The first such display was the 1909 Schweizerische Heimarbeitausstellung (Swiss Exhibition of Cottage Industries), held in Zürich and Basel. It was inspired by a similar presentation in Berlin[10] three years earlier that was also devoted to the conditions of home-based production. In 1953, to commemorate the 150th anniversary of the canton joining the Swiss Confederation, the women's organisations of the Canton Sankt Gallen initiated an extensive exhibition at the city museum. Entitled 150 Jahre Frauenarbeit im Kanton St. Gallen (150 Years Women's Work in the Canton St. Gallen), it drew attention to women's achievements in the professional and private sectors, that is, as housewives, farmers, teachers, artists, graduates of universities, industrial workers and members of women's associations.[11]

In 1928, the first SAFFA, which took place in Bern, the Swiss capital, had been a pioneering event and, until 1958, served as the highpoint of the display of women's work and culture in this nation. For the 1928 exhibition,

8 The full motto concluded with an appeal to women: "Let's help to make it more homelike." Cf. Krähenbühl (1991); Die Linie. Bilder und Texte der „Linien" an der Saffa 1958 (1958); Cf. also Joris/Witzig (eds.) (1986), 167–273.

9 Cf. Krähenbühl (2000), 203–205.

10 The Berlin exhibition was entitled: Deutsche Heimarbeit-Ausstellung 1906.

11 Cf., Heiss/Koppel (eds.) (1906); Lorenz (1909); „Von der Heimarbeit-Ausstellung in Zürich" (1909); Ausstellung 150 Jahre Frauenarbeit im Kanton St. Gallen, Abteilung Kunst/Kunsthandwerk. Katalog (1953); Archiv für Frauen-, Geschlechter- und Sozialgeschichte Ostschweiz (ed.) (2010).

women architects and designers erected boldly articulated pavilions on the national fairgrounds. The exhibits drew attention to the professional work and skilled labor performed by women, and the endeavour was a great popular and financial success. Although it advocated for cottage industries as appropriate remunerated activities for women, due to commercial interests, presentations also addressed women as consumers. The presence of such gender-directed advertising there served as the main argument for allowing for similar sponsorship at *SAFFA 1958*.[12]

The organizers of *SAFFA 1928* intended to make men aware of the scope of feminine talents and abilities; their ultimate goal was to gain suffrage and equal rights for women. Considering the restrained calls for emancipation that accompanied the event and the support of it by female activists who were involved in the socialist movement, this proved to be a naïve proposition.

Even the organizers of *SAFFA 1928* could not deny the snail's pace with which women's suffrage was pursued in Switzerland, drawing attention to this situation in the inaugural ceremonies.[13] The great success of *SAFFA 1928* notwithstanding, for the planning and realization of the *Landi 39* a decade later, their competence and know-how was apparently not required. The subject of women was relegated to a small pavilion, located apart from the main promenade, with wall paintings on the interior by the Zürich artist Berta Tappolet.[14]

Whereas *SAFFA 1928* displayed feminine production in a typical exhibition format,[15] *SAFFA 1958* intended to present a more complex and comprehensive review of the everyday lives of women and the kinds of work under-

---

12 Cf. Voegeli (1988); Arnold (ed.) (2001), 112.

13 In 1928, an oversized sculpture of a snail labeled the "Progress of Women's Suffrage in Switzerland" was prominently displayed in the parade for women's suffrage in Bern. At the *SAFFA 1958* exhibition, however, this sculpture was not tolerated at the main entrance to the fair and was relegated to the remote edge of the surrounding forest. Cf. Ruckstuhl/ Benz-Burger (1986), 31.

14 Cf. Arnold (ed.) (2001), 111.

15 The professions undertaken by women ("Frauenberufe") on display were divided in 14 categories, including: domestic economy, kitchen and laundry, the life of the countrywomen, traditional costumes, amateur works and education and nursing. There were also sections for fine arts, arts and crafts, as well as science and culture and the work of Swiss women abroad. Cf. Arnold (ed.) (2001), 113.

taken by them. In 1958, statistics showed that approximatively 700,000 Swiss women or 35% of the adult female population were employed outside of the home. Nevertheless, the political and economic forces shaping post-war Europe caused organizers to evoke nationalist sentiments to frame their gendered show of life and work. Taking place at the start of the Cold War and as a period of economic expansion was unfolding, *SAFFA 1958* turned to the recent past and referenced the Swiss National Exhibition of 1939. The *Landi 39* was orchestrated during a moment of social and political transition on the eve of the Second World War and had promoted the patriotic position known as *Geistige Landesverteidigung* (national intellectual defence). Nineteen years later, the *SAFFA 1958* committee underscored their affinity to common national values of pragmatism and frugality, implying that it was a *Landi* of the Cold War period. Beyond ideology, other similarities—including the exhibition site, the disposition of the buildings and the program—were in evidence. In addition to demonstrating their willingness to be engaged citizens and their commitment to national defence, the women of *SAFFA 1958* tried out a strategy to blunt criticism of their demands for equal rights and suffrage by adopting Cold War rhetoric and favouring general declarations with humanist intent over overt statements about women's political issues.[16]

Nevertheless, the Swiss Federal Government only supported *SAFFA 1958* with the modest amount of 550,000 Swiss Francs, while delegating the sum of nine million Swiss Francs to the all-male national contribution to the concurrent World Exhibition in Brussels. The remaining funds came from the cantons, local institutions, private industry, individual donations and merchandising. It is therefore all the remarkable that the *SAFFA 1958* management closed its books with a net-profit of two million Swiss Francs.[17]

Approximately 500 women were employed in various capacities, such as members of commissions and as remunerated professionals. In this regard, *SAFFA 1958* turned out to be a powerful development program, giving many young women, artists, architects, graphic and object designers, writers, journalists and so on their first commissions. (Figure 2) Through documenting their accomplishments and introducing them to the public at large, *SAFFA 1958* also succeeded, as no other national event of the post-war era in

---

16 Cf. Krähenbühl (2000).

17 Cf. „SAFFA 1958: Reingewinn von 2 Millionen Schweizerfranken" (2000), 983–984; Krähenbühl (2000), 207.

Switzerland, in presenting a representative cross section of the artistic and creative work of Swiss women. On display one year before the failed attempt to gain female suffrage, *SAFFA 1958* was an event of national importance that hosted nearly two million visitors, or slightly less than forty percent of Switzerland's population at that time.[18]

Teamwork – A miracle of cooperation and logistics

The great number of women who actively participated in shaping the aesthetic contours of *SAFFA 1958*—33 architects, 7 interior architects, 2 landscape architects, 38 graphic designers, one engineer, over 30 artists—whose names have mostly been forgotten by Swiss art and architecture history, represent a real challenge for present-day researchers as the documentation of women's intellectual, artistic and technical contributions to the post-war cultural and art history of Switzerland is still in a nascent stage.

The organizers were well aware that the physical realization of the exhibition, notably the quality of the architecture in addition to the materials and the details, would communicate the achievements of women and highlight their professional abilities. Therefore, the choice of the chief architect was decisive. Nonetheless, the person they selected revealed the ambiguous attitude towards female professionalism on the part of the organizing committee.[19] In May 1956, after the committee agreed to the provisory program and drew up a planning chart, they appointed Annemarie Hubacher as the chief architect of *SAFFA 1958*.[20]

Annemarie Hubacher (1921-2012)[21] represented the perfect choice for the conservative organizers: at that time, she ran an office in Zurich with her husband, Hans Hubacher. As rumours go, this fact was decisive for the organizing committee because it was assumed that if she failed, he could step in to help. Hans Hofmann, the chief architect of the *Landi 1939*, had been con-

18 Cf. the data on visitors in: SAFFA 1958 (1960), Appendix IX/79.

19 Minutes of the meeting of the building commission, March 26, 1956. Schweizerisches Sozialarchiv Zürich.

20 SAFFA 1958 (1960), 3.

21 On Annemarie Hubacher-Constam cf. Walther (1990), 43–46; Maurer (2000), 7; Schindler (2012); Hubacher (2014) and Perotti (2016).

sulted and he could have suggested Annemarie, who was his former student and wife of his former assistant, Hans. Moreover, she belonged to the local architectural establishment: she was the granddaughter of Gustav Gull, who was city architect of Zürich (1895-1900) and a professor at the ETH (1900-1929), whose public buildings, like the National Museum, prominently figure in the modern-day city. In addition, Annemarie Hubacher had been in practice since 1944 and had successfully planned temporary exhibitions (such as the stands for the Swiss center for commerce at the international fairs in Brussels in 1950 and in Milan in 1951)[22] and popular, celebratory events, like the sexacentennial commemoration of the canton of Zürich joining the Swiss Confederation in 1951, which her husband, acting as chief architect, directed.[23]

In an interview with Mariette Beyeler in 1994, Annemarie Hubacher recalled that in Spring 1956 she had been invited to comment on the master plan for *SAFFA 1958* designed by the Swiss architects Berta Rahm and Lisbeth Sachs the year before.[24] In fact, at the beginning of 1955, when the BSF decided to organize the exhibition, the study commission approached the architects Berta Rahm and Lisbeth Sachs and asked them for a non-binding, schematic proposal for the exhibition.[25]

The nomination of Annemarie Hubacher deeply affected Berta Rahm (1910-1998), who interpreted it as a rejection of unmarried women, like herself, as architects.[26] Berta Rahm, who had studied architecture at the ETH, was a pioneering woman professional and struggled throughout her life for recognition as an architect. Among her innovative interests, she proposed new forms of housing and communal living among individuals based on mutual affection and interests or the desire to economize. She called these people "incomplete families", meaning those who were widowed, divorced or single parents with children; grandparents with grandchildren; sisters and

---

22 Cf. „Die Schweizer Abteilung an der Internationalen Messe in Brüssel 1950" (1951).

23 Roth (1951).

24 Cf. SAFFA 1958 (1960), 2; Beyeler (1999); Hartmann Schweizer (2020), 180–181.

25 Only the proposal by Lisbeth Sachs is known. For the most part, Berta Rahm's professional papers that record her architectural oeuvre have been lost or were destroyed during her eventful life.

26 On Berta Rahm cf. also Lang Jakob (1999); Lang (1992), 431–471; Köchli (1993).

brothers; or friends and colleagues.[27] An avowed feminist, she was actively involved in women's organizations and in 1963 participated in the founding of the International Union of Women Architects (UIFA) in Paris.[28] Persistent conflicts with municipal building authorities caused her to leave architecture and establish the ALA publishing house in Zurich, focusing on feminist questions and reissuing books by forgotten women writers.[29] In the end, Rahm's participation in *SAFFA 1958* was reduced to the design and realization of an annex to the club pavilion by the Italian architect Carlo Pagani.

Lisbeth Sachs (1914-2002) also studied architecture at the ETH and had worked in Stockholm as well as in Helsinki at the office of Alvar and Aino Aalto.[30] Shortly after receiving her diploma in 1939, she won the competition for the *Kurtheater* (health resort theatre) in her hometown, Baden. She completed it after the Second World War, the first building of this typology in post-war Switzerland.[31] Sachs was a successful independent architect and had a strong interest in the arts. She supervised the construction of Le Corbusier's final project, the 1967 house for Heidi Weber in Zürich, was active as an architectural critic and publicist in addition to lecturing at the F+F School for Art and Design in Zürich.[32]

Drawing upon *SAFFA 1928*, Lisbeth Sachs proposed in her master plan a tower and a suggested that the site be enlarged, ideas that the organisers integrated into the final scheme but without acknowledging her contribution. Eventually, she only received the commission to design and construct the *Kunsthalle* (art pavilion). Even within the limits of an extremely modest budget, Sachs was able to design a striking new building, which harmonized with the overall aesthetic of the exhibition.

The reaction of Berta Rahm to the nomination of Annemarie Hubacher brings up a generational conflict: Rahm, like Sachs, belonged to the older generation of women architects in Switzerland who had to choose between family and career. For this reason, many remained single. Hubacher's

---

27 Rahm (1950).

28 Rahm (1963).

29 Howald (1990).

30 On Lisbeth Sachs cf. Maurer (2003); Jakob (1994); Lang (1992), 535–574; Rey/Wanner (1980), 14–17; Hartmann Schweizer (2020).

31 The building was completed in 1951-52. „Das neue Kurtheater in Baden" (1952).

32 Cf. Rey/Wanner (1980), 14–17.

younger generation, meanwhile, tried to reconcile these choices: all were married, with one exception, to architects.[33] As perhaps fitting to the exhibition's contradictory message, the organizers, who condemned professional activity for women with families, chose as chief architect a woman who was expecting her third child.

The selection of the supporting architects is also interesting: the building commission recommended that contracts be awarded to a dozen women, mostly from an older generation, who had been considered for the position of chief architect.[34] In addition, Annemarie Hubacher probably lobbied for projects to be given to many younger colleagues. For this up-and-coming generation, participation in *SAFFA 1958* was an important opportunity, as it introduced them to a large audience and enabled them to acquire other commissions after the event. Annemarie Hubacher acted as an important intermediary between the organizers and the young architects who did not embrace the "three phase" notion about how women should lead their lives. However, the organizers were well aware that drawing attention to these young, married women who had families yet were able to design and oversee the construction of the exhibition was good publicity; they were independent, liberal, creative, self-assured and—most important of all—none were feminists.[35] According to the organizers, Annemarie Hubacher epitomized the ideal modern woman because she collaborated with men and did not act as their rival.[36]

Advertising post-war Modernity in Switzerland:
International style and technological excellence

In view of the organizers' conservative ideology, their conciliatory strategy, their ambition to emulate the success of *SAFFA 1928* and, in particular, their profound fear of economic failure, the realization of the exhibition repre-

---

33 For a comparison of the architects' biographies, see: Beyeler (1999), 46–47.

34 Cf. Minutes of the meeting the building commission 23.04.1956. Schweizerisches Sozialarchiv Zürich.

35 Cf. B. (1958).

36 Cf. Die Frauen-Landi. Die Gastgeberin Annemarie Hubacher-Constam, dipl. Arch. ETH (1958).

sented an on-going challenge for the chief architect. From the beginning, an economy of means was imperative, and this prerequisite dictated the use of cheap, prefabricated, recycled wooden frames for the structural supports of the temporary structures.[37] Over the course of the planning, several pavilions had to be eliminated for economic reasons because the organizers were more concerned with the budget than with the architectural quality or coherence of the exhibition route. Arguably, their fear of financial deficits implied that they themselves were not convinced that the exhibition would be a success. The chief architect was thus challenged to produce a representative public event with extremely limited resources.[38]

For her part, Annemare Hubacher desired to create an ensemble that was on par with contemporary international exhibition architecture. Despite budget constraints, she achieved her goal.[39] With the exception of the chapel at the entrance, many of the most important structures that she designed were located in the main part of the fairgrounds on the Landiwiese. This included the tower, the movie theatre, the kiosks, the entry pavilions as well as the administrative and service buildings. Thus, her aesthetic predilections determined the architectural image of the exhibition. Moreover, her favourite part of the scheme, an artificial island, which she had planned from the inception of the event, was intended to remain after the close of the exhibition.[40] If, in the collective memory, the exhibition site is still associated with the *Landi 39*, the island is known today as the *SAFFA-Insel* (SAFFA Island), even though many people are not aware of the origin of its name.

The structural wooden frames that were used throughout the exhibition were known in the German-speaking world as *Bierzelt* (tent for drinking beer) construction, an association that the chief architect consciously wanted to avoid. Instead of arranging the frames to form long, low rectangular halls for drinking beer, she assembled the frames to form round pavilions, which was a new and unconventional application.[41] (Figure 3) The roof surfaces were pitched toward the centre of each pavilion to facilitate drainage and to fur-

---

37 Hubacher/Sachs (1958), 352.

38 Ibid.

39 Cf. Hubacher (1958a).

40 Cf. Beyeler (1999), 86.

41 Cf. Annemarie Hubacher, quoted in Wyss (1958), 245–246.

ther distinguish them from a *Bierzelt*. To achieve unity, the chief architect also selected materials and designed elements that appeared throughout the thematic sections. These consisted of white canvas; rough horizontal timber planks; recycled panes of glass; fiber cement boards and a special panel system made by intertwining the white canvas and highlighting it with a metal stem, which lent the surfaces of the pavilions plasticity and could be enlivened by the play of sunlight.[42] Despite the interventions of many different architects, the use of canvas, a cheap and ordinary material, allowed for a formal unity; in 1964. the Swiss national exhibition in Lausanne subsequently adopted it for their representative architecture.[43]

A tower was already present in the master plan by Lisbeth Sachs and recalled the prominent landmark that stood at the entrance to the first *SAFFA* in 1928. A contemporaneous reference was the cylindrical, glazed tower that recalled a tubular electric lamp at the 1958 World's Fair in Brussels. Like Hubacher's structure, visitors rode an elevator directly to the topmost level, from which they descended via stairs while inspecting the displays in the floors below.[44] Although the exhibition at the *SAFFA 1958* focused on domesticity and modern interior design, the tower served another function. Located on the public space of the *Landi 39*, known as Celebration Square, the tall structure provided a point of orientation that was visible from every part of the site, directing visitors to the center of the fairground. Frequently photographed, it became the symbol of the exhibition, its transparent facade revealing visitors moving downwards during the day and featuring a more suggestive illuminated version at night. Demonstrating her technical know-how and ability to work with extreme economic constrains, Annemarie Hubacher built the 40-meter-tall tower using only four types of steel profiles. These parts were bolted together, since the construction company Zschokke had lent them free of charge under the condition that they could be dismantled and reused.[45] (Figure 4)

---

42 Cf. Hubacher/Sachs (1958), 352.

43 Cf. Landesausstellung, under the direction of Camenzind, Alberto (ed.) (1965), 202.

44 Hubacher/Sachs (1958)

45 Ibid.

Figure 3: Detail, round exhibition halls, SAFFA 1958. Source: Bequest Annemarie und Hans Hubacher (gta Archives, ETH Zürich).

Figure 4: Detail, SAFFA Tower, 1958. Source: Neue Schweizerische Illustrierte Zeitung, no. 30, 21.-27.1958 (Open access).

On the island, Hubacher wanted to build a light, seemingly floating enclosure to shelter the restaurant. She selected a demountable tensile membrane structure developed by the architect and engineer Frei Otto that was first used for the café at the *Interbau 1957* exhibition in West Berlin.[46] It was not only an attractive architectural solution, but also a technical novelty because such a structure had not been previously constructed in Switzerland. At the *Interbau 1957*, Annemarie Hubacher and her assistant Anna Cordes also encountered the technically sophisticated and aesthetically pleasing Mero construction system. It allowed for the easy and quick assembly of tubular steel elements using connective nodes to create wide spans without intermediary vertical supports and was well suited for exhibition architecture.[47]

Elsa Burkhardt-Blum and Jeanne Bueche wished to employ this system for their respective pavilions, the House of the Cantons and the Restaurant Romand, but due to budget limitations they made do partly with the aforementioned wooden frames. In the end, only the chief architect was able to take advantage of the Mero system.[48]

The *SAFFA 1958* engaged contemporaneous international architectural discourses in different ways: it presented inventive designs for temporary exhibition pavilions; employed the global language of the International Style; largely avoided national references to local building traditions; and, last but not least, demonstrated an informed and aesthetically refined commitment to advanced construction technology. At the same time, its content and ideology drew upon very conservative and conventional beliefs, a dichotomy that was not unusual for many of the great European exhibitions and fairs of the 1950s and cannot be exclusively reduced to the Swiss situation and the vexing question of women's suffrage there.

---

46 Hubacher (1958b), 2–7.

47 Ibid, 2.

48 Ibid.

Literature

Archiv für Frauen-, Geschlechter- und Sozialgeschichte Ostschweiz (ed.) (2010), *Frauensache: das Archiv für Frauen-, Geschlechter- und Sozialgeschichte Ostschweiz*, Baden: Hier + Jetzt.

Arnold, Martin (ed.) (2001), *Von der Landi zur Arteplage: Schweizer Landes- und Weltausstellungen (19.–21. Jh.). Hintergründe und Erinnerungen*, Zürich: Orell Füssli.

Ausstellung 150 Jahre Frauenarbeit im Kanton St. Gallen, Abteilung Kunst/ Kunsthandwerk. Katalog (1953), exhibition catalogue, s.l.: s.n.

B., C. (1958), „SAFFA '58," in: *Die Tat*, no. 195, 19.7.1958.

Beyeler, Mariette (1999), *La SAFFA (Schweizerische Ausstellung für Frauenarbeit) de 1958 à Zurich. Son architecture et ses architectes*, PhD, École Polytechnique Fédérale de Lausanne.

Landesausstellung, under the direction of Camenzind, Alberto (ed.) (1965), *Construire une exposition. Eine Ausstellung bauen. Building an exhibition*, Lausanne: Marguerat.

„Das neue Kurtheater in Baden" (1952), in: *Werk*, vol. 39, Sept. 1952, 286–290.

„Die Frauen-Landi. Die Gastgeberin Annemarie Hubacher-Constam, dipl. Arch. ETH" (1958), in: *National-Zeitung*, Supplement, no. 343, 29.7.1958, n. p.

Die Linie. Bilder und Texte der „Linien" an der Saffa 1958 (1958) [Bilder: Warja Honegger-Lavater; Text: Marga Bührig; Mitarbeit und Grafik: Helen Sarasin], Zürich, Europa Verlag.

„Die Schweizer Abteilung an der Internationalen Messe in Brüssel 1950" (1951), in: *Werk*, no. 9, Sept. 1951, 113–114.

Hartmann Schweizer, Rahel, (2020), *Lisbeth Sachs. Architektin, Forscherin, Publizistin*, Zürich: gta Verlag.

Heiss, Clemens/Koppel, August (eds.) (1906), *Deutsche Heimarbeit-Ausstellung, Berlin 1906. Im Auftrage des Bureaus für Sozialpolitik, Deutsche Heimarbeit-Ausstellung*, Berlin: H.S. Hermann.

Howald, Stefan (1990), „Eine Pionierin der Frauenemanzipation. Berta Rahm wird 80," in: *Tages-Anzeiger*, 4.10.1990, 12.

Hubacher, Annemarie/Sachs, Lisbeth (1958), „SAFFA 1958 in Zürich. 2. Ausstellung ‚Die Schweizerfrau, ihr Leben, ihre Arbeit'," in: *Werk*, vol. 45, no. 10, 1958, 352–363.

Hubacher, Annemarie (1958a), „SAFFA 1958 in Zürich. 2. Ausstellung ‚Die Schweizerfrau, ihr Leben, ihre Arbeit.‘ Anmerkungen der Chefarchitektin zur Aufgabe,“ in: *Werk*, vol. 45, no. 10, 1958, 352.

Hubacher, Annemarie (1958b), *SAFFA'58. Schlussbericht der Baukommission*, Zürich: s. n.

Hubacher, Matthias (2014), *Hubacher und Issler Architekten. Hans Hubacher, Annemarie Hubacher-Constam, Peter Issler. Ausgewählte Bauten 1946-1987*, Zürich: Blurb.

Jakob, Ursina (1994), „Ein Frauenleben für die Architektur. Lisbeth Sachs zum 80. Geburtstag,“ in: *Werk, Bauen + Wohnen. Balkone, Terrassen*, vol. 81, no. 8, 78.

Joris, Elisabeth/Witzig, Heidi (eds.) (1986), *Frauengeschichte(n). Dokumente aus zwei Jahrhunderten zur Situation der Frauen in der Schweiz*, Zürich: Limmat Verlag.

Joris, Elisabeth (2011), „Geschlechtergeschichte von der Spurensuche zur thematisch ausdifferenzierten Analyse gesellschaftlicher Verhältnisse,“ in: *Traverse. Zeitschrift für Geschichte*, vol. 18, 238–269.

Joris, Elisabeth (2018), „Eigenständig und emanzipatorisch: Pionierinnen der feministischen Selbstermächtigung,“ in: Keeling, Regula Schmid/Hürlimann, Gisela/Hebeisen, Erika (eds.) (2018), *Reformen jenseits der Revolte. Zürich in den langen Sechzigern. Mitteilungen der Antiquarischen Gesellschaft in Zürich*, 58, Zürich: Chronos, 95–106.

Köchli, Yvonne-Denise (1993), „Wie soll denn eine Frau mit Behörden verhandeln?,“ in: *Die Weltwoche*, no. 19, 13.5.1993, 81.

Krähenbühl, Eva (1991), *„Unsere neue Wohnstube ist die Welt—Helfen wir mit, dass sie wohnlich wird". Das Frauenleitbild der SAFFA 1958, zweite nationale Ausstellung: Die Schweizer Frau, ihr Leben, ihre Arbeit*, licentiate, Universität Zürich.

Krähenbühl, Eva (2000), „SAFFA 1958 - die Landi der Frauen" (Bundesarchiv Dossier 12), in: *expos.ch. Ideen, Interessen, Irritationen*, Bern: Schweizerisches Bundesarchiv, 201–218.

Lang, Evelyne (1992), *Les premières femmes architectes de Suisse*, PhD, École polytechnique fédérale de Lausanne.

Lang Jakob, Evelyne (1999), "Recent Acquisitions. Swiss Women of the First Generation: Berta Rahm and Claire Rufer," in: *International Archive of Women in Architecture Newsletter*, no. 11, Fall 1999, 1–3.

Lorenz, Jacob (1909), *Führer durch die Schweizerische Heimarbeit-Ausstellung 1909*, Basel: Kommissionsverlag der Buchhandlung des Schweizerischen Grütlivereins.

Lustig, Beat P. (1958), *Frauen bauen mit: Lebensprobleme der berufstätigen Frau*, Zürich: OFMCap.

Maurer, Bruno (2000), „Zürcher Architektinnen. Zwölf Porträts—elf Bauten," in: *Das kleine Forum in der Stadelhofer Passage. Zweiundzwangzigste Plakatausstellung in der Stadelhofer-Passage Zürich*, Zürich: Colliers CSL AG, 7.

Maurer, Bruno (2003), „Lisbeth Sachs. 1914-2002," in: *Badener Neujahrsblätter*, vol. 78, 2003, 222–226.

Mesmer, Beatrix (2007), *Staatsbürgerinnen ohne Stimmrecht. Die Politik der schweizerischen Frauenverbände 1914–1971*, Zürich: Chronos.

Morell-Vögtli, Nelly (1958), „Die Frau in der sozialen Arbeit," in: Neue Helvetische Gesellschaft (ed.), *Die Schweiz. Ein nationales Jahrbuch*, vol. 29, Bern: Jahrbuch-Verlag, 61–69.

Oettli, Mascha (1958), „Probleme der Frauenarbeit in der Wirtschaft," in: Neue Helvetische Gesellschaft (ed.), *Die Schweiz. Ein nationales Jahrbuch*, vol. 29, Bern: Jahrbuch-Verlag, 47–56.

Perotti, Eliana (2016), "Annemarie Constam Hubacher," in: García, Ana Fernández/ Franchini, Caterina/Garda, Emilia/Serazin, Helena (eds.), *MoMoWo. 100 Works in 100 Years. European Women in Architecture and Design, 1918–2018*, Ljubljana, Turin: Založbe ZRC, 103.

Rahm, Berta (1950), „Wohnmöglichkeiten für Alleinstehende," in: *Das Werk*, vol. 37, no. 11, Nov. 1950, 325–334.

Rahm, Berta (1963), „Der erste internationale Architektinnenkongress in Paris 1963," in: *Schweizerische Bauzeitung*, vol. 81, no. 39, 1963, 687–688.

Rey, Charlotte/Wanner, Katharina (1980), „Man muss einfach besser sein als die Männer. Gespräche mit Schweizer Architektinnen. Trix Haussmann-Högl, Lisbeth Sachs, Beate Schnitter, Flora Ruchat," in: *Aktuelles Bauen*, vol. 16, no. 8, 1980, 9–17.

Roth, Alfred (1951), „Der städtebauliche Rahmen der 600 Jahrfeier Zürichs," in: *Werk*, no. 10, Oct. 1951, 289–291.

Ruckstuhl, Lotti/Benz-Burger, Lydia (1986), *Frauen sprengen Fesseln. Hindernislauf zum Frauenstimmrecht in der Schweiz*, Bonstetten: Interfeminas.

Saffa 1958 (1958a). *Offizieller Führer mit Ausstellerverzeichnis und Orientierungsplan. 2. Ausstellung. Die Schweizer Frau, ihr Leben, ihre Arbeit. Zürich 17.7.–15.9.1958*, Zürich: Schweizerische Ausstellung für Frauenarbeit.

Saffa 1958 (1958b). *Zürich. Katalog. Offizieller Führer mit Ausstellerverzeichnis und Orientierungsplan*, Zürich: s. n.

SAFFA 1958 (1960), 2. *Ausstellung: Die Schweizerfrau, ihr Leben, ihre Arbeit, in Zürich. 17. Juli-15. September 1958. Schlussbericht*, Zürich: Saffa 1958.

„SAFFA 1958: Reingewinn von 2 Millionen Schweizerfranken" (2000), in: Gosteli, Marte (ed.), *Vergessene Geschichte. Illustrierte Chronik der Frauenbewegung 1914–1963/Histoire oubliée. Chronique illustrée du mouvement féministe 1914-1963*, vol. 2, Bern: Stämpfli Verlag, 983–984.

Schindler, Anna (2012), „Annemarie Hubacher. Leitfigur für Architektinnen," in: *Neue Zürcher Zeitung*, 13.7.2012, 17.

Voegeli, Yvonne (1988), „„Man legte dar, erzählte, pries, und wich dem Kampfe aus'. SAFFA 1928, SAFFA 1958," in: *Verflixt und zugenäht! Frauenberufsbildung, Frauenerwerbsarbeit 1888–1988*, exhibition catalogue Bernisches Historisches Museum, October 1988, Zürich: Chronos, 121–141.

„Von der Heimarbeit-Ausstellung in Zürich" (1909), in: *Die Vorkämpferin*, vol. 4, no. 6, 1.8.1909, 1–5.

Walther, Marianne (1990), *Die SAFFA 1958 und ihre Architektinnen*, Diploma Thesis, ETH Zürich.

„Was bedeutet das SAFFA-Zeichen?" (1958), in: *Tagesanzeiger*, no. 182, August 5, 1958.

Wyss, Lore (1958), „SAFFA 58, Schweizerische Ausstellung für Frauenarbeit in Zürich," in: *Schweizerische Bauzeitung*, 19.04.1958, 243–247.

Internet Sources

Women's Research Group DEDRA http://www.dedra.ch, accessed on June 28, 2022.

SAFFA 1958 http://www.saffa1958-snf.ch, accessed on June 28, 2022.

Archives

gta Archive, ETH Zürich, Zürich, Switzerland
Schweizerisches Sozialarchiv Zürich, Zürich, Switzerland

"I do not assert myself."
Women architects in State Socialist Hungary

Mariann Simon

State socialism existed for almost half a century in Hungary. During this
time, the imposition of socialist ideology was uneven, and different manifestations of this political system came into being. After a brief period of
multi-party democracy, the Hungarian Communist Party gained power in
1949. The country embarked on rapid and extensive industrialization which
led to an uprising against the communist rule in 1956. The ensuing three
decades, known as the Kádár Era after the first secretary of the Hungarian Socialist Workers Party, János Kádár, was characterized by an unwrit-
ten social contract: the communist government was not to be criticized or
opposed openly and, in return, individuals were allowed more freedom from
the state than they had previously enjoyed. As a result, whereas socialist ideology had a decisive impact on the status of women, the peculiarities of the
architectural profession in Hungary together with this country's rigid attitudes towards gender only limited the effectiveness of this attempt at social
transformation.

In the first part of this chapter, I discuss the situation of women in general under the period in question and present the position of women architects that was closely connected to the economic and political changes taking
place during the years of state socialism. In the second part, I consider Hungarian women architects of the period using a typical framework for gender
research: How did they balance career and family? How did they interpret
success? Did they achieve recognition according to the normative standards
of this period? And, can it be assumed that women architects were most
successful in architectural specializations that were perceived as being marginal or less prestigious?

State Socialism

Immediately following the cessation of the Second World War, the electoral law of 1945 granted women the same rights as men in Hungary. Thus, women gained suffrage and could stand for election—although men and women used envelopes of different colours at the first joint election. Just one year later, in 1946 all universities admitted women without restrictions, including the architectural faculty at the Technical University of Budapest.[1] As these changes were carried out during the so-called coalition times, they are usually interpreted as a part of the long-overdue modernization of Hungary.

The 1949 constitution, which conformed to the prevailing communist ideology, proclaimed the equal rights of women. Like the new family law, which came into effect in 1953, it declared that "the socialist marriage is a community built on the mutual affection of two free and equal human beings."[2] Women gained the same legal rights as men, but their freedom to work outside of the home was more than a possibility: now it was an imperative. Thus, remunerative labour by female citizens was not only an ideological position, but the government also expected it to be carried out. The communist regime subsequently intensified industrial production in reaction to the build-up of Cold War armament programs. The country needed women tractor drivers for the extensive agricultural production along with women engineers for industry, including architects, to design and build for the construction sector.

Compared to some European nations, women appeared in the architectural profession in Hungary at a rather late date, only after the First World War. Nevertheless, universities actively limited the number of women students. Those who were able to enroll at the architecture faculty usually came from a middle-class family, with a father who was an architect or a building contractor. Although the first woman architect graduated from the Technical University of Budapest in 1924, a recent publication on this theme lists only four women who went on to practice this profession in Hungary prior

---

1 University-level architectural education started in Budapest in 1873. The architecture faculty was integrated into the Technical University of Budapest in 1949. During the investigated period it was the only institution in Hungary where a university degree could be obtained in architecture.

2 Schadt (2002), 18.

to 1940. The names of a few others appear in a university publication, but no information exists about whether they completed their studies or had careers.[3] After 1946, women gained unrestricted access to the architectural faculty, but the number of women graduates increased slowly. Because architecture was considered to be an engineering subject and, as has been noted, the government needed engineers for rapid industrialization, the university accepted almost all applicants. Between 1949 and 1961, the average number of graduates in architecture per year was five times higher than the interwar period. Women, however, only comprised a modest 13% of the total.[4]

Female equality was a key component of state socialist ideology, and political propaganda took advantage of every opportunity to publicize the progress made in this area. A brochure, published in 1960 and devoted to the 50th anniversary of International Women's Day, declared that: "In our country work for women is not an act of coercion but a social need."[5] And: "Equal wages are due to women who perform the same jobs as men."[6] The positive report was illustrated with images of smiling and happy women from all walks of life successfully participating in different kinds of work, from politics to science, industry and finally to the assembly line. This situation was possible because the state provided them with childcare services, public laundries, cafeterias at their place of employment, semi-prepared food and so on. In the same year, the first statistics were published on Hungarian women. This data highlighted the changes that took place in the 20th century and drew attention to the radical development occurring between 1949 and 1958, that is, during the socialist era. Yet, in contrast to the impressive supporting materials and the general tone of optimism, the report also acknowledged one problem. Namely, there was an inverse relationship between the level of wages and the proportion of women in a given profession or line of work: the higher a position regarding its status and responsibility, the fewer the number of women who could be found there. The brochure also published data about the situation of women engineers, noting that women in

---

3 Prakfalvi/Ritoók (2011), 297–302.

4 Between 1949 and 1961, 2330 architectural degrees were awarded. Only 314 were given to women. Az Építőipari és Közlekedési Műszaki Egyetem évkönyve (1949-1960/1961), passim.

5 The liberated women of Hungary (1960), 5.

6 Ibid, 6.

this group received 31% lower wages than their male colleagues.[7] The author explained that this inequality came about for two reasons. Most important was the fact that women had less experience, as the average age of women engineers was significantly lower than that of their male colleagues. Secondly it noted that women tended towards less-demanding jobs because they were still expected to carry out household tasks when they returned home.

We do not have contemporary information about how women experienced the extreme changes that upended their lives throughout the 1950s because, up until 1963—when the stabilization of the Kádár Era resulted in an easing of ideological controls—, the field of sociology as well as the practice of social research had been abandoned in Hungary. However, the majority of university-educated women architects were satisfied with their work, and they were proud of their newly attained equality. "The situation, opportunities and wages of Hungarian women architects are equal to those of their male colleagues. They do the same work as men and they are able to reconcile their family life and career, thanks to social infrastructure like mending services, laundries and restaurants," said Éva Spiró at the first congress of the International Union of Women Architects (UIFA) in 1963 in Paris, the perfect venue to express such sentiment.[8] Even if we take into consideration that the representative of a socialist nation at an international conference had to think very carefully about what she said in public, we have to assume that in this situation, she really believed her words.

After the collapse of the Iron Curtain in 1989/90, research about the system of State Socialism has proposed different conceptual frameworks to portray the experience of women in Central and Eastern Europe. "State feminism," "socialist emancipation," "forced emancipation" and "emancipation from above" are just a few variants which describe a condition where women ostensibly did not have to struggle to attain equal rights. This circumstance was taken as one of the possible explanations to clarify why newly constituted women's movements were weak and disappeared quickly in the former socialist states after the changes of 1989/90.[9] However—at least from the

---

7 A nők helyzete régen és most (1960), 34.

8 1st UIFA Congress Report, 1963. Gertrud Galster Publications, Ms2009-054, 6–7.

9 A study discovered that the so-called democratic opposition of the 1970s and 1980s in Hungary was male dominated despite having several female members and the gender question was never raised. (Acsády (2016)).

perspective of the United States—socialist emancipation did produce lasting results. As scholars of modern Europe, Kristen R. Ghodsee and Julia Mead, note: "And yet, by most every measure, women had a degree of education, economic independence, and legal standing that their Western peers would not have until much later and, once won, always seem on the verge of losing."[10] The authors of this quotation refer to the level of education and the relative economic independence that women attained under socialism as being crucial factors, which made a lasting difference and enabled them to adapt to the new post-socialist society. Another reason can be found in the heterogeneity of female experience and the relatively privileged place that those at the top—as women architects tended to be—occupy in this spectrum. As sociologist Mária Adamik discovered while looking for reasons to explain the lack of feminist movements in post-socialist Hungary, the "liberated women" never constituted a coherent group. Under socialism, women's ability to take advantage of professional opportunities depended upon their economic situation, with the most affluent women, "amongst whom at the expense of some self-delusion it was always easier to maintain a universal (female) identity (work, sex, children) that was not class dependent in the past, was undoubtedly equal with the most advantageous group of men."[11] Those women with the highest educational levels measured themselves in relation to the normative behaviour of the male world, even at the expense of uncritically adopting masculine attitudes towards professional work and private life.

Hungarian women architects

Several recent interviews with women architects who were active during the period of state socialism confirm these observations. Accompanying the change of political system in 1949, architectural practice in Hungary was reorganized, and all architects found employment in large, state-run offices. Soon after they left the university, the first generation of women architects received a job and had the opportunity to carry out responsible architectural work; most of their designs were realized. They had the sense that they

---

10 Ghodsee/Mead (2018).

11 Adamik (2001), 195.

were building up socialism and, even if they did not support the communist party, they felt that they were contributing to the modernization of the
nation. Large state design offices desperately needed the skills of women
architects. Although the office managers were male, some incidents reveal
that a few supported female equality. One interviewee told me that when she
asked the manager if she should sign her first independent design with "Mrs."
and followed by her married name, or with "Ms." and her maiden one, he
answered that she received her degree as Sára Juhász, so she surely had to
use her name before marriage.[12] Nevertheless, women architects strove to
relate to the profession in a gender-neutral manner, that is, they compared
their architecture to the buildings produced by men. In a somewhat similar
manner, another interviewee, who was extremely active in the International
Union of Women Architects (UIFA) during the state socialist period, recalled
that she and her female colleagues viewed the congresses as an opportunity
to present their buildings to a large audience and to prove that they were able
to produce architecture that was equal to the work of men.[13] On the basis of
politically declared ideology as well as a deeply internalized sense of gender
equality, Hungarian women architects felt their attitudes towards work and
the nature of their architecture were equivalent to the outlook and products of men. They did not want to appear inferior to their male colleagues by
asserting that their work might be feminine or embody gender-specific qualities. However, it was exactly this attitude which informed the manner in
which most male architects viewed the architectural production of women.

A gradual change can be detected in the situation of women architects
in the second part of the period in question. Around the middle of the 1960s,
the years of economic growth came to an end. Politicians realized that they
needed fewer people in the workforce, especially those who were less well-educated. At the same time, they wanted to increase the birth rate. Women,
who in the 1950s were considered to be a supplemental labour reserve, now
were sent back to the household—so to speak. In 1967, a childcare benefit,
lasting up to three years, was introduced to secure a woman's workplace if
she took time off to care for her offspring. Although the benefit was targeted
at those with modest education and training, all women took advantage of
it. Even though university educated women usually did not use the full three

12 Interview Sára Juhász, 2018.
13 Interview Mária Fejes, 2014.

Figure 1: Apartment house, Budapest 1961. Architect: Olga Mináry (1929-2000). Minary received the Ybl Prize for this building in 1964. Source: Magyar Építőművészet 1961, 1, 11.

years of leave, the officially propagated "double vocation" only amplified the deeply ingrained attitudes toward women's traditional roles as mothers and housekeepers. For women architects in managerial positions, interrupting their career to care for children removed them from the workforce for long periods and diminished their status within the office hierarchy.

Women architects who graduated in the 1970s had to wrestle with another problem. Those who graduated in the 1950s and in the early 1960s quickly received commissions and were able to build their own designs while they were young and active. Although the number of architecture students who completed their degrees decreased to approximately 140 per year in the 1960s and about 120 in the 1970s, the ratio of women graduates steadily increased to 35%. Translated into contemporary language: just as the number of women architects increased, the market for architectural work, particularly large buildings and representative structures, decreased. At the same time, women architects were being devalued because of their officially declared "double vocation" as professionals who also required time to be mothers and housewives.

Because of the lack of commissions and the fact that many important positions in the large state offices were already occupied, the above-mentioned economic changes affected a whole generation of architects, both men and women. Sociological research about the recent architecture graduates during the 1970s revealed that they felt that their intellectual and creative capacities were unused.[14] Despite the fact they could find a job, as everyone, excluding women who took leave to care for children, was required to be employed, young architects had to wait for a very long time to work on their own projects and assume responsibility. To compensate for the lack of challenging work, young architects participated in design competitions in their free time. The sociological research mentioned earlier did not explicitly investigate gender, but at this point in the study, the author felt it was important to note that significantly fewer women regularly took part in these competitions. According to the researcher, the underrepresentation of women in architectural competitions "is only partly explained by differences in their abilities, but women's lower self-confidence should also play a role." This observation leads us to the second part of this paper: namely to family matters, to how women perceived success and to architectural specialities that had a significant proportion of women.

Areas of specialization of women architects

When turning to the areas of architectural practice that women architects specialized in, I find it necessary to first discuss how they balanced the competing demands of career and family. As Laura Weissmüller's essay in the *Frau Architekt* catalogue notes, women professionals have struggled with this issue, regardless if they were active in a capitalist or in a socialist society.[15] In the absence of relevant research, we have to rely on general information published about women and the fragmentary documentation that exists about those members of the first generation who gained professional recognition: they are known because a publication of an important building

---

14 Szilágyi (1976).

15 Weissmüller (2017).

Figure 2: Machine Tool Plant, Esztergom 1966. Architect: Sára Cs. Juhász (1926-2020). Juhász received the Ybl Prize for this building complex in 1966. Source: The children of Sára Cs. Juhász.

Figure 3: Hotel, Balatonfüred 1968. Architect: Margit V. Pázmándi (1930-1995). Pázmándi received the Ybl Prize for this building in 1968. Source: Fortepan No 65685 http://download.fortepan. hu/?search=65685, accessed on August 23, 2020.

that they designed exists; they won an architectural prize; or had a leading position in the Association of Hungarian Architects. They were few in number, but they served as role models for the following generation of women architects. Those who were married usually had a husband who was also an architect. If he was not an architect, he usually had a university degree and a profession that required academic training. Although the Hungarian government increased the number of childcare facilities in the 1950s, the long, inflexible working hours in the state-run offices were an impediment to the participation of women architects. For this reason, the exemplary women architects of the first generation either had no children, only one or, at the very most, two. Similar information about those women who graduated later and received professional recognition does not exist. Based on the extant research, it is clear that women architects overwhelmingly chose architects as their husbands.

Several studies have been published about how architects, and especially women architects, interpret professional success. On this topic, there are few relevant sources. The afore-mentioned sociologist, who surveyed young architects in the 1970s and later extended her research to those who graduated in the 1980s, returned to both groups in the 1990s.[16] In the interviews, she focused on the architects' rhetoric and their understanding of achievement. She concluded that those who graduated in the 1970s maintained notions about architectural success—which had been impressed upon them during their university years—throughout their careers. For them, professional accomplishment meant the built object, the completed HOUSE (in capital letters), the larger the project the better. In short, success meant productivity, quality and creativity, and, of course, professional and social recognition. As the researcher put it: the architectural ideal overshadowed existential prosperity. The ensuing economic changes, that is, the recession of the 1970s accompanied by the weakening of political power, made it possible for architects to start smaller private practices in the 1980s. However, the idea of architectural achievement hardly changed. In the 1980s success in architecture was still measured in terms of a completed building, creativity and social recognition while the profitability of a practice was seen as a by-product. There were men and women among the interviewees of the

---

16 Szilágyi (1999).

study, but the fact that the researcher did not separate their answers by gender suggests that there were no significant differences.

Around the millennium, I made a series of interviews with Hungarian women architects.[17] The aim of the project was to investigate women architects who already had professional recognition but represented the different generations who were active in the second half of the twentieth century. They graduated between 1957 and 1996, so their activity spanned almost 40 years in architecture. I put the same question to all of them: "What does success mean for you?" Regardless of their age and the different political and economic situations during their years in practice, my interviewees almost unanimously mentioned the joy and satisfaction they found in the design process itself, the intellectual challenge of architecture and—of course—the excitement of experiencing a completed building. Some of them also mentioned that they were able to balance professional and familial responsibilities. It should be noted that the women who I selected as interviewees were all present in the public sphere. They achieved recognition in design competitions, taught at universities and were active in professional organizations, but they interpreted these activities rather as the expression of an internal need, and not primarily as a means to draw attention to themselves. All of them denied that they worked exclusively to be successful in the normative sense. As the architect Judit Z. Halmágyi stated: "I do not assert myself, but if something happens, that could take the country's standard ahead, and I know about it, I pick up the phone and announce that everybody should know. I bustle about to shake up my colleagues."[18]

A typical indication of success is professional recognition: a higher position in the design office, a prize-winning competition entry, or an international or national architectural award. The highest professional recognition in Hungary, the Ybl Prize, was established in 1953.[19] The first woman architect won the prize in 1964, which is consistent with the fact that women had a delayed entry into the profession and the ratio of graduated women architects grew steadily at that time. (Figure 1) If we consider the period between 1964 and 1990, 263 architects were awarded the prize and only 26 were women.

17 Simon (2003).
18 Judit Z. Halmágyi, quoted in: Simon (2003), 110.
19 Schéry (ed.) (1995), passim.

Women won 10% of the prizes, averaging one female awardee per year. In actuality, the Association of Hungarian Architects, the professional organization that nominated the candidates and the Ministry of Building Affairs, the official body that chose the prize winners, adhered to the following rule: one women architect per year must receive an award.

A recurring assumption is that women are better suited to carry out small-scale projects and domestic designs: dwellings, community buildings and monument protection. Data is not available to determine if this statement is valid for Hungary, so I turned to the aforementioned Ybl Prize winners. 13 of the 26 women received the award for residential or public buildings. However, among the public buildings, we also find larger ones, like hotels, a hospital and a sports hall. One award was given for the design of industrial buildings and three were granted to urban designers. (Figures 2–3) The remaining nine Ybl Prize winners received recognition for their work in monument preservation. The approximately 35% ratio of monument preservation awardees, however, did not reflect the total amount of monument preservation work within the total completed construction during the period in question. The explanation regarding this discrepancy is simple: for women, it was easier to work in monument preservation at a time when the majority of architects in Hungary were striving to build a new, modern house.

Finally, we should turn to the women architects who were employed as university lecturers. During the 26 years in question (1964-1990), 13 Ybl Prizes were awarded to university professors. All are men. The change of the political system did not alter this trend: over the last 30 years, other university professors have received this award. Not one is a female professor of architecture. After all, this is understandable: since they entered the profession, women architects have held teaching positions at the architectural faculty of the Technical University of Budapest, but, up until the present day, women have not been appointed to the highest academic rank, the full professor. The issue of gender equality remains problematic in Hungary.

Literature

A nők helyzete régen és most (1960). Budapest: Central Statistics Office.

Acsády, Judit (2016), „Megtettük-e azt, amit az eszményeink szerint meg kellett volna, hogy tegyünk?" Az államszocializmus demokratikus ellenzékének elmaradt nőemancipáció-reflexióiról," in: *Socio.hu, Társadalomtudományi Szemle*, DoI:10.18030/socio.hu.2016.2.173.

Adamik, Mária (2001), "The Greatest Promise—the Greatest Humiliation," in: Jähnert, Gabriele/Nickel, Hildegard/Gohrisch, Jana et al. (eds.), *Gender in Transition in Eastern and Central Europe Proceedings*, Berlin: Trafo Verlag 2001, 190–199.

Az Építőipari és Közlekedési Műszaki Egyetem évkönyve (1949-1960/1961), Budapest: Tankönyvkiadó.

Ghodsee, Kristen R./Mead, Julia (2018), "What has Socialism Ever Done for Women?," *Catalyst*, vol. 2, no. 2, 2018, 101–133.

Prakfalvi, Endre/Ritoók, Pál (2011), „Építésznő van néhány": Építésznők a két világháború közötti Magyarországon," in: *Tanulmányok Bibó István 70. születésnapjára*, Budapest: CentrArt, 297–302.

Schadt, Mária (2003), *Feltörekvő dolgozó nő": Nők az ötvenes években*, Pécs: Pannónia Könyvek.

Schéry, Gábor (ed.) (1995), *Évek, művek, alkotók: Ybl Miklós-díjasok és műveik 1953-1994*, Budapest: Építésügyi Tájékoztatási Központ Kft.

Simon, Mariann (2003), *Valami más. Beszélgetések építésznőkkel*, Budapest: Terc.

Váriné Szilágyi, Ibolya, Pályakezdő építészek szemlélete, *Valóság*, vol. 21, no. 10, 1978, 87–96.

Váriné Szilágyi, Ibolya (1999), „Az építészek sikerképe és retorikája a 70-es, 80-as és a 90-es években," in: Solymosi, Zsuzsa/Lengyel, Zsuzsanna/Váriné Szilágyi, Ibolya (eds.), *A siker lélektana*, Budapest: Hatodik Síp Alapítvány-Új Mandátum, 177–203.

The liberated women of Hungary (1960), Budapest: Athenaeum 1960.

Weissmüller, Laura (2017), "Die unsichtbare Architektin/The invisible Female Architect," in: Pepchinski, Mary/Budde, Christina/Voigt, Wolfgang/Schmal, Peter C. (eds.), *Frau Architekt. Seit mehr als 100 Jahren: Frauen im Architekturberuf/Frau Architekt. Over 100 Years of Women in Architecture*, Ausstellungskatalog/Exhibition Catalogue, Deutsches Architekturmu-

seum (DAM), Frankfurt-am-Main (30.09.2017-08.03.2018), Tübingen/
Berlin: Wasmuth, 17–23.

Interviews

Interview with Sára Juhász (1926-2020), August 28, 2018.
Interview with Mária Fejes (1931-2021), July 22, 2014.

Archives

IAWA – International Archive of Women in Architecture, Gertrud Galster
    Publications, Ms2009-054, Special Collections, Virginia Polytechnic
    Institute and State University, Blacksburg, Virginia, USA.

Maria Schwarz
Architect, wife, widow

Annette Krapp

Maria Schwarz, née Lang, was born in Aachen on October 3, 1921, to Josef and Else Lang, the second of their three children. Starting in 1946, she practiced architecture until shortly before her death on February 15, 2018.[1] In 1951, she married Rudolf Schwarz, the educator, theoretician and noted architect of Roman Catholic churches.[2] They embarked on an intense professional collaboration until his passing on April 3, 1961. Subsequently Maria Schwarz directed his office and, beginning in 1992, continued in partnership with Dagmar Drese and Jutta Stiens. (Figure 1)

During her more than seven decades in architecture, Maria Schwarz primarily carried out commissions for the Roman Catholic church, creating a significant and, for a woman in the post-war years in West Germany, highly unusual body of work. However, she chose not to draw attention to her contribution to the architecture that is attributed to Rudolf Schwarz, preferring a less prominent public role while remaining deeply convinced of the importance of her work.

Upon occasion, Maria Schwarz engaged in publicity, but only to protect the buildings by the office of Rudolf Schwarz when they were endangered. Prominent examples include St. Paul's Church, a 19th century edifice in Frankfurt-am-Main, and the *Gürzenich*, a medieval trade and festival hall in

---

1 Unless otherwise specified, all biographical information about Maria Lang Schwarz and details about her architecture and collaboration with Rudolf Schwarz are taken from: Krapp (2015).

2 Rudolf Schwarz (1897–1961) was a German architect, theoretician and educator. His office completed a number of Roman Catholic churches, and he played an influential role in post-war architecture and urban planning in West Germany. See: Caruso/Thomas (2018) and Stegers (2020, orig. 2000).

Cologne, both of which were damaged during the Second World War. In the immediate post-war years, Rudolf Schwarz had overseen the reconstruction of the exteriors while introducing contemporary design to the interiors. In the 1980s, when plans were put forth to remove the post-war refurbishments, as was the situation in Frankfurt-am-Main, or heavily modify them, as in Cologne, she successfully fought to preserve the post-war architecture. Her greatest defeat was the demolition of the Church of St. Raphael in Berlin-Gatow at the beginning of July 2015, one day before it was to receive official protection as a historic monument.

In her struggle to preserve not only these projects but also the many churches by the office of Rudolf Schwarz, Maria Schwarz launched a contentious debate about the value of the architecture of the immediate post-war years. Such engagement shaped her public persona, and she became known as the *Witwe* (widow) of Rudolf Schwarz. Architectural circles considered her to be the *Mädchen* (little girl), who first worked in the master's office and then became the *Gralshüterin* (female guardian of the holy grail) who administered her husband's estate and maintained his legacy after his death. She was never taken seriously as a woman architect with her own, independent body of work.

When I began to research Maria Schwarz, I expected to write about her life and work just like that of a male architect. However, my firm resolve to discover her own oeuvre, and not see her merely as the wife and widow of Rudolf Schwarz, proved to be impossible. During their ten-year long collaboration from 1951 to 1961, their architecture was so closely interconnected and, for Maria Schwarz, the contact to Rudolf Schwarz and his body of thought was so intense, that her later endeavors cannot be separated from the creative and intellectual labor of her husband. Over the ensuing decades, Maria Schwarz also kept abreast of the condition of their buildings, all the while choosing to remain in the shadow of her husband. Shaped as I am by the self-understanding of the generation of the grandchildren, who were born during the last third of the 20th century and know a very different world from their grandparents, this was difficult for me to comprehend. It took a long time to realize that this apparent reticence was actually a very clever strategy. Whereas the *widow* of Rudolf Schwarz could receive commissions to complete the churches that had been planned before her husband's death as well as invitations to design church towers, community centers or

Figure 1: Maria Schwarz, 2011. Source: © Elke Wetzig.

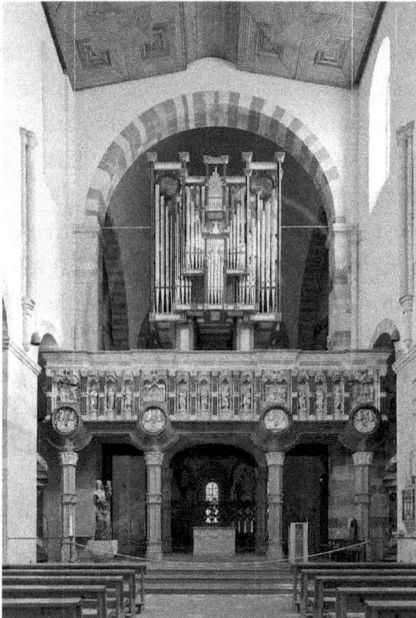

*Figure 2: Lettner-Orgel (choir screen organ),
St. Mary's in the Capitol, Cologne, 1991.
Source: © Holger Klaes.*

ecclesiastic interiors, this would never have been possible for the *independent woman architect* named Maria Schwarz.

In the 1990s, following the completion of the organ cases for two Romanesque churches in Cologne, Maria Schwarz finally emerged from her husband's shadow. The *Lettner-Orgel* (choir screen organ) in St. Mary's in the Capitol, the city's largest church from this period, along with the organ for St. Andreas church lead us to the question: Who in fact is this Maria Schwarz, the designer of such magnificent constructions which fit harmoniously into the naves of churches that were not originally planned to accommodate such a monumental instrument? (Figure 2)

The female student

Maria Schwarz belonged to a generation where it was unusual for a woman to study architecture. Her father had completed a degree in this subject and, although he never practiced, he conveyed his enthusiasm for designing and building to his children. Even though her older brother Elmar was studying architecture at the *Technische Hochschule* (TH or technical university) in Aachen, the family's middle child had to fight hard to pursue her career choice. Her father's reaction to her decision—"This is not possible!"—is symptomatic for the period around 1940.

Between 1903 and 1909, the German states admitted women to their universities.[3] The first female student enrolled at the TH Aachen, where Maria Schwarz studied, in 1915.[4] Throughout Germany, their numbers rose conspicuously during the First World War, but beginning in 1919 new restrictions limited their enrollment. The demobilization law of March 28, 1919 aimed to free up places at universities for the returning soldiers.[5] Against the backdrop of inflation and rising unemployment, a law was passed in 1923 to restrict the "double earners," that is, a married couple where both partners are gainfully employed, which became even more prohibitive in 1933. An academic career was now out of reach for many women, and the

3 Maasberg/Prinz (2015), 31.

4 Mertens (1991), 119.

5 Maasberg/Prinz (2015), 20.

number of female students declined.[6] Some women did study architecture, yet their male classmates hardly viewed them as equals. In 1931 one young man attending the TH Berlin stated that the female students were awkward, unfeminine and extraordinarily hardworking. Although they "brilliantly master everything connected to technology," they do this "in a formulaic manner" and "rarely grasp the essence of technical problems." Nevertheless, they could become "the hardworking and conscientious employee of a man."[7]

Starting in 1936, it became easier for women to attend universities. With the introduction of the first four-year plan and the preparations for war, the National Socialists encouraged women to pursue higher education, and the enrollment of female students increased.[8] Accordingly, Maria Schwarz's desire to seek a career came at an auspicious time. In 1941, she enrolled in the Department of Architecture at the TH Aachen, alongside three female and 25 male students. Trained by a faculty that propagated *Heimatschutzarchitektur* (Homeland Conservation Architecture), a type of modern design that oriented new building on regional forms and materials, the instruction was demanding. Yet the war years could also be a time of opportunity. Maria Schwarz was employed as a student helper and, starting in 1945, as a teaching assistant. She was drawn to René von Schöfer, a professor of architectural design and an archeologist, under whom she completed her final diploma project,[9] and Hans Schwippert, an adjunct instructor who became a prominent architect in the Federal Republic of Germany.

At the close of the war, the vast destruction and urgent need for rebuilding presented staggering challenges. Universities initially reduced their enrollments and returning soldiers were given priority. Sometimes female students had to wait for several semesters until they could continue their education.[10] For a short time, however, those women architects who had recently finished their education profited from a lack of male competition and gained valuable professional experience. As time went by, this genera-

---

6 Frauengruppe Faschismusforschung (ed.)(1981), 142.

7 Erich D. cand. Phys. Techn. (1931). Quoted in: Dörhöfer (2004), 176.

8 Kuhn/Mühlenbruch/Rothe (1996), 69.

9 The theme of the diploma project was a hotel in Gmünd. For the sake of brevity, I refer to the designs by Maria Schwarz without reference to primary sources. For a list of sources up to 2014, see: Krapp (2015).

10 Frauengruppe Faschismusforschung (1981), 162.

tion disappeared from public view because they, just as the Berlin student had predicted in 1931 and just like Maria Schwarz, went on to become the "hardworking and conscientious employees" of their husbands. Their own independent creativity was submerged in a spousal collaboration.

The young woman architect and reconstruction after 1945

At the start of post-war reconstruction, the most pressing tasks concerned the need to develop long-term concepts to rebuild the destroyed cities and house the millions of homeless. Aachen was the first German city to be occupied by the Allies, who entered it on October 21, 1944. As a border city, it had been fiercely contested and lay in ruin. Maria Schwarz worked under Hans Schwippert and René von Schöfer in the initial efforts, and then followed René von Schöfer to Jülich, a small city roughly 30 kilometers northeast of Aachen, where she carried out similar tasks and planned shelters for the homeless.

In January 1949, on the basis of this experience, she was hired by the Reconstruction Limited Liability Company for the City of Cologne. Directed by Rudolf Schwarz, the staff included many male architects who would go on to play a leading role in West German architecture.[11] Here she worked on the preservation of several historical churches,[12] and joined the effort to reconstruct the *Gürzenich*. This monument had been extensively damaged during the Second World War, and the City of Cologne issued a competition to rebuild it as a venue for public events. A team consisting of Josef Bernhard with Rudolf Schwarz and Karl Band with Hans Schilling won the commission. They promptly established a planning consortium, inviting artists and craftspeople to rebuild the *Gürzenich* as a "dancing house [...] all the way down to the last doorknob."[13] Here the notion of the *Werkhütte* (work cottage or work lodge), a holistic community where architects and members of

---

11 Among others: Josef Bernard, Gottfried Böhm, Kurt Jatho, Wilhelm Kleinertz, Hermann Pfeifer and Fritz Schaller.

12 *St. Mechtern* in Cologne-Ehrenfeld, *St. Marien* in Cologne-Kalk and the *Liebfrauenkirche* in Cologne-Mülheim.

13 Rudolf Schwarz speaking on the completion of the rebuilding of the *Gürzenich* before the Cologne City Council in October 1955. Manuscript, HAEK; Pfotenhauer (1993), 53–56.

diverse trades labor collectively, and which Rudolf Schwarz had propagated during his brief directorship of the Applied Arts School in Aachen in the late 1920s and early 1930s, came to fruition in an exemplary manner. This early experience with collective design remained important to Maria Schwarz for the rest of her life, as it reinforced her conviction that the identification of the different contributors to a project, that is so beloved in art history, does not make sense, because in the creative process one idea gives rise to the next and, in a best-case scenario, who suggested what idea is unimportant. Yet she remained deeply disappointed throughout her life that only the male architects were publicly acknowledged at the opening ceremony for the reconstructed *Gürzenich*.[14] Surviving drawings indicate that Maria Schwarz devised innovative details for the long, curved gallery in the foyer and, together with Marianne Hagen-Weyres, was largely responsible for the arrangement of the main stairway. And it is these two elements, when seen from the central foyer, that connect all the representative spaces and make the notion of a "dancing house" come alive. With this in mind, her struggle to preserve this interior remodeling in the 1980s takes on a whole other meaning.

The wife and female colleague

Not only the architectural detailing of his young assistant, but also her personality deeply impressed Rudolf Schwarz. In June 1951, Maria and Rudolf Schwarz married, commencing a professional collaboration and private union that lasted almost ten years. They primarily built churches that today are associated with the name of Rudolf Schwarz, although Maria Schwarz's contribution to thirty of these buildings is clearly documented.

In the immediate post-war years, the need for new Protestant and Roman Catholic churches was a pressing task for architects in West Germany. During the 1920s and 1930s, Germans regularly attended houses of worship. After 1945, newly built churches lent physical orientation to the destroyed cities and towns while enabling their congregations to find spiritual direction and solace. Through participating in weekly services, celebrating holidays or taking part in rituals like baptisms, marriages or funerals, churchgoing enabled

---

14 Maria Schwarz, quoted in: Kier (2000), Manuscript.

people to restore a sense of normalcy to their everyday lives and continue the cultural and religious practices of the interwar years.[15]

How the design process in Rudolf Schwarz's offices in Cologne and Frankfurt was structured; the nature of the collaboration between Maria and Rudolf Schwarz; and the manner in which Maria Schwarz assumed more authority in this practice can be gleaned from the archival documents.[16] As a rule, Rudolf Schwarz made a rough sketch of the concept for a building, and the architects in the office were free to develop it further. For example, for the renovation of the church of the Archabbey at Beuron, Rudolf and Maria Schwarz and their collaborators made hundreds of sketches until the final plans slowly emerged. Besides drawing, each project was the subject of intense discussions. In their house in Cologne-Müngersdorf, the living room and work area occupied the same space, seamlessly uniting professional tasks and private life. "Our buildings were our children," said Maria Schwarz.

Rudolf Schwarz's letters to his wife reveal the intimacy of their collaboration and what deep meaning it had for him.[17] Writing about the church of St. Michael in Frankfurt in a letter dated January 23, 1953, he expressed his profound happiness that they had created the church together, and observed that the interior resembled the *Aareschlucht*,[18] an idea that Maria Schwartz had put forth.[19] Describing the interior of this edifice for a public context in 1960, he explained the significance of this geological formation, noting, "We understood the passage through the gorge as a universal human condition that we then built in *St. Michael*."[20] The same confluence of sensibilities can be observed in the church of St. Anna in Düren where Maria Schwarz's contribution is even more pronounced. Writing to his wife, Rudolf Schwarz described his visit to the bishop in Aachen to present the new orientation of the plan of the church. He recalled that the bishop enthusiastic about the

15 James-Chakraborty (2018), 36–39, and the sources referenced there.

16 Since January 2019, the papers of Maria Schwarz are located in the Historisches Archiv des Erzbistum Köln (HAEK).

17 For excerpts from the letters by Rudolf Schwarz to Maria Schwarz concerning their collaboration, see: Krapp (2015), 39–54; 56–118.

18 The *Aareschlucht* is the limestone gorge along the river Aare, near Meiringen, Switzerland. It is a popular area for hiking.

19 Letter from Rudolf Schwarz to Maria Schwarz from January 23, 1953. In possession of the Lang family. See: Krapp (2015), 39–54; 56–118.

20 Rudolf Schwarz, quoted in: Schwarz/Gerhards/Rüenauver (2007), 221.

change and was delighted to learn that Maria Schwarz was responsible for the clever adjustment and the overall design.[21] In fact, not only this information but also the extant sketches and plans indicate that Maria Schwarz exerted considerable influence on the development of St. Anna in Düren. On one drawing, the signature "M. Schwarz" appears under the office stamp "The Architect Prof. Dr.-Ing. Rudolf Schwarz."[22] This autograph is rare, because, as a rule, Maria Schwarz always signed the drawings with her last name.

In another letter to Maria Schwarz, Rudolf Schwarz expressed his great pleasure that the plan of St. Anna in Düren is from her, and that he would like this fact to be made known widely.[23] At this point one must ask the question why is only St. Anna in Düren considered to have joint authorship? Why not all the other churches that were produced by the office of Rudolf Schwarz from 1951 to 1961 as well? Indeed, in the 1950s in West Germany, women were appearing in greater numbers as partners of architectural offices, usually in collaboration with a husband.[24] After the death of her husband in 1961, Maria Schwarz could have changed the name of the office, but declined to do so. In the exhibition catalogues about the architecture of Rudolf Schwarz from 1963[25] and 1981[26] and which she co-edited, she always referred to herself as a *Mitarbeiterin* (female assistant), the same status as the other architects in their office.

21 Letter from Rudolf Schwarz to Maria Schwarz, undated, on stationery from Josef Lang. In possession of the Lang family. See: Krapp (2015), 39–54; 56–118.

22 HAEK PK67/4 Bl. 10a.

23 Letter from Rudolf Schwarz to Maria Schwarz from October 2, 1952. In possession of the Lang family. See also: Krapp (2015), 39–54; 56–118.

24 "The fifties seemed to be the best time for married couples in architecture: they appeared in large numbers, became imprinted on people's minds as couples, won competitions and built." Schmidt-Thomsen (1986), 20. She lists a number of women architects in partnership with their husbands in various West German cities at that time.

25 Schwarz/Rosiny/Schürmann/Ungers (1963).

26 Sundermann/Lang/Schwarz (1981).

The widow: The inheritor and the woman architect who completed her husband's final buildings

In the spring of 1961, Maria Schwarz took charge of the offices in Cologne and Frankfurt. She retained the name "Architecture Office Rudolf Schwarz" until 1992, when she established a partnership with Dagmar Drese and Jutta Stiens, her long-term employees, calling themselves "Architecture Office Schwarz & Partner." She never used the name Maria Schwarz to designate her practice.

Until her death in 2018, Maria Schwarz was occupied with additions, changes, modernizations, repairs and measures to adapt and reuse the buildings that were executed under the name of Rudolf Schwarz. For more than half a century, she acted as a consultant to many of the churches that their office had built, striving to remain as loyal as possible to their ideas about religious architecture. Maria Schwarz deeply admired her husband and always emphasized that without him, she never would have become the architect that she became in later years. But without his wife, Rudolf Schwarz never would have occupied the place in architectural history that he enjoys today. Starting in the early 1960s, Maria Schwarz assumed another life-long task, namely the administration and the dissemination of the drawn and written legacy of her husband. She was extremely hospitable to students and researchers, staying in touch with them, advising them on their projects and explaining the ideas and buildings of their office. Through influential exhibitions[27] and the reissuance of seminal texts by Rudolf Schwarz, she introduced his work to a wide public.

Until 1967, the offices in Frankfurt and Cologne concentrated on completing the architectural legacy of Rudolf Schwarz. Upon his death, ten churches were in different stages of planning and construction. Even though Maria Schwarz was known as being an experienced architect who was extremely familiar with her husband's body of thought, during the early 1960s she had to fight hard to be given the responsibility to finish some of these buildings. This was not a problem for St. Theresia in Linz, Christ König

---

27 The exhibition, *Rudolf Schwarz - Architekt einer anderen Moderne* (Rudolf Schwarz – Architect of another Modernism), curated by Wolfgang Pehnt and Hilde Strohl, took place at the *Museum für Angewandte Kunst* in Cologne, from May 16 to August 3, 1997 and at the *Architekturzentrum Wien* from December 1, 1998 to January 10, 1999.

in Weinbach-Gräveneck, St. Pius in Hausen, St. Bonifatius in Aachen and St. Bonifatius in Wetzlar. From the very beginning, she was accepted as a competent assistant; in Linz and Aachen she was acknowledged as being the co-designer. It was also fairly uncomplicated to be given the responsibility to complete St. Florian in Vienna and St. Pius in Wuppertal. Yet even until today it is important to note that all these buildings are officially recognized as churches by Rudolf Schwarz. It goes without saying that when I began my research at the start of the 21st century, my desire to research Maria Schwarz's contribution to this collective oeuvre was not always warmly received.

Returning to the early 1960s: When it came to the churches of St. Raphael in Berlin-Gatow and the Heilig Kreuz in Soest, however, Maria Schwarz encountered massive resistance. Hilde Strohl, an employee in their office, had been entrusted by Rudolf Schwarz before his death to plan both churches and she eventually finished them under Maria Schwarz's supervision. In Berlin-Gatow, various authorities had fundamental problems with the design. The local bishop found the church tower to be too small and the passage through the church confusing. Meanwhile the city building department felt the edifice was too big and did not suit the village-like context of Gatow. In the end, Hans Scharoun intervened in support of the project. In Soest, the leaders of the congregation expressly wanted one of the "stars" of ecclesiastical architecture, either Gottfried Böhm or Rudolf Schwarz. Upon the death of the latter, they began negotiations with Gottfried Böhm. The support of both the chief architect of the diocese of Paderborn, Josef Rüenauver, as well as the Archbishop of Paderborn, Lorenz Jaeger, paved the way for the church "according to the plans of Rudolf Schwarz" to be realized by Maria Schwarz. Nevertheless, Maria Schwarz and Hilde Strohl had to submit new drawings at regular intervals over a four-year period until, in 1965, they received approval for a church that was slightly modified from the original scheme.

The circumstances surrounding two other projects, the Liebfrauen in Oberursel and St. Franziskus in Osnabrück, were equally absurd. Shortly before his death, Rudolf Schwarz had received commissions for both churches. Preliminary ideas existed, but there were no final schemes. Maria Schwarz was awarded the contracts under the condition that the designs were from Rudolf Schwarz. Thus, when the official drawings were finished, she signed them under the stamp "The Architect Rudolf Schwarz" using only her last name and listing herself as one of the collaborators on the project.

At the consecration of the Church of the Liebfrauen in Oberursel, the speakers even thanked him for his wonderful plans.[28] Furthermore, in 1965, the Minister of Finance from the Federal State of Hesse and the Association of German Architects honored the Church of the Liebfrauen in Oberursel as an exemplary work of architecture. (Figure 3)

The woman church builder?

In the 1960s and 1970s, Maria Schwarz submitted designs to seven competitions for churches; in some instances, her participation was explicitly requested. However, she was not able to realize any of these projects. It was not always a question of not wanting a woman architect, as the designs that were selected and built seemed to be better suited to their time than those offered by Maria Schwarz.[29] Nonetheless, if one reviews the church architecture of the 20th century up to the present, women architects rarely make an appearance.

There are a few husband-wife architect pairs who built churches, and the authorship of both is acknowledged in the most recent literature. Concerning Roman Catholic churches of the 1960s and 1970s in West Germany, in addition to Maria and Rudolf Schwarz, these include: Elisabeth and Gottfried Böhm; Stephan Legge and Ursula Legge-Suwelack; Joachim and Margot Schürmann; as well as Anton and Marianne Weischer. The few independent women architects that are known to me and who built a church in the 1950s or 1960s are: Lucy Hillebrand, Hanna Kluth and Sigrid Kressmann-Zschach. Lucy Hillebrand, who studied under the church architect Dominikus Böhm in the 1920s and established an atelier in Göttingen in 1945, built the Roman Catholic Church of St. Nikolaus of the Dunes on the island of Langeoog in 1961 and the chapel of the dormitory complex for Catholic students in Göttingen in 1965. Hanna Kluth established her office in 1961 in Hamburg and, between 1962 and 1964, realized the Protestant Cornelius Church in Hamburg-Fischbeck. The West Berlin architect Sigrid Kressmann-Zschach was responsible for another Protestant church, the Jerusalem Church, in West Berlin, and completed in 1968. Only Hanna Kluth received additional commissions from

---

28 Compare, the file on the Liebfrauen Church, HAEK.
29 For Maria Schwarz's competition designs for churches, see Krapp (2015).

the Roman Catholic Church.[30] On an international level, Jeanne Bueche built eight Roman Catholic churches and was involved in approximately 30 church renovations in the 1950s and the early 1960s in the Swiss Jura, a region where she was born and raised. During the 1970s in Brazil, the Italian-Brazilian architect Lina Bo Bardi realized the small Franciscan cloister, the *Espirito Santo do Cerrado*, and the Chapel of *Santa Maria dos Anjos*. How these projects came about is the result of their specific circumstances, and these very few exceptions only prove the rule.

If it is possible to ascribe the small number of women architects who designed churches from the 1950s until the 1970s to their general scarcity at that time, then today this is no longer the case. At German universities women students are now in the majority and women architects have long proven their competence. In the line-up of the architectural stars, however, they are still an exception. They tend to work as partners in larger offices or in husband-and-wife teams, although today the contribution of both is clearly communicated. Yet I have found very few independent women architects who have built a Protestant or Catholic church under their own name. One notable recent project is the small St. Paulus Church of the German-speaking Roman Catholic congregation in Brussels, designed by Catherine de Bie and completed in 2001.[31] Hopefully, this small "rear courtyard church" points to

---

30 During the preparation of this chapter, more information about the architect Gerti Elliger-Gonser has come to light. She opened her own practice in the late 1940s and completed the Protestant Church of Reconciliation in Münster in 1963 with her brother, the architect Hans-Jörg Gonser, who worked for her. The church was demolished in 2018. See, Wolfgang Voigt's chapter in this volume.

31 The Protestant Church in Germany generally has been more willing to accept changing gender roles, and has allowed women to assume positions of authority, such as vicars, bishops and even the head of the church; this is perhaps one reason why there are more Protestant churches by women architects in Germany. The short list that follows can certainly be extended by one name or the other, but it is noteworthy that the Roman Catholic Church in Germany, which does not accept women in positions of authority, rarely commissions women architects. See Gerhards (2002), 30; also: *Das Münster 54* (2001), 297–299. Since the 1990s, women architects who have built Protestant churches in Germany include: Nike Fiedler (Chapel of the Evangelical Academy in Bad Boll, 1994); Ute Grindel (Evangelical Church of the Reconciliation in Moosburg an der Isar, 2000); Jutta Heinze (Protestant community house with a church room in Duisburg, 2005; the Protestant community house with childcare center in Dinslaken, 2010); and Gesine Weinmiller, Weinmiller Großmann Architects (Genezareth Church Aachen, 2018). Three notable recent churches by architect pairs are: Louisa Hutton and Matthias Sauerbruch (Immanuel

Figure 3: Liebfrauenkirche, Oberursel, 1961–1965. Source: © Foto Artur Pfau, Maria Schwarz Papers, HAEK.

future opportunities. But for Maria Schwarz's generation, women architects almost never had a chance to build for the Roman Catholic Church.

In the post-war years, this religion's stance towards women's role in the modern world closely aligned with the prevailing attitudes in West Germany, where traditional gender roles were deeply entrenched. In the early 1960's, the Second Vatican Council's attempts to reform the Roman Catholic Church resulted in the modernization of liturgical practices and greater ecumenism, but not a fundamental reconsideration of the role of women in secular or religious life. Indeed, the last books placed on the Vatican's List of Prohibited Books were *The Second Sex* (1949) and *The Mandarins* (1954), both by the French feminist, Simone de Beauvoir, due to their perceived threat to religious faith

Church and community center, Cologne 2014); Gesche Grabenhorst and Roger Ahrens (Renovation of the Christus Church for use as a church and a choir center, Hannover 2015); and Julia Klumpp and Hermann Klumpp (Roman Catholic Church of St. Paulus in Balingen-Frommern, 2015).

and moral sensibilities. It may have been easier for women to skirt these constraints when practicing in remote places, such as Jeanne Buche in the Swiss Jura or Lina Bo Bardi in Brazil. But Maria Schwarz's architectural office was in Cologne, a city that was home to the wealthy and powerful Diocese of Cologne, which occupied a key place at the center of Roman Catholicism in Germany and was closely aligned with the Vatican in Rome. Considering this context, for the independent woman architect Maria Schwarz, it certainly was beneficial to affirm the image a selfless widow in service of her husband's legacy. As shifting attitudes towards sexuality and changing cultural mores began to upend everyday life in the 1960s, one wonders: Could her reluctance to assume a more pronounced public identity be seen as a bulwark against behavior that appeared to be threatening or disruptive to traditional notions about gender and society as well?[32]

And nonetheless: A woman architect in service of the Roman Catholic Church

Maria Schwarz faced this situation in 1967, when she completed the final church that was begun while Rudolf Schwarz was still alive. The demand for new Roman Catholic churches in West Germany after the Second World War was largely fulfilled and few additional ones were needed. Nevertheless, Maria Schwarz continued building for the Roman Catholic Church for the next half century. Under her direction, the office of Rudolf Schwarz completed various additions, including rectories, parish halls, day care centers and church towers. Following the reforms set down by the Second Vatican Council (1962-1965), Maria Schwarz also received commissions for the redesign of chancels, a task that included the repositioning of the altar and the ambo; the removal of the benches to receive communion; and, in most cases, changes to or the relocation of the baptismal font. When she approached these tasks, she acknowledged the existing architectural and liturgical requirements, while devising practical solutions that did not detract from the original spatial conception of a church. Maria Schwarz acquired a reputation for her sensitive remodeling projects and was awarded commissions for churches that were not connected to the name of Rudolf Schwarz. In her

---

32 For the situation in divided Germany, see: Droste/Huning (2017).

final years, one especially disheartening task involved the decreasing role of religion in daily life, which led to the closing of many churches. Several buildings from the office of Rudolf Schwarz were impacted by this development, and Maria Schwarz strove to identify new, appropriate uses for them.

As an architect, Maria Schwarz was first and foremost concerned about the work at hand. For her, a church had profound meaning, being a point of orientation in a city and a place for solace, prayer and renewal.[33] This quality, to be able to comprehend a situation in its totality, was the precondition that allowed Maria Schwarz, as an independent woman architect in the second half of the 20th century, to be able to work almost exclusively for the Roman Catholic Church. In this way she created an extensive body of work, that reflects, in an exemplary way, the transformation of ecclesiastical architecture since the 1950s.

Translated by Mary Pepchinski

Literature

Caruso, Adam/Thomas, Helen (eds.)(2018), *Rudolf Schwarz and the Monumental Order of Things*, Zurich: gta.

D., Erich cand. Phys. Techn. (1931), „Frl. stud. Ing. setzt sich durch! Eine Umfrage bei Studentinnen der Technischen Hochschule Berlin," *Scherl's Magazin*, no. 2, 1931, 170–174.

Das Münster 54 (2001), 297–299.

Dörhöfer, Kerstin (2004), *Pionierinnen der Architektur*, Tübingen: Wasmuth.

Droste, Christiane/Huning, Sandra (2017), "Ms. Woman Architect and Ms. Architect. Social Frameworks for the Careers of Women Architects in West and East Germany," in: Pepchinski, Mary/Budde, Christina/Voigt, Wolfgang/Schmal, Peter C. (eds.), *Frau Architekt. Seit mehr als 100 Jahren: Frauen im Architekturberuf/Frau Architekt. Over 100 Years of Women in Architecture*, Ausstellungskatalog/Exhibition Catalogue, Deutsches Architekturmuseum (DAM), Frankfurt-am-Main (30.09.2017-08.03.2018), Tübingen/Berlin: Wasmuth, 59–67.

---

33 Schwarz (2006), 164.

Frauengruppe Faschismusforschung (ed.)(1981), *Mutterkreuz und Arbeitsbuch. Zur Geschichte der Frauen in der Weimarer Republik und im Nationalsozialismus*, Frankfurt-am-Main: Fischer Taschenbuch.

Gerhards, Albert (2002), „Räume für eine tätige Teilnahme. Katholischer Kirchenbau aus theologisch-liturgischer Sicht," in: Stock, Wolfgang Jean (ed.), *Europäischer Kirchenbau 1950-2000*, Munich: Prestel.

James-Chakraborty, Kathleen (2018), *Modernism as Memory. Building Identity in the Federal Republic of Germany*, Minneapolis: University of Minnesota Press.

Kier, Hiltrud (2000), „Laudatio anlässlich der Verleihung der AIV-Ehrenplakette an Dipl. Ing. Elisabeth Böhm, Dipl. Ing. Margot Schürmann und Dipl. Ing. Maria Schwarz," Köln 1. Dezember 2000". Manuscript.

Krapp, Annette (2015), *Die Architektin Maria Schwarz. Ein Leben für den Kirchenbau*, Regensburg: Schnell & Steiner.

Kuhn, Annette/Mühlenbruch, Brigitte/Rothe, Valentine (eds.)(1996), *100 Jahre Frauenstudium, Frauen an der Rheinischen Friedrich-Wilhelms-Universität Bonn*. Exhibition catalogue, Dortmund: Edition Ebersbach.

Maasberg, Ute/Prinz, Regina (eds.)(2005), *Die Neuen kommen! Weibliche Avantgarde in der Architektur der zwanziger Jahre*, Hamburg: Junius.

Mertens, Lothar (1991), *Vernachlässigte Töchter der Alma Mater. Ein sozialhistorischer und bildungssoziologischer Beitrag zur strukturellen Entwicklung des Frauenstudiums in Deutschland seit der Jahrhundertwende* (Sozialwissenschaftliche Schriften 20), Berlin: Duncker & Humblot.

Pfotenhauer, Angela (1993), *Köln. Der Gürzenich und Alt St. Alban*, Köln: Bachem.

Schmidt-Thomsen, Helga (1986), "Women in architecture—new professional paths since the turn of the century," in: Union Internationale des Femmes Architectes Sektion Bundesrepublik e. V. (ed.), *About the History of Women Architects and Designers in the Twentieth Century. A first Survey. Exhibition catalogue*, Berlin: UIFA Berlin/Sabine Konopka Verlag für Architektur- und Kunstpublikationen, 13–21.

Schwarz, Maria/Rosiny, Nikolaus/Schürmann, Joachim/Ungers, Oswald Mathias (eds.)(1963), *Rudolf Schwarz. Denken und Bauen. Schriften und Bauwerke*. Exhibition catalogue, Heidelberg: Kerle.

Schwarz, Maria (2006), „Erbe verpflichtet," *Jahrbuch 2004–2006. Verein Ausstellungshaus für christliche Kunst*, Regensburg: Schnell & Steiner.

Schwarz, Maria/ Gerhards, Albert/Rüenauver, Josef (ed.)(2007), *Rudolf Schwarz, Kirchenbau. Welt vor der Schwelle* (reprint of the 1st edition from 1960 with a foreword by Maria Schwarz), Regensburg: Schnell & Steiner.
Stegers, Rudolf (2020, orig. 2000), *Räume der Wandlung, Wände und Wege, Studien zum Werk von Rudolf Schwarz* (Bauwelt Fundamente 114), Berlin/ Basel: Birkhäuser.
Sundermann, Manfred/Lang, Claudia/Schwarz, Maria (ed.)(1981), *Rudolf Schwarz*. Exhibition catalogue. Düsseldorf: Akademie der Architekten-kammer Nordrhein-Westfalen/Bonn: Deutsche UNESCO-Kommission/ Architektur und Denkmalpflege, vol. 17.

Archives

Lang family, private archive, Aachen, Germany
Maria Schwarz Papers, Historisches Archiv des Erzbistum Köln (HAEK), Cologne, Germany

Denise Scott Brown and Zaha Hadid
Peripheries and centers[1]

Kathleen James-Chakraborty

Denise Scott Brown and Zaha Hadid are two of the most celebrated architects of the last half century. They would not immediately appear to have
much in common besides being among the few women to have achieved that
status. Scott Brown is one of the most important theorists of postmodern
architecture. She is best known for her advocacy of what she and Robert
Venturi term decorated sheds, rather than ducks, and for her championing
of the "ugly and ordinary."[2] Nearly two decades Scott Brown's junior, Hadid
first achieved fame as an apostle of deconstructivism.[3] More recently her
parametric approach has resulted in something like the revival of the late
modernist duck, albeit in ways that have only been buildable since the onset
of digital design, which Hadid consistently pushed to new limits.[4]

Biography is out of fashion as a means of writing architectural history,
but when it comes to understanding how some women are able to be influential in the teeth of discrimination, and even harassment, it can still be a
useful tool. Among the many things Scott Brown and Hadid shared were
privileged upbringings on the fringes of the British Empire, educations that
included the Architectural Association in London, careers initially defined
more by teaching than by building, temperaments that, as Scott Brown notes

1 This chapter was written with the assistance of a grant from the Humanities Institute, University College Dublin. I am deeply indebted to Denise Scott Brown for her careful review
and edit of this essay. All otherwise unattributed quotes are from a draft she returned to
me on February 2, 2021.
2 Venturi/Scott Brown/Izenour (1972).
3 Johnson/Wigley (1988), 68–79.
4 Schumacher (2016).

are "called difficult in women and assertive in men," and belated recognition as crucial role models. They also exploited, although very differently, the way in which their habitus, to use Pierre Bourdieu's term for the social conditioning common across a group, as women raised to believe that architecture and design were appropriate domains for women equipped them to cut across the grain of modernist theory and understand how architecture could be used to construct identity.[5]

A number of the twentieth century's most celebrated architects, including Erich Mendelsohn and Louis Kahn, came from very modest, even impoverished backgrounds.[6] Such origins posed obstacles that they were able to overcome at the cost of the educational and professional prospects of their sisters. Until very recently, however, almost all women architects were raised in comfortable circumstances. Exploring their family backgrounds, including the patronage of architecture, oppositional political stances and locations on the supposed periphery in which modernism actually flourished helps to explain the attitudes Scott Brown and Hadid brought with them to the Architectural Association, at which they arrived in their early twenties.

The two women came from well-off families who were on the move. Scott Brown was born Denise Lakofski in Nkana, a copper mining town in what was then Northern Rhodesia and is today Zambia. Located close to the border with the former Belgian Congo, today the Democratic Republic of Congo, Nkana is now part of the city of Kitwe, itself founded only in 1936 after the Lakofskis had decamped to Johannesburg, in part because of worries about young Denise's health. Her parents came from modest backgrounds in what is now South Africa and Zimbabwe to which their German-speaking parents had moved from what had been the Duchy of Courland in Czarist Russia and is now Latvia.[7] Hadid's family were originally from Mosul and moved to Baghdad only after it became the capital of Iraq, a country formed after World War I from three former Ottoman provinces.[8]

5 Bourdieu (1977).

6 Morgenthaler (1999), 10; Lesser (2017), 48–59.

7 "Oral history interview with Denise Scott Brown, 1990 October 25—1991 November 9," Archives of American Art, https://www.aaa.si.edu/collections/interviews/oral-history-interview-denise-scott-brown-13059#transcript, accessed on May 20, 2018.

8 Hadid (2014), 42.

The badges of family prosperity and progressive politics included the houses in which the two future architects grew up. Scott Brown's mother Phyllis Lakofski commissioned a house from Norman Hanson, her former classmate at the architecture school at the University of Witwatersrand, the program in which her daughter would later enroll.[9] Here the Lakofskis welcomed a wide variety of intellectuals, as well as fellow Jews fleeing even more terrifying persecution than the pogroms that had prompted their own parents to leave Europe. Phyllis Lakofski had not completed her degree because she ran out of money. Hers was one of the first houses in sub-Saharan Africa to display the obvious influence of Le Corbusier and Walter Gropius (Gropius's own house in Lincoln, Massachusetts, was designed only after the Lakofski house was completed).[10] Its architect had been to Europe where he had seen their work for himself. One of the most respected South African architects of his generation, he eventually left the country to teach at the University of Manchester, where Scott Brown later visited him.[11]

Scott Brown grew up assuming that architecture was an appropriate field for women, and she was familiar with cutting-edge design. She said of the house in a 1990 interview:

I don't have the sentimental memories of the attic and the steps up to the attic, and the oak paneling. What I have is strip windows, which have walls that don't come quite up to the window, and there's a little piece between that you can peep through and listen through. I have mild steel columns that are piloti, that you can climb up, and a fantastic deck, which came out like a deck of a ship, with a spiral stair coming down to the ground floor, where I could play ships. And we could climb up on the roof and play on the garage roof and play ...[12]

The house in which Hadid grew up had in the 1930s been as much of a showpiece of modern architecture in Baghdad as the Lakofski house was in Johan-

9 Venturi/Scott Brown (2004), 106; Herbert (1975), 136.

10 Murphy (2011), 308-29.

11 Norman Leonard Hanson, Artefacts, https://www.artefacts.co.za/main/Buildings/arch frames.php?archid=691, accessed on April 13, 2018.

12 "Oral history interview with Denise Scott Brown, 1990 October 25—1991 November 9".

nesburg.[13] Although Badri Qadah's work, which included a house for Kamil Chadirji, one of Hadid's closest political associates and the father of Rifat Chadirji, the most important Baghdad-based architect of the next generation and a friend of Scott Brown and Venturi's, was arguably more Art Deco than International Style, it is representative of the popularity that a clear break with the past had with progressively minded elites across the Middle East, Asia, and indeed also Latin America already in the 1930s.[14]

Hadid's father was representative of this group. His mother and his wife came from the two of Ottoman-era Mosul's wealthiest and most powerful families. Educated at the London School of Economics, where he was attracted to Fabian Socialism, Mohammed Hadid was for many years a leading political figure in Iraq and participated as Finance Minister in the government that assumed power after a bloody coup in 1958.[15]

For Zaha Hadid, architecture was both an appropriate profession for women and a means of expressing modernity. In an interview, she remembered that in Iraq there had been many women architects and the impact upon her when she was six of watching the architect of a house her aunt was building in Mosul present drawings and models of it.[16] She also recalled:

I used to draw a lot. And my father knew many architects, they used to come and visit us. If you think back, there was incredible development and new ideas in the Sixties – it was when they built Brasilia. And there was another issue too – in South America and the Middle East, architecture began to represent a new era, a new level of independence, and move away from colonialism to modernity. We had Gropius building the university campus – there was a lot going on.[17]

13 Chadriji (1991), 510. I thank Amin Alsaden for his help in locating information about it and explaining its Iraqi context to me.

14 More work needs to be done on the importance of upper middle class and elite patronage to the dissemination of modern architecture internationally and especially in the Global South. See, for instance, Akcan (2012), and Oshima (2010).

15 Hadid (2014).

16 Qureshi (2018).

17 Barber (2008).

The university was officially the work of The Architects Collaborative, two of whose eight founding partners were women.[18]

Scott Brown and Hadid were born far from the cities in Europe and the United States in which modernism was forged, but Johannesburg and Baghdad were also places where historical and historicist buildings were not as important as they were in most of Europe. Johannesburg was established in Scott Brown's words as "a fast-growing, highly segregated, gold mining center" only half a century before her family moved there.[19] Hadid's hometown, Baghdad, was a much older city, but its population roughly quadruped in the two decades following her birth in 1950.[20] Both architects in consequence approached modernism in ways that were very different from those of Europeans who associated it, not necessarily accurately, with socialist politics between the wars and reconstruction afterwards. Although neither Scott Brown nor Hadid had access growing up to buildings as skilled and subtle as the best recent work of the starchitects of the day, they experienced modernism as the backdrop to daily life.

Moreover, their privileged social positions were supported by the presence of servants, meaning that even as children, they grew up accustomed to commanding others. Furthermore, from an early age they must have been acutely aware of cultural and political difference. Although Scott Brown is Jewish and Hadid Muslim, they attended academically rigorous and socially prestigious private schools, Anglican in Scott Brown's case and Catholic in Hadid's, although Scott Brown remembers that a Jewish teacher gave lessons on the modern history of Judaism, and that she herself prompted the school to invite a Muslim scholar to address the students. Mohammed Hadid was usually in opposition to governments he regarded as insufficiently independent of British influence, while the Lakofskis, like many South African Jews, did not support the 1948 apartheid law.[21]

These experiences informed the positions the two women took as architects. Increasing attention is now being paid, for instance, to the South African roots of Scott Brown's predilection for Pop, which signifi-

---

18 Kubo (2013).

19 Beavon (2005).

20 "Population estimates for Baghdad, 1950-2015," https://books.mongabay.com/popula tion_estimates/full/Baghdad-Iraq.html, accessed on May 20, 2018.

21 McGetrick (2012).

cantly preceded her exposure to the Independent Group once she arrived in London. She has written of her youth, "Our racial conflicts degraded and dishonored us all . . . But the clash had another dimension. For me African folk artists' adaptations of Johannesburg far outstrip European artists' interpretations of Africa, interesting though these are. 'Debased' African folk-pop was an inspiration for our study of roadside America."[22] The Africa that she experienced while growing up, documented in contemporary photographs by Constance Stuart Larrabee, was far removed from the African architecture fawned over in the 1950s and sixties by Aldo van Eyck and Bernard Rudofsky.[23] The two European men turned to African and other so-called primitive cultures for a supposed authenticity that they believed the industrial revolution, and very specifically its commercialism rather than its industry and engineering, had destroyed. Scott Brown, on the other hand, believed in the modernity of black Africans, and understood that they had the same right to fashionable clothes and to urban space as she did. Having accepted this for them, she could also allow, with help, she acknowledges from the American urban sociologist Herbert J. Gans, that working and middle class Americans, whether or not their taste agreed with her own, should not be dismissed out of hand with the air of cultured superiority that characterized, for instance, Peter Blake's book *God's Own Junkyard: The Planned Deterioration of the American Landscape*, published in 1964, at just the time that she was applying her interest in popular culture to Las Vegas.[24] Scott Brown's experiences growing up in an increasingly racially divided society left her with a respect for the tastes of working and lower middle-class people, which was unusual at a time when advocates of modern architecture tended to espouse it as the expression of the power of the masses, but used it to define their own cultural sophistication.

Scott Brown arrived at the Architectural Association on Bedford Square in 1952; Hadid exactly twenty years later. It is not clear whether either knew at the time that the surrounds of the doors they entered for the next phase of their education had been manufactured by Britain's most successful eigh-

---

22 Scott Brown (2011), 10.

23 Larrabee in collaboration with Paton (1985); McCarter (1985), 120–21; Rudofsky (1964).

24 Blake (1964); see also Stierli (2013), 219–23.

teenth-century businesswoman, Eleanor Coade.[25] No matter. Here they acquired some of the tools they needed to become among the most influential architects of their time.

Growing up in and around innovative houses, including some commissioned by female relatives, was certainly empowering, but so was having the means to travel. Scott Brown made her first family visit to Europe as a toddler; Hadid attended boarding schools in England and Switzerland and earned her undergraduate degree from the American University in Beirut. Mobility is too often overlooked as a crucial factor in the careers of successful women artists and architects. In a famous essay written nearly half a century ago, the late Linda Nochlin answered the question, "Why have there been no great women artists?" by pointing to the impossibility of respectable women studying the nude figure, but the ability to travel has been at least of equal importance.[26] Scott Brown and Hadid, scions of families with strong international networks, were thus from a very young age able to go abroad, at first with family, but eventually also unaccompanied. The strong sense of independence that followed directly from their zest for exploration remained with them for life.

Moving from South Africa to London to Philadelphia in Scott Brown's case and from Baghdad to London in Hadid's took them to the places that fostered the theoretical discourse about the architecture they had grown up with at home. It also wrenched them away from the gendered conventions of the cultures into which they were born, while leaving them relatively independent of those of their adopted homelands, in which they remained slightly alien. And it left them unusually adept at working in cultural contexts outside of those typical for the architects who had trained beside them in London and, in Scott-Brown's case, also in Philadelphia.

In London Scott Brown was joined in 1954 by her former South African classmate, Robert Scott Brown, who became her first husband. In 1958, after traveling and working in Europe, and briefly returning to South Africa, the couple went to the United States, where they enrolled at the University of Pennsylvania. Widowed after his death in a car crash, she completed a master's degree in urban planning and another in architecture. In 1960 she began to teach, holding a joint appointment at Penn in architecture and planning.

25 Kelly (1985), 71–101.
26 Nochlin (1988), 147–58.

In 1965, she headed west to Berkeley, just as the free speech movement was reaching its height, and UCLA. Along the way she stopped at Las Vegas, which her parents had already enjoyed visiting, as her father loved theme parks.[27] The following year she invited her former colleague Robert Venturi to Los Angeles to be a guest critic at her studio jury and took him as well to Las Vegas, to which she had already returned twice. In 1967 the pair married, and Scott Brown returned to Philadelphia to join his practice. Her professional breakthrough came in 1972, with the publication of *Learning from Las Vegas*, based on a studio they had team-taught at Yale. In addition to displaying her fascination with the "ugly and ordinary," the book also bore the clear imprint of her writing skills.

While most of the other American architects to whom the postmodernist label is frequently assigned eschewed social engagement, Scott Brown has always insisted not only on understanding the way in which architecture conveys meaning but also acknowledged and respected the social context in which this happens. Her sensitivity to race also manifested itself in her "joining with," as she puts it "and advocating for low-income communities put at risk by Philadelphia's plan to build an expressway on South Street." It would have created a barrier between black neighborhoods to the south and the more prosperous, largely white city to the north.[28] Her close observation of the recent American vernaculars can also be seen in her firm's 1976 exhibition *Signs of Life: Symbols in the American City* at Washington's Renwick Gallery, on which she collaborated with Robert Venturi and Steven Izenour, who served as the exhibit designer. (Figure 1) The labels argued that "people are more interested in representing their ideals and aspirations through architecture than they are in noticing how well a building expresses its structure and function."[29] This argument was buttressed by thoughtful analyses of what the critic Ada Louise Huxtable in a rave review published in the *New York Times* termed "a revealing picture of today's aesthetic standards that has everything to do with what is, and little to do with what anyone thinks should be."[30]

---

27 "Oral history interview with Denise Scott Brown, 1990 October 25—1991 November 9"; "Interview with Denise Scott Brown and Robert Venturi: Is and Ought" (2008).

28 Haumann (2009), 35–48.

29 Huxtable (1976), 84.

30 Ibid.

Figure 1: Signs of Life: Symbols of the American City, Denise Scott Brown and Steven Izenour, Renwick Gallery, Washington, 1976. Source: Courtesy of Venturi, Scott Brown and Associates, Inc.

Scott Brown built her career around her ability to take the ordinary seriously and to decode the messages it communicated to those far removed from architecture culture. Some of the skills this required undoubtedly came from being an outsider who did not take row-houses like the ones that clustered near South Street nor the ways in which their interiors were decorated for granted (these houses were as likely to be inhabited by African-American as Polish or Italian-American families). It also indicated an almost uncanny ability to understand how women without either her highly tuned sense of irony or her top-drawer professional training used their culturally sanctioned role in choosing their families' interior decor. Scott Brown acknowledged that they furnished their homes to say something about who they were and what they valued. In taking their choices seriously, she accorded them real respect. This was an unusual position for an American architect in the 1970s, when the specter of the so-called silent majority's support for the Vietnam War still hung over the American left, but this did not deter Scott Brown. The sympathetic Huxtable concluded "This is the kind of show that changes the way you look at the world", but most of the architectural profession, including others who would be termed postmodernists, remained appalled.[31]

In 1976 the connection between this position and female experience went unarticulated except in Huxtable's review, which noted the relationship between the most genteel of the exhibited interiors and the pages of *House Beautiful*. Edited by a series of influential women, including Ethel Power (the partner of pioneering American architect Eleanor Raymond), and Elizabeth

---

31 Ibid.

188 Kathleen James-Chakraborty

Gordon (who famously backed Edith Farnsworth over Ludwig Mies van der Rohe in their conflict about the suitability and functionality of his house for her), for most of the period 1913 to 1969, although less consistently since, this is one of the many magazines that targets women as consumers of interior design as much as architecture.[32] Although, as Gordon's Cold War-infused condemnation of Mies made clear, the shelter press seldom backed cutting edge design, it has, in addition to employing female editors and journalists, encouraged middle class women around the world to view themselves as knowledgeable about an area in which they were often able to assert considerable agency in their own lives.[33]

After the publication of *Learning from Las Vegas* established her as one of the most original and influential architectural theorists in the English-speaking world (it would take time for the book to have a significant readership elsewhere), Scott Brown struggled to achieve similar recognition for her design work.[34] She notes that "though their shared creativity had been beneficial in mutual ways, her husband received most of the credit for their contributions, and she received almost none." Her name appeared in that of the firm only in 1980. In 1989 she published her famous essay "Room at the Top? Sexism and the Star System in Architecture" in which she detailed the degree to which her husband had received credit for her contributions and the other outright sexism she had faced.[35] This made her a feminist icon, a status that was only enhanced when after Venturi won the Pritzker prize in 1991 she declined to attend the awards ceremony, and again two decades later when a grassroots campaign failed to get her the Pritzker but did result in changes to the American Institute of Architects Gold Medal that resulted in their receiving the award jointly in 2016.[36]

---

32 Penick (2017); See also: Corbett (2010); Friedman (1997),140–41 and Gruskin (2003),146–62.

33 I strongly believe that these women editors often had real agency that the architecture profession sought to ignore and/or undermine. See: James-Chakraborty (2019), 465–80.

34 It appeared in German in 1979 as *Lernen von Las Vegas: Zur Ikonographie und Architektursymbolik der Geschäftsstadt* (Berlin: Bauwelt), but in French as *L'enseignement de Las Vegas our le symbolism oublié de la forme architecturale* (Bruxelles: P. Mardaga) in 1987 and in Spanish as *Aprendiendo de Las Vegas: El simbolismo olvidado de la forma arquitectónica* (Barcelona: Gustavo Gil) only in 1998.

35 Scott Brown (1989), 237–46.

36 Etherington (2013); "2016 AIA Gold Medal awarded to Denise Scott Brown & Robert Venturi" (2015).

Fame, if not opportunities to build, came more quickly to Hadid. After working briefly for Rem Koolhaas, she established her own practice in 1979, when she was only thirty, more than a decade younger than Scott Brown had been when *Learning from Las Vegas* was published.[37] Hadid's victory in the Hong Kong Peak competition three years later quickly established her as among the world's most formidable and original design talents.[38] It would take more than another decade, however, before she completed a building, the Vitra Fire Station in Weil-am-Rhein, here in Germany.[39] Throughout the 1980s and well into the 1990s, she relied upon teaching and lecture gigs in order to support herself and her fledgling practice.[40]

When success came, she found it abroad. The sad saga of the Cardiff Bay Opera House competition, which began in 1994, demonstrates the hostility that Hadid faced in Britain. Nearly twenty years after she won the first of three rounds (she triumphed in the second and third as well) she was not sure whether what she termed the "resistance and prejudice" she had faced had been because she was a woman or because she was a foreigner.[41] She had no major work in Britain until the Glasgow Museum of Transport opened in 2011 and in England until the completion of the Aquatics Center for the London Olympics the following year.[42]

Scott Brown and Hadid faced similar hostility, exacerbated in Hadid's case undoubtedly by the fact that she was an Arab Muslim (long after she obtained British citizenship, newspapers there typically described her as Iraqi), but they addressed them from very different personal situations.[43]

---

37 Kimmelman (2016) and http://www.zaha-hadid.com/people/zaha-hadid/, accessed on May 20, 2018, which gives 1979 as the date that she established the practice, although most published sources state it was 1980.

38 Johnson /Wigley (1988), 68–79. See also http://www.zaha-hadid.com/architecture/the-peak-leisure-club/, accessed on May 22, 2018.

39 Márquez Cecilia/Levene/Hadid (2004), 250–61. See also http://www.zaha-hadid.com/architecture/vitra-fire-station-2/, accessed on May 22, 2018.

40 Barber (2008).

41 Rowland (2013).

42 For a discussion of local press coverage of the Transport Museum see James-Chakraborty (2018a), 397–405.

43 For instance, "Z marks the spot for Transport Museum's journey into the future/Glasgow chooses gravity-defying design by Iraqi architect" (2004), and "Work on new £74m transport museum set to begin within weeks" (2007).

Scott Brown both benefited and suffered from being married to one of the most heralded and scorned architects of her generation.[44] Across the twentieth century and into the twenty-first most successful female architects have been married to their professional partners.[45] Hadid, however, remained single, and for all public purposes, unattached. Lacking a man at the helm to reassure nervous clients, she was slow to build, despite being one of the most talked about architects in the profession. Once she finally did begin to receive major commissions, however, her single status played in her favor, leaving her in control of her own image, even after her practice expanded to a scale in which she was no longer responsible for the details of each and every project. Her office eventually far surpassed Venturi Scott Brown in size, but, despite the key role that Patrik Schumacher played in it, it was far less openly collaborative.[46] Moreover, being childless enabled her to be constantly on the move. Scott Brown, by contrast, was for a long time more tethered to Philadelphia, where in the 1970s and eighties she had a son to help raise.[47]

Denied substantive commissions in Britain, Hadid depended in the first decade of this century for work upon three quite different constituencies outside it. All were for "people [who] are more interested in representing their ideals and aspirations through architecture than they are in noticing how well a building expresses its structure and function," to repeat Scott Brown, although these ideals and aspirations were now more typically conditioned by attentiveness to public relations and corporate identity than Scott Brown could have foreseen when she addressed American domesticity in 1976. The first included European clients in search of imaginative visions of the new. Companies like Volkswagen, whose Auto-

---

44 A measure of the low regard in which Venturi was held by many of his American peers is that fact that he was elected a fellow of the American Institute of Architects only in 1978, by which point he was already one of the most influential members of the organization. The American Institute of Architects: College of Fellows History & Directory (2017), 396. Scott Brown shared in the receipt of the 2016 Gold Medal without ever having been elected to fellowship.

45 Searing (1998).

46 Schumacher quickly, however, attracted considerable public attention almost immediately after Hadid's death. See for instance, Renn (2018). And for the size of her office, which in 2018 was still the third biggest in the United Kingdom, see Douglas (2018).

47 "Oral history interview with Denise Scott Brown, 1990 October 25-1991 November 9".

stadt and original factory, the Phaeno, her science museum in Wolfsburg, Germany, faces, and BMW, for which she built an administration building in Leipzig as well as the founders of the MAXXI, a national museum of contemporary art in Rome, turned to Hadid, much as Vitra already had, to advertise their ability to stay atop art and design trends.[48] This happened at precisely the time when Muslim culture, and particularly its supposed treatment of women, was being widely disparaged in Germany as part of the discussion of *Leitkultur*.[49] Hiring Hadid was not necessarily an expression of support for multiculturalism, but it did have the added benefit of bestowing an air of cosmopolitanism upon clients seeking global recognition.

A second group were attracted to Hadid specifically because, as an Arab woman, she understood the desire of wealthy Middle Eastern and Chinese clients for landmarks that communicated newly achieved modernity at home and abroad. She proved extremely effective at working across cultures, but there were also cases when Muslims clearly cherished bestowing opportunities on one of their own. Furthermore, she understood what they wanted. For instance, on the office website, the Sheik Zeyed Bridge is described as being "intended to serve as a catalyst for further growth in Abu Dhabi," while of the Heydar Aliyev Centre it says, "The Center, designed to become the primary building for the nation's cultural programs, breaks from the rigid and often monumental Soviet architecture that is so prevalent in Baku, aspiring instead to express the sensibilities of Azeri culture and the optimism of a nation that looks to the future."[50] Such marketing language masks the conditions of production of these buildings, with allegations of human trafficking and other human rights abuses surrounding the construction industry in both cities.[51]

---

48 For an expanded version of this discussion see James-Chakraborty (2018b), 231–34.

49 For an introduction to German-Turkish issues at the time see Göktürk/Gramling/Kaes (eds.) (2007).

50 http://www.zaha-hadid.com/architecture/sheikh-zayed-bridge/ and http://www.zaha-hadid.com/2013/11/14/heydar-aliyev-center-baku-azerbaijan/, accessed on May 22, 2018.

51 Wainwright (2014); Ray (2015).

Figure 2: Zaha Hadid in Heydar Aliyev Cultural Center in Baku, November 2013. Source: Photograph by Dmitry Ternovoy, courtesy of Wikipedia Commons at https://en.wikipedia.org/wiki/File:ZahaHadid_in_Heydar_Aliyev_Cultural_ center_in_Baku_nov_2013.jpg.

Figure 3: Denise Scott Brown at home, 1978. Source: © Lynn Gilbert, courtesy of Wikipedia Commons at https://en.wikipedia.org/wiki/Denise_Scott_Brown#/ media/File:Denise_Scott_Brown_1978_©_Lynn_Gilbert.jpg.

The final constituency was the fashion industry. Piers Gough, a juror on the committee that awarded the Hedar Aliyev Center the Design of the Year from London's Design Museum, described it as being "as pure and sexy as Marilyn's blown skirt."[52] This is clearly sexist, but in the final years of her career, Hadid willingly exploited the relationship between fashion and architecture, so often used to trivialize women's accomplishments, to her advantage. It helped that she epitomized the star system that Scott Brown scorned. Often described as a diva, a term, of course that is never applied to men, Hadid also garnered attention in ways that were uniquely available to her as a woman, without ever appearing sexual or submissive. Fashion became a means to both build her own brand and to get work.[53] Posing for fashion shoots, being profiled in women's magazines, designing shoes, and working with companies such as Chanel and Louis Vuitton helped offset the blatant sexism that characterized much of the writing and gossip about her.[54]

Hadid's effectiveness as a fashion icon was enhanced by the fact that she clearly enjoyed clothes. Although she favored skirts and tunics over leggings, very few of her outfits were in any way feminine or conventionally revealing. Instead they often appeared to operate as shields, celebrating her engagement with avant-garde design while floating relatively free of her actual body.[55] (Figure 2) They thus announced her talent while denying her availability. In comparison Scott Brown was often self-consciously ordinary, even slightly prim. (Figure 3)

Fashion matters, not because these women's achievements should or indeed can be reduced to the clothes that they wore, but because women schooled to make decisions about self-presentation through dress have also often made decisions about the appearance of interiors and gardens, about what kind of house to buy or build, about the buildings—including public libraries, hospitals, schools, and churches—where their participation has long

---

52 Wainwright (2014).

53 McKenzie (2014).

54 For her pavilion for Chanel see http://www.zaha-hadid.com/architecture/chanel-art-pa
    vilion/, accessed on May 30, 2018. For a selection of her handbag and shoe designs see
    Périer (2017).

55 See, for instance, the photograph of her published in Andrew Wilshere and Zahra Hankir,
    "9 Reasons We Love Zaha Hadid – Introducing the UX Academy Hadid Cohort", https://
    trydesignlab.com/blog/9-reasons-we-love-zaha-hadid-ux-academy/, accessed on Febru-
    ary 18, 2021.

been sanctioned, and in other less gender constrained circumstances as well, as in the case of what was originally South America's tallest building.[56] While these possibilities have always been inscribed by class, they are real even if too many historians, like the male architects whose careers they validate, have been reluctant to assign agency to women who were wielded real authority.

Scott Brown and Hadid grew up in families where modernism was simultaneously an expression of social and economic status and of progressive politics. From societies in which class trumped gender, they further expanded their horizons by building careers abroad. Their self-consciousness about the way in which consumerism encouraged many women of their own and previous generations to construct identities through dress and design assisted them in carving out spaces for personal emancipation through creative expression. The challenge before us as historians is to recover the contributions many less celebrated women, including Scott Brown's mother and Hadid's aunt, have long made to architectural culture. As people, however, it is to empower those who lack the privilege required to launch Scott Brown and Hadid and to build the relationship between architecture and substantive political change they shrewdly realized had been much exaggerated.

Literature

"2016 AIA Gold Medal awarded to Denise Scott Brown & Robert Venturi," (2015), AIA press release, December 3, 2015, https://www.aia.org/press-releases/2316-2016-aia-gold-medal-awarded-to-denise-scott-b:26, accessed on May 22, 2018.

"9 Reasons We Love Zaha Hadid – Introducing the UX Academy Hadid Cohort," *Design Lab*, http://trydesignlab.com/blog/9-reasons-we-love-zaha-hadid-ux-academy/, accessed on May 30, 2018.

Akcan, Esra (2012), *Architecture in Translation: Germany, Turkey and the Modern House*, Durham: Duke University Press.

Barber, Lynn (2008), "Interview: Zaha Hadid," *The Guardian*, March 9, 2008, https://www.theguardian.com/lifeandstyle/2008/mar/09/women.architecture, accessed on May 20, 2018.

---

56 The Edificio Kavanagh in Buenos Aires completed in 1936. See Carranza/Lara (2015), 55, 83.

Beavon, Keith (2005), *Johannesburg: The Making and Shaping of the City*, Pretoria: Unisa.

Blake, Peter (1964), *God's Own Junkyard: The Planned Deterioration of America's Landscape*, New York: Holt, Rinehart and Winston.

Bourdieu, Pierre (1977), *Outline of a Theory of Practice*, Cambridge: Cambridge University Press.

Chadriji, Rifat (1991), *Al-Ukhayḍir wa-al-Qaṣr al-Ballūrī: nushū' al-naẓarīyah al-jadalīyah fī-al-'imārah*, London: Riyāḍ al-Rayyis.

Carranza, Luis E./Luiz Lara, Fernando (2015), *Modern Architecture in Latin America: Art, Technology, and Utopia*, Austin: University of Texas Press, 55, 83.

Corbett, Kathleen (2010), *Tilting at Modern: Elizabeth Gordon's "The Threat to the Next America,"* Dissertation, University of California, Berkeley, Berkeley, California USA.

Douglas, Mary (2018), "Gender pay gap: Zaha Hadid Architects announces 20% disparity," *The Architect's Journal*, April 3, 2018, https://www.architectsjournal.co.uk/news/gender-pay-gap-zaha-hadid-architects-announces-20-disparity/10029672.article, accessed on May 22, 2018.

Etherington, Rose (2013), "Denise Scott Brown petition for Pritzker recognition rejected," *Dezeen*, June 14, 2013, https://www.dezeen.com/2013/06/14/pritzker-jury-rejects-denise-scott-brown-petition/, accessed on May 22, 2018.

Friedman, Alice (1997), *Women and the Making of the Modern House*, New York: Abrams.

Göktürk, Deniz/Gramling, David/Kaes, Anton (eds.), (2007), *Germany in Transit: Nation and Migration, 1955-2005*, Berkeley: University of California Press.

Gruskin, Nancy (2003), "Designing Women: Writing about Eleanor Raymond," in: Frederickson, Kristen/Webb, Sarah E. (eds.), *Singular Women: Writing the Artist*, Berkeley: University of California Press, 146–62.

Hadid, Foulath (2014), *Iraq's Democratic Moment*, London: Hurst.

Haumann, Sebastian (2009), "Vernacular Architecture as Self-Determination: Venturi, Scott Brown and the Controversy over Philadelphia's Crosstown Expressway, 1967-1973," *Footprint* (Spring 2009), 35–48.

Herbert, Gilbert (1975), *Martienssen & the International Style: The Modern Movement in South African Architecture*, Cape Town: AA Bakema.

Huxtable, Ada Louise (1976), "The Pop World of the Strip and the Sprawl," *New York Times*, March 21, 1976, 84.

"Interview with Denise Scott Brown and Robert Venturi: Is and Ought," *Perspecta* 41 (2008)39.

James-Chakraborty, Kathleen (2018a), "Architecture, its histories and their audiences," *Journal of the Society of Architectural Historians*, 77(4), 2018, 397–405.

James-Chakraborty, Kathleen (2018b), *Modernism as Memory: Building Identity in the Federal Republic of Germany*, Minneapolis: University of Minnesota Press.

James-Chakraborty, Kathleen (2019), "The Diversity of Women's Engagement with Modern Architecture and Design: Three Case Studies," *The Plan Journal*, 4 (2019), 465–80.

Johnson, Philip/Wigley, Mark (1988), *Deconstructivist Architecture*, New York: Museum of Modern Art.

Kelly, Alison (1985), "Coade Stone in Georgian Architecture," *Architectural History* 28 (1985): 71–101.

Kimmelman, Michael (2016), "Zaha Hadid, Groundbreaking Architect, Dies at 65," *New York Times*, March 31, 2016.

Kubo, Michael (2013), "The Cambridge School: What went on at 46 Brattle Street," *Architecture Boston* 16.2 (2013), https://www.architects.org/architectureboston/articles/cambridge-school, accessed on May 20, 2018.

Larrabee, Constance Stuart in collaboration with Paton, Alan (1985), *Go well my child*, Washington: Smithsonian Institution Press.

Lesser, Wendy (2017), *You Say to Brick: The Life of Louis Kahn*, New York: Farrer, Straus and Giroux.

Márquez, Cecilia Fernando/Levene, Richard C./Hadid, Zaha (2004)(eds), *Zaha Hadid, 1983-2001*, Madrid: Croquis Editorial.

McCarter, Robert (1985), *Aldo van Eyck*, New Haven: Yale University Press.

McGetrick, Brendon (2012), "Denise's recollections ¼," *Domus*, November 30, 2012, https://www.domusweb.it/en/interviews/2012/11/30/denise-s-recollections-1-4.html, accessed on April 13, 2018.

McKenzie, Sheena (2014), "Zaha Hadid: 'Would they still call me a diva if I was a man?'," CNN, August 21, 2014.

Morgenthaler, Hans R. (1999), "'Why should we be laymen with respect to art?': The Formative Years 1910-1918," in: Stephan, Regina (ed.), *Erich Mendelsohn: Architect 1887-1953*, New York: Monacelli.

Murphy, Kevin D. (2011), "The Vernacular Moment: Eleanor Raymond, Walter Gropius, and New England between the Wars," *Journal of the Society of Architectural* Historians 70(3), (2011), 308–29.

Nochlin, Linda (1988), *Women, Art and Power and Other Essays*, Boulder: Westview Press, 147–58.

"Oral history interview with Denise Scott Brown, 1990 October 25–1991 November 9," Archives of American Art, https://www.aaa.si.edu/collections/interviews/oral-history-interview-denise-scott-brown-13059#transcript, accessed on May 20, 2018.

Oshima, Ken Tadashi (2010), *International Architecture in Interwar Japan: Constructing Kokusai Kenchiku*, Seattle: University of Washington Press.

Qureshi, Huma (2012), "Zaha Hadid: 'Being an Arab and a woman is a double-edged sword'," *The Guardian*, November 14, 2012, https://www.theguardian.com/lifeandstyle/2012/nov/14/zaha-hadid-woman-arab-double-edged-sword, accessed on May 20, 2018.

Penick, Monica (2017), *Tastemaker: Elizabeth Gordon, House Beautiful and the American Home*, New Haven: Yale University Press.

Périer, Marie (2017), "Fashion and architecture: 8 must-see Zaha Hadid collaborations," *Vogue*, November 20, 2017.

Ray, Debika (2015), "What can architects do about workers' rights in the Gulf?," *Icon*, March 26, 2015, https://www.iconeye.com/architecture/features/item/11715-what-can-architects-do-about-worker-rights-in-the-gulf, accessed on May 22, 2018.

Renn, Aaron M. (2018), "Architect Patrik Schumacher: 'I've been depicted as a fascist'," *The Guardian*, January 17, 2018.

Rowland, Paul (2013), "Award winning businesswoman Zaha Hadid hits out at 'prejudice' over doomed Cardiff Bay Opera House Project," *Wales Online*, April 23, 2013, https://www.walesonline.co.uk/news/wales-news/zaha-hadid-hits-out-prejudice-2996109, accessed on May 22, 2018.

Rudofsky, Bernard (1964), *Architecture without Architects: A Short Introduction to Non-Pedigreed Architecture*, Garden City: Doubleday.

Schumacher, Patrik (2016), *Parametricism 2.0: Rethinking Architecture's Agenda for the 21st Century*, London: Academy Press.

Scott Brown, Denise (1989), "Room at the Top? Sexism and the Star System in Architecture," in: Berkeley, Ellen Perry/McQuaid, Matilda (eds.), *Architecture: A Place for Women*, Washington: Smithsonian Institution Press, 237–46.

Scott Brown, Denise (2011), "To the University of Witwatersrand from Denise Scott Brown: 21 July 2011," *Architecture South Africa* (September/October 2011), 10.

Searing, Helen (1998), *Equal Partners: Men and Women Principals in Contemporary Architectural Practice*, Northampton: Smith College Museum of Art.

Stierli, Martino (2013), *Las Vegas in the Rearview Mirror: The City in Theory, Photography and Film*, Los Angeles: Getty Research Institute.

The American Institute of Architects: College of Fellows History & Directory (2017), Washington: American Institute of Architects.

Venturi, Robert/Scott Brown, Denise/Izenour, Steven (1972), *Learning from Las Vegas*, Cambridge: MIT Press.

Venturi, Robert/Scott Brown, Denise (2004), *Architecture as Signs and Systems for a Mannerist Time*, Cambridge: Belknap Press.

Wainwright, Oliver (2014), "Wave of protest over Zaha Hadid's Baku prize-winner," *The Guardian*, June 30, 2014.

"Work on new £74m transport museum set to begin within weeks," *Herald* (Glasgow), October 8, 2007.

"Z marks the spot for Transport Museum's journey into the future; Glasgow chooses gravity-defying design by Iraqi architect," *Herald* (Glasgow), October 12, 2004.

Internet Sources

American Institute of Architects https://www.aia.org/press-releases/2316-2016-aia-gold-medal-awarded-to-denise-scott-b:26

Archives of American Art https://www.aaa.si.edu/collections/interviews/oral-history-interview-denise-scott-brown-13059#transcript

Design Lab https://trydesignlab.com/blog/9-reasons-we-love-zaha-hadid-ux-academy/

Mongabay https://books.mongabay.com/population_estimates/full/Baghdad-Iraq.html

Norman Leonard Hanson https://www.artefacts.co.za/main/Buildings/archframes.php?archid=691

Zaha Hadid http://www.zaha-hadid.com/

Recording and Reflecting
On AAXX100AA Women in Architecture 1917-2017

Elizabeth Darling & Lynne Walker

The AAXX100 project was established in 2013 to tell the story of women at the Architectural Association School of Architecture (AA) in London. Founded in 1847 by a group of young men disgruntled by the then dominant method of architectural training in Britain, that of pupillage, the Association was intended partly as a club and mutual meeting ground, and a place where they could teach themselves on the model of the European *Beaux-Arts* system. This soon evolved into a more formal school and the AA became one of the earliest places in the UK to offer a systematic architectural training. By the early 1900s the AA had gained a reputation for being one of the best places in the country to study architecture. In 1917 it made the decision to open its doors to women, and it was from a desire to commemorate this centenary that the AAXX100 project was born. When it started, we did not even know the names of the first students, but by its completion we did, and so much more. It became clear to us through our research that the history of AA women in architecture is at once a history of women's presence within an educational institution, a history of women's presence within a profession—architecture—and a part of the history of architecture in both Britain and the wider world.

The project unfolded over a four-year period and was originated by the architect Yasmin Shariff and Brett Steele (the AA's then director). It was carried out by a team led by Elizabeth Darling, Lynne Walker, Manijeh Verghese, Ed Bottoms, Eleanor Gawne and Ellen Leopold, working alongside AA students, architect members and other staff. It was a multi-faceted project and featured an annual lecture series under the AAXX100 "brand," and an oral history project led by Ed Bottoms that saw AA alumnae filmed and interviewed. It culminated in 2017 with the publication of the book, *AA Women in Architecture 1917-2017*, which accompanied the exhibition *AAXX100: AA Women in Architecture 1917-2017*, which ran from October to December 2017, and which is the focus of the discussion here. Our aim is to document the exhibition (which we co-curated, as well as co-editing the project book) and, in so doing, reflect on how our research questions and approach to curation were framed in relation to the institution and our position as feminist historians.

The curatorial process

Some early decisions shaped the form that the exhibition would take. The primary one was a reluctance to curate a display of individual women and their projects, which is usual for architecture exhibitions. This, we felt, would have replicated the myth of the lone architectural genius on which a sexist architectural history is based, and which is often ahistorical. Instead, we adopted a thematic approach. This allowed us to achieve two things, first to link the work of AA women to broader developments in 20th and 21st century world architecture. Second, and at the same time, to represent key practitioners and projects and to show how they were shaped by the AA *and* historical conditions, especially changing ideas about gender and women's place in architecture. Our aim was not to downplay the importance of individuals and their architectural productions but to weave them into a wider and more complex history. By stressing this interweaving, we found a way to show that while women's presence in architecture may not have been ordinary, it certainly was not untypical or exceptional, which a focus on the individual alone can suggest.

Another factor that shaped our curating was the fact that for the AA to even have an exhibition about women and architecture was something entirely new (and, indeed, untypical of wider exhibition practice). Making AA women, past and present, visible within the institution became a key strategy for us. This we did by occupying as much space as possible at the AA: not just the main gallery on the ground floor (Figure 1), but the entrance hall and grand staircase up to the piano nobile (Figure 2), where we used the main rooms. As a parallel to this, our designers Eva Jiricna and Georgina Papathanasiou created settings that let the individual exhibits speak for themselves:

subtle framing, plain materials and spacious layouts gave an underlying gravitas and respect to the work on display.

Our research led us to formulate the following themes to organise the display: 1917; Politics of Practice; Public Practice/Public Service; Beyond the Drawing Board; Collaborations; Local/Global; AA Spirit and 21st Century Women (we also had sections devoted to the AAXX100 Oral History Project and a series of portrait photographs of AA women on site or in their offices on the staircase walls and a slide show of AA women in the bar). These distributed themselves fairly logically and, for the most part, chronologically across the building but an early challenge came with the untimely death of Dame Zaha Hadid in early 2016. Up to that point we had envisioned that her highly successful career would have been represented within the theme of Local/Global and would have served as a good example of linking an individual—very much a "starchitect"—to the wider context which shaped her. The fact of her death suggested that her radical architecture perhaps warranted more of a commemoration and a central place in the exhibition narrative. Our initial solution was to give her pride of place but keep her in the Local/Global section where she rightly belonged, by reconstructing part of her 1983 installation "Planetary Architecture Two" which had filled the same space. Practicalities, however, overtook us and the insurance value of the exhibits meant we could not show them in this un-invigilated, first-floor space. This required us to step outside the chronology of the exhibits and move her work downstairs to the main gallery and potentially do what we had been striving so hard to avoid, the separation of individual from historical context. However, the new position of the exhibit, which now comprised the model for the Hong Kong Peak project and a characteristic painting of a project for Trafalgar Square and related drawings, worked out in collaboration with Zaha Hadid Architects, in fact suggested another narrative. It faced the opening section of the exhibition which focused on 1917, that moment when women were first admitted to the AA. We therefore had the radical act of women entering a hitherto all-male school, faced by the radical work of arguably the 20th and 21st-century's most important architect, a woman. It also underlined how far women had come in a century of practice. (Figure 3)

Figure 1: Detail, main exhibition room; exhibition AAXX100: AA Women in Architecture 1917-2017, October to December 2017, The Architectural Association, Bedford Square, London. Source: M. Pepchinski.

Figure 2: Detail, staircase with portraits and model; exhibition
AAXX100: AA Women in Architecture 1917-2017, October to
December 2017, The Architectural Association, Bedford Square,
London. Source: Courtesy The Architectural Association Archive/
AAXX100.

The exhibition

Visitors' first encounter with the exhibition was in the entrance hall of the AA's building at 36 Bedford Square in Bloomsbury, central London. There we placed on facing walls two photographs which demonstrated the way the AA had evolved since women were admitted. The first, taken in 1896, showed male students dressed in drag and blacked up for a pantomime performance to the all-male student body. The other was a photograph of the 2016 graduating class. This showed the diverse ethnicity of the school population today and the gender balance in which women now exceed men.

From these "scene setters," visitors entered the main gallery where the first display was "1917." This explored the life and work of the four women who joined the school in October 1917, the conditions they encountered there, their spirited reaction to those circumstances and their life after graduation. A key exhibit was a series of silhouettes, which showed them as the "Future Heads of the Profession: Lady Students at the AA," and which appeared in a 1918 edition of the *Architectural Association Journal*. When we began our research, we did not know the names of all these first students—the records from 1917 are missing—and which student went with which "head". But with a few clues which emerged, and the help of their families, we identified them: Winifred Ryle (Maddock), Ruth Lowy (Gollancz), Gillian Cooke (Harrison) and Irene Graves (Garforth). Of the original four students, two married AA students and set up in successful husband and wife practices and two left, having married non-architects.

Researching the lives of these individual women allowed us to draw more general conclusions about how women's entry into the sort of systematic architectural education that was offered at the AA was facilitated by the Women's Movement and its advocacy for equal access to education and the professions. Many had family members who were active in the Suffrage Movement and all came from well-to-do, upper middle-class families, a reminder of a class profile that has dominated architectural education and practice more or less ever since. What also became apparent was the preference of these early graduates and many of the generations who followed in the 1920s and 1930s to work collaboratively either with a marital partner or other women, and often for women clients.

This was evident in the first building designed by an AA woman graduate which was a village hall in the Sussex countryside, a typically modest project. Such small-scale work dominated the work of these first alumnae, but as early as 1927 it became clear that women were not going to allow themselves to be stereotyped as domestic designers. In that year Elisabeth Whitworth Scott, a recent graduate (1924), won the anonymous international competition to design the Shakespeare Memorial Theatre at Stratford-upon-Avon (1927-32). This was seen as a victory for all women and confirmation of their ability to design large-scale public buildings. Exhibition research revealed that Scott saw this great achievement from a feminist perspective and made a specific decision to employ women, particularly AA alumnae, to work with her on the scheme.

Another landmark was the election of Cooke in 1931 as the first woman FRIBA, Fellow of the Royal Institute of British Architects, the major professional body of architecture in Britain. This showed the way that women understood themselves to be part of the profession (and we showed a copy of her Diploma certificate) and that they could and should play an active role in its organisation and discourse. This concern for an identification with the profession and with the nature of practice would become stronger in the later 1920s and the next several decades, themes that shaped the curation of the next two sections of the exhibition: Politics of Practice and Public Practice/Public Service.

Here we focused on how creativity allied to social commitment, and the desire to shape the profession accordingly was manifested in the work of many AA women. (Figure 4) There was very much the sense that the privilege of their education required of them some form of service to society. We found that, continuing the theme of collaboration noted above, AA alumnae worked frequently with women reformers from outside the school, using their skills as designers to argue for social change. In the 1930s, this related mostly to the issue of housing with graduates such as Janet Fletcher, Mary Crowley, Judith Ledeboer and Justin Blanco White working with the reform group "New Homes for Old" to oppose what they saw as an unimaginative state housing policy and to advocate for a slum clearance programme which proposed modern, well-designed flats alongside amenities such as nursery schools, playgrounds and allotments.

This willingness to stand against the mainstream and be fiercely critical of the status quo can be found five decades later in the work of Matrix, to which the second half of the Politics of Practice display was devoted. This feminist architectural cooperative was formed in 1980 by women practitioners, several AA graduates among them. Cutting across the decades in one display was a deliberate strategy, as we wanted to draw attention to the persistent strand of feminist and social activist commitment among AA alumnae. Like those involved with "New Homes for Old," Matrix's concern was to empower people who had little influence over the formation of the built environment, and they did this in a number of ways: writing, exhibitions and through developing new modes of practice. Documented in their 1984 book, *Making Space, Women and the Manmade Environment* (a very battered library copy of which was on display, to show how much of an inspiration it was to students), their approach stressed the architect as a facilitator, listener, mediator, of working with and not against clients to get the buildings that worked best for users. We also exhibited material relating to their best-known project, the Jagonari Educational Centre, Whitechapel, East London, completed 1987, and designed with the participation of their Bangladeshi women clients.

Our emphasis on Matrix in the exhibition was also a statement about how their approach and activities are now more than ever relevant, and a model for contemporary practice. Such thinking also underpinned, to some extent, the next section, Public Practice/Public Service. This continued the themes laid down in Politics of Practice and showed how the ideas of 1930s AA women were absolutely instrumental in ensuring that the idea of well-planned environments from region to city to town to neighbourhood unit to home became an integral part of the post-war reconstruction programme. In fact, it was not just their ideas that shaped the architecture of the Welfare State, but the women themselves.

Most notable of these was Mary Medd who became the leading figure in the theory and practice of school design after 1945; we exhibited photographs of Burleigh Infants School, Cheshunt, Hertfordshire (1946-7), one of her earliest and collaboratively designed schools. And again, to make the point that a commitment to public architecture and the public realm has not withered, despite our neo-liberal age, we included the work of Julia Barfield (working with her husband David Marks) and their primary school in Cambridge. This innovative project, completed 2013, is the first training school set up by a University (Cambridge) to provide teacher training, research and teaching on one site. The concept of a school, where every voice matters, divided into small communities, yet unified as a whole, led to a circular plan building, which is non-hierarchical and inclusive, built around an open courtyard into which every classroom opens.

Figure 3: Opening room, 1917 with the Zaha Hadid commemorative section; exhibition AAXX100: AA Women in Architecture 1917-2017, October to December 2017, The Architectural Association, Bedford Square, London. Source: Courtesy The Architectural Association/Photographer: Sue Barr.

Such projects showed how within a decade or so of first entering the school, AA women were engaging with architecture at all scales, often working collaboratively and with real social commitment. Our research also revealed different or unexpected ways in which women used their design training and allowed us to show how architecture exhibitions do not just have to comprise solely of two-dimensional representations of buildings. This might be a model (such as the Hong Peak maquette in the Zaha Hadid display), books by designers, RIBA registration certificates, the miniature furniture used by Mary Medd to promote discussion about school design but also work that we categorised as "Beyond the Drawing Board." The school seems to have a particular track record in graduates who train and then practise in diverse fields, often to remarkable effect and impact, so we placed a large vitrine in the space between Politics of Practice and Public Practice/Public Service, to feature the work of women who had trained at the AA but not pursued an explicitly architectural career.

This theme allowed us to enliven the exhibition with the use of film, an important outlet for AA graduates—the Oscar winning art director Carmen Dillon, Sylvia Moberly who worked for Walt Disney, and much more recently Susanne Bier, the director, whose film, *A Better World* won an Oscar in 2011. Also included was the work of the textile designer Marian Pepler and the furniture and textile designer Florence Knoll. Her company, which survives her, generously loaned us two of her pieces of furniture which served both as exhibits and places for visitors to sit and reflect. We also used the vitrine to reflect on the way students were taught to design, showing a selection of drawing implements that would have been used by AA students for much of the preceding century. Now virtually historic artefacts they included a slide rule, Rotring pen, compasses and a T-square. In contrast a working model of the Universal Constructor designed by Julia Frazer and John Frazer was on display, this was an early example of the CAD systems that now dominate practice.

Beyond the Drawing Board completed the displays in the main gallery. Visitors then proceeded up the main staircase to the suite of rooms on the first floor. This staircase is the main thoroughfare of the school, and we wanted to populate its walls with photographic portraits of AA women (and the curators!) to remind everyone on a daily basis of women's presence in the institution and in the profession.

In approaching the curation of the first-floor spaces, an initial problem seemed to be that they are "public" and social spaces for the school, comprising the front and back members room and student bar. On reflection, however, we realised that the co-mingling of exhibits and today's students working on their current projects in these rooms offered a wonderful sense of how contemporary women students are building on and connecting with the work of their antecedents. This was reinforced by the fact that most of the exhibits in these spaces focused on works from the 1960s onwards. In the front members room two themes were explored: Collaborations and Local/ Global. Again, a problem arose because we could not use original material in these spaces apart from two very robust and well protected models of the Hopkins house (Hampstead, London, 1976) by Patty and Michael Hopkins and the Faculty of Science Building, University of Lagos (Lagos, Nigeria, 1972) by Gillian Hopwood and John Godwin. We realised that this could be used to the exhibition's advantage through the use of digital materials, interactive oral histories and the creation of thematic slideshows to represent a wider array of women. That also allowed us to add in the theme of 21st Century women (curated by Hannah Durham, Albane Duvillier, and Ye Jin Lee), a series devoted to work in the present day by AA students and recent graduates. Rather than select and privilege a few in this process, an open call was held and 70 submissions were received and edited into a slideshow. Some historic student work was shown in the back members room as a complement to these most recent projects.

One of the key themes that emerged from the research for AAXX100 is the collaborative nature of architecture, which the section Collaborations highlighted. Architects' teamwork with other professions, engineers, artists, surveyors, contractors, building workers and so on is vital, but in the exhibition we focused on portraying diverse partnerships among and between architects, especially men and women working together on individual projects or in firms of architects or in partnerships of women. Most numerous were husband and wife teams from the mid-20th and 21st century. We represented a series of practices from the 1950s to the present day and used our labels and panel texts to raise questions around authorship between married couples. These, as we reminded visitors, are questions rarely asked of male collaborators like Herzog and de Meuron: Who designed what? Who does the designing? Is design the most important part of architecture? Whose name is on the practice? Who gets the credit? The question of authorship is

Figure 4: Politics of Practice section; exhibition AAXX100: AA Women in Architecture 1917-2017, October to December 2017, The Architectural Association, Bedford Square, London. Source: Courtesy The Architectural Association Archive/AAXX100.

further fraught with gendered cultural assumptions—"he must have been the designer/lead/responsible for the concept"—while recognising individual contributions is complicated by the partners' inevitable claim that credit should be shared equally.

We were also able to show that these intimate and creative collaborations have produced significant public architecture such as the extensive work at the Festival of Britain, 1951, by Jane Drew and Maxwell Fry; the Glyndebourne Opera House, 1994, designed by Patty and Michael Hopkins; the London Eye, 2000, from the practice of Julia Barfield and David Marks; and Tate St Ives, 1993, created by Eldred Evans and David Shalev. These married couples are among the architects who with their "significant others" have designed architecture, urban space and landscape, which in our view warranted space in an exhibition of women architects. Significantly from the curatorial perspective, which emphasised the collaborative nature of architecture, we did not insist on the (misnamed) "sole practitioner" or exclude women who practised with their spouses.

Local/Global was conceived from our research discovery that since 1917 women from all over the world have come to Bedford Square to study architecture, working alongside British-born students. In the 1920s several students were from empire families in India and Kenya; while a steady stream of students came from former colonies, Australia and New Zealand in particular. In 1930 the first Asian women students arrived from the colony of Malaya (Malaysia), the remarkable Yuen sisters who were of Chinese descent. (Figure 5) The post-war colonies and Commonwealth contributed students again: notably Minnette de Silva from Ceylon (Sri Lanka) and Denise Scott Brown (South Africa), and another wave of Australians in the 1970s. Today women make up 52 per cent of the student body, 90 per cent of which is from outside the UK.

Local/Global therefore explored the trajectories taken by AA alumnae as they returned home from the locale of Bedford Square and set up their own practices. It also followed UK-based former students who have designed projects all over the world or used the local to inspire their designs. We showed a project by Salma Samar Damluji in which she reconstructed and rehabilitated 12 mud-built houses in the fortified town of Masna'at Urh in Wadi Daw'an, Yemen (2007-10).

Local/Global can also mean working in and from London in the global marketplace. In 2017, AA alumna Amanda Levete's practice, AL_A, unveiled the Museum of Art, Architecture and Technology (MAAT) in Lisbon and, during the exhibition, their new Exhibition Road entrance and galleries opened at the Victoria & Albert Museum in London. It is rare that two major museum projects are completed within the same year by a single architect, so it seemed especially important to have these in our display.

In an attempt to reach the spiritual home of the AA and its occupants, we decorated the bar with a photomontage of images of student life across the past 100 years. This expressed the spirit and exuberance for which AA students and the institution are known and created a setting in which ideas provoked by the exhibition could be debated.

The exhibition was not merely a discrete event. We very much wanted it to be a springboard for discussion and to have a legacy which addresses and promotes women's presence in architectural culture. An international conference, "AA Women and Architecture in Context, 1917-2017," convened in partnership with the Paul Mellon Centre for Studies in British Art was held in November 2017. The three-day event was followed by a two-day coach tour of buildings designed by women architects in London and Cambridge, co-organised with the Twentieth Century Society. Looking to the future of practice and of history, a workshop for sixth formers, many of whom were considering their career options, was arranged with the organisation "Art History in Schools." Comprising talks and drawing sessions in the exhibition, many of the young women left decided on pursuing architectural training.

In conclusion

This was a large-scale project, completed in 2017. We are still reflecting on what we have learnt from our research, but already we recognise that certain themes were examined insufficiently in the exhibition. The interweaving of colonial and post-colonial discourse throughout the lifetime of this institution, and in the work that its graduates produced, was too little examined and is deserving of fuller attention and articulation. Similarly, while we were able to address issues around institutional sexism, with abundant evidence thereof (a key exhibit was a minute book that noted a decision to introduce a restrictive quota for women students in 1930), personal sexuality itself proved a more elusive topic to pursue. Nevertheless, the exhibition had many strengths, which we have sought to present here, most importantly making visible the work of so many women across 100 years of practice.

Figure 5: Detail, Local/Global; section of the exhibition: Elizabeth Darling and Lynne Walker, exhibition curators photographed alongside the exhibition showing the students Angeline Yuen Mo-Ting and Esther Yuen Mo-Yow, AAXX100: AA Women in Architecture 1917-2017, October to December 2017, The Architectural Association, Bedford Square, London. Source: Courtesy The Architectural Association Archive/AAXX100 & Ivan Ho.

Literature

Darling, Elizabeth/Walker, Lynne (eds.)(2017), *AA Women in Architecture 1917-2017*, London: AA Publications.

Frau Architekt
Two reasons and a résumé

Christina Budde

For all intents and purposes there were two reasons to organize the exhibition *Frau Architekt*. One was a result of in-house discussions which acknowledged that we, as the *Deutsches Architekturmuseum* (German Architecture Museum or DAM), a major architectural institution in Frankfurt-am-Main, were a part of the problem. Given the fact that there is a broad consensus about architecture being a masculine domain, it has the tendency to remain male-dominated where it is appreciated, debated and exhibited. As is well known, the perceived state of being of any given thing determines not only how we regard it, but also the themes we choose to discuss as much as those we would rather ignore. Up until today this is particularly true for architecture museums.

The masculine habitus

Since it was established in 1984, DAM has shown approximately 400 exhibitions. Whereas roughly 100 focused on a male architect, only 4 were dedicated to a female architect: the Irish-French designer Eileen Gray (1996); Margarete Schütte-Lihotzky, the first woman architect in Austria and a collaborator on Ernst May's "New Frankfurt" team (1997); the architect and feminist Verena Dietrich (2006); and Galina Balaschowa, the architect and interior designer for the Russian aerospace industry (2014). Even where it would have been appropriate to include a female partner, she was either not mentioned or only referred to in passing. Such was the fate of Ray Eames in the exhibition about Charles Eames (1991) or Marlene Moeschke-Poelzig in the one dedicated to Hans Poelzig (2008). This was by no means malicious intent or particularly misogynist, but historically and culturally the *state of the art*. And DAM, too, was formed by a masculine habitus in architecture which marginalizes women. Therefore, it is not surprising that the architecture museum of the Technical University of Munich has even more room for improvement: its highly regarded exhibition about Lina Bo Bardi (2014) remains the only show dedicated solely to a woman architect since it was founded in 1977.

In 1991, the American architect Robert Venturi received the Pritzker Prize in acknowledgment of his life's work, for, among other things, the influential 1972 publication about Post Modernism, *Learning from Las Vegas*. His longstanding partner, the urbanist Denise Scott Brown, who was actually the main author of this study, came away empty-handed. Even a petition that was set in motion in 2013 and signed by numerous highly regarded colleagues and experts to retroactively award the prize to Denise Scott Brown has so far remained unsuccessful. Established in 1979, the Pritzker Prize was given exclusively to male architects for twenty-five years, until the first woman, Zaha Hadid, was honored in 2004. The German practice of awarding prizes does not look any different. In 2013, Matthias Sauerbruch, of the Berlin-based office Sauerbruch Hutton, received the Gottfried Semper Prize of the Saxon Academy of the Arts, while his partner, Louisa Hutton, was ignored. The prize was only conferred on her after a sustained outcry.

The dry statistics

The flagrant marginalization of women architects, of which DAM has been a willing participant, was one reason for the *Frau Architekt* exhibition. The other, namely the dry statistics, was equally disquieting: since 2006, female and male students have been studying architecture in equal numbers.[1] Since 2016, women, at 58%, are now overtaking the men,[2] a tendency that is steadily increasing. Nonetheless, in spite of a remarkably low dropout rate and, for the most part, outstanding qualifications, according to the most recent statistics of the Federal Chamber of Architects, barely 36% of female

---

1 Kaufmann/Ihsen/Braslavsky (2019), 5.

2 Ibid.

graduates actually start practicing and become licensed.[3] Many do not even enter the profession and others leave after a short time. There is a "missing group" of more than 20%. What happens to these women and where are they? Even those who carry on rarely make the jump to the top tiers of professional practice. Shaped by the star system, the image of the genius, the alpha animal in a black suit wearing a distinctive pair of designer eyeglasses, architecture remains a masculine domain. In a *New York Times* interview, Yen Ha, the founder of the New York architecture office Front Studio, succinctly described this situation: "I'm not white, wearing black, funky glasses, tall or male. I'm none of the preconceptions of what an architect might be, and that means that every time I introduce myself as an architect, I have to push through the initial assumptions."[4] Reason enough for DAM to tackle the project *Frau Architekt. Over 100 years of women in the profession of architecture* and to finally examine the root causes of this masculine habitus, particularly in our own ranks. It is a matter of nothing less than the commitment to stop being the problem, and to start becoming the solution. (Figures 1–2)

Frau Architekt: Catalogue, exhibition, films

The catalogue and exhibition of *Frau Architekt* presented 22 women architects who were active in the 20th century; as a group, they embraced modernity, discarded conventions and entered a profession that previously had been closed to them. The lives of these women played out against the tumultuous decades of recent German history, starting around 1900 when the first female architects emerged, and continued through empire, republic and dictatorship; the years of German division, reunification and the first decades of the 21st century. Taken together, this collection attempts to write architecture history in a new manner, namely from the perspective of female protagonists. The biographical approach is the concept; history does not exist exclusively in the collective singular, but is always a construction of many personal, individual and subjective stories. Since the student uprisings of

---

3 https://www.bak.de/architekten/wirtschaft-arbeitsmarkt/ausbildung/ accessed on February 20, 2021.

4 Quoted in Pogrebin (2016).

1968 and the emergence of the "second wave" women's movement at the very latest, the notion that the private is always political has become mainstream.

The 22 women architects that were portrayed were chosen according to the best curatorial knowledge and convictions, but even the most careful selection cannot compensate for the omissions that nonetheless exist in a limited and subjective collection of stories. Because it would have been possible to write a similar history using the lives of other women, the exhibition was expanded to include nine interviews that were captured in seven films, in order to render "architecture histories" more comprehensible and to give other women architects, especially those who are active in the here and now, a forum. The films could be seen in our *Frauenzimmer*[5], that is, the transformed "house in house," that the Cologne architect Oswald Mathias Ungers inserted into the upper-floor galleries as the programmatic centerpiece of DAM. (Figure 3)

These short films introduce contemporary witnesses as they examine questions that concern women in architecture in recent history and up until the present day. Cutting across different generations, the selection affords a personal, utterly subjective impression of the past century, its different political systems, everyday realities and the kinds of careers that were available. Born between 1930 and 1995, these women recount their lives in in West Germany or in East Germany; during the years immediately after reunification; and today. Their stories recall decades of professional and personal experiences in the male-dominated profession of architecture and give insight into their accomplishments in a wide spectrum of specializations.

In 1960, Iris Dullin-Grund won the competition for the *Haus der Kultur und Bildung* (House of Culture and Education) in Neubrandenburg in East Germany. Ten years later she became this municipality's chief city architect—the most important position that an architect could attain in East Germany—and worked in this capacity until the change of the political system in 1989/90. In 1982, a jury selected the design by Ingeborg Kuhler over those submitted by a large number her colleagues, overwhelmingly male, for the *Landesmuseum für Technik und Arbeit* (State Museum for Technology and Work)[6] and

---

5 In this context, the German word *Frauenzimmer* is a wordplay. Originally *Frauenzimmer* denoted a domestic room for use by noble women in the early modern times. Later it also meant a wench or a loose woman but can also refer to a woman in general.

6 Today it is known as the *Technoseum*.

Figure 1: Poster, Frau Architekt (DAM). Source: DAM.

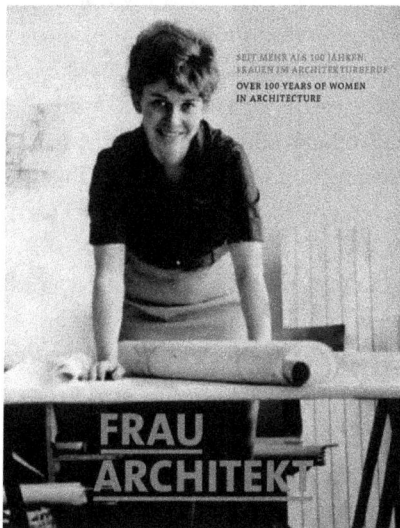

Figure 2: Catalogue, Frau Architekt (DAM). Source: Wasmuth & Zohlen/DAM.

the neighboring building for the *Süddeutsche Rundfunk* (Southern German Radio Broadcasting Service). In 1984 she became the first tenured female professor for architectural design at a West German architecture faculty at the university level, namely at the *Hochschule der Künste* (College of the Arts or HdK[7]) in West Berlin, where she taught until her retirement in 2008. As a single mother and an independent practitioner, the architect Marie-Theres Deutsch, based in Frankfurt-am-Main, has left numerous architectural traces in this city, notably the Portikus, the exhibition hall of the *Städelschule* (Staedel School or Academy of Fine Arts) and various measures to revitalize the banks along the Main River. In 2001, Susanne Hofmann established an office, the *Baupiloten*[8] in Berlin, focusing on educational and cultural facilities. To foster the participation of users in the design process and to communicate with them on an equal level, she developed sophisticated methods that are adapted to age or other aspects of personal identity. Since she completed her architectural degree in 2004, the Bavarian architect Anna Heringer builds chiefly in Bangladesh, always taking into consideration traditional building forms and materials. She has received many prizes for her work, among others the Aga Khan Award in 2007. Cathrin Schultz and Kathrin Sievers are the youngest architects in this series. Since they established their office in 2009 in Bremerhaven, far away from the large metropolitan centers, they have worked successfully as a two-woman team. In 2014 they received the local BDA (*Bund Deutscher Architekten* or Association of German Architects) prize for the greater area of Bremen. Aylin Akgöz and Meike Kimmel, students at the Technical University of Darmstadt and the Frankfurt University of Applied Sciences, respectively, both almost finished with their education, reflect upon this stage of their lives and what they expect from their future careers.

A young female filmmaker, Sophia Edschmid,[9] who is based in Frankfurt-am-Main, was hired to produce and direct these films. As she did not have close proximity to the subject matter, she was able to interview the women with a trained "view from the outside." As a result, very personal portraits

---

7   Today it is known as the *Universität der Künste* or University of the Arts (UdK).

8   *Baupiloten* is a made-up word meaning "building pilots" or "architecture navigators".

9   Sophia Edschmid, Director; Holger Priedemuth, Camera; Philipp Kehm, Sound. Film portraits of: Iris Dullin-Grund, Ingeborg Kuhler, Marie-Theres Deutsch, Susanne Hofmann, Anna Heringer, Cathrin Schultz & Kathrin Sievers, Aylin Akgöz & Meike Kimmel.

emerged, which blended reflections about their work, life, memories and anecdotes in a distinctive manner that are well worth seeing. For example, when asked about their experiences with inequality in everyday professional life, all recounted extreme instances of discrimination and their self-confident means of dealing with it. The older the woman the more intensely she was affected by such aggressive behavior, regardless if she worked in East or West Germany. The grand old lady of East German architecture, Iris Dullin-Grund, recalled the opening ceremony for her cultural and social center in Neubrandenburg, which took place in front of the assembled political *Nomenklatura* including the East German head of state, Walter Ulbricht, but not with her—they had forgotten to invite the architect.

Ingeborg Kuhler lamented that the media cared little about her architectural accomplishments and more about her gender, with statements like: "she looked like Caesar" or "a woman won the race." At the same time, she emphasized the freedom that women have because there are no strongly established expectations about "how a woman [architect] should be." In a similar way, Marie-Theres Deutsch talked about her conscious attempts to appear like a man ("Of course I smoked the cigar that was offered"), but also about the benefit of being the exotic female on the building site. She also observed that for women today, the need to prove themselves is much greater than in the 1980s when she started her career. Anna Heringer, approximately twenty years younger, is committed to sustainable building with mud brick. She meanwhile refuses to submit to the unspoken rule of proving herself by participating in "aggressive" competitions, which require long hours of hard work through the night and on weekends and are incompatible with family life. In doing so, she has consciously renounced the expectation that it is necessary to pursue prestigious, large-scale commissions in this manner.

It is striking that all the interviewees point out that women in architecture, as soon as they are professionally active, always must accomplish more than their male colleagues in order to survive the fierce competition. This inequality does not appear to exist during their studies. Aylin Akgöz and Meike Kimmel emphasize that women students are now in the majority at departments of architecture—in the university context they are an accepted fact.

Frau Architekt: Engaging the public sphere

Both the necessity for and the implicit mission of *Frau Architekt*—namely to render women in architecture more visible—led to a discourse that was further developed in a variety of events that took place at DAM and other locations. Two large symposia, lasting several days, with academics and architects from Austria, Belgium, Germany, Great Britain, Hungary, Israel, Sweden, Switzerland and the United States, addressed the current state of gender-research and provided insight into recent projects undertaken by women architects who are professionally active world-wide.

A comprehensive program with highly differentiated formats and equally heterogeneous partners provided an extension of the exhibition and gave many additional women architects a platform—through lectures, seminars, podium discussions, film evenings, a Pecha-Kucha night organized by students attending the universities in the Rhine-Main area and a national meeting to foster networking among women architects that was organized by the n-ails group in Berlin—to name but a few. As expected, the majority of the events focused on women architects and dealt with issues like finding solutions to make family and professional life more compatible; identifying the habitus and methods of exclusion that determine architectural professionalism; or defining the conditions that are needed for the better representation of women in leadership positions and as tenured professors at universities.

Others took a more macrosocial view of the situation and participated in lively and engaged debates about power, dominance and the gender-specific pre-conditions for a more equitable society. The lectures series *Stadtplus* (City plus), that DAM has presented once a month for many years, provided one outlet for these reflections. For example, with her topic "The City and Feminism—How the Women's Movement changed/changes Frankfurt,"[10] Dörthe Jung, the sociologist and co-founder of the Frankfurt *Weiberrat,*[11] focused on the second women's movement in West Germany, whose starting point was the legendary "tomato throwing incident." In September 1968, only male members of the *Sozialistischer Deutschen Studentenbundes* (SDS or Socialist German Students Federation) were chosen to address a delegate

---

10 Lecture by Dörthe Jung in the DAM series „*Stadtplus*": „*Die Stadt + der Feminismus – Wie die Frauenbewegung Frankfurt bewegt(e),*" October 4, 2017, DAM Auditorium.

11 *Rat* means council and *Weiber* is slang for old hags, women, wives, broads, etc.

conference at the Frankfurt Student House. They declared that the social oppression of women was at most a peripheral issue, irrelevant to the greater revolutionary struggle. In reaction, a visibly pregnant female delegate from Berlin, expressing the outrage of the other women in the audience, threw tomatoes at the speaker's platform, one meeting the chief theoretician of the federation.[12]

The film director Heike Sander spoke about the role of women in the SDS, who typed leaflets and cared for their children and household in private, while the decision-making lay in the hands of men outside the home. Issues about the private sphere, as it were, had been marginalized, but now were emerging, for the first time, as political themes. In the wake of the profound silence that followed the "tomato throwing incident," she launched her own activism. Two decades of political work in autonomous initiatives as well as the fight to end the prohibition on abortion culminated in the creation of the Frankfurt *Frauenreferat* (Frankfurt Department of Women's Affairs).

Among the many visitors, there were women activists of this era, who aligned themselves with the notion of solidarity with all women and, once again, articulated the need for political agendas rooted in feminism. The podium discussion, "The cowardice of women,"[13] with Bascha Mika, the author of the eponymous book and the editor-in-chief of the *Frankfurter Rundschau*, and Tanja Paulitz, Professor of Cultural Sociology and the Sociology of Knowledge at the Technical University of Darmstadt, was an evening of controversy. "The cowardice of women" is a provocative accusation aimed at well-educated women, who do not leave their "comfort zones" and all too often fall into old role models. In both of these extremely well attended events, the willingness of the audience, who came from a wide spectrum of society, to engage with the issues at hand, was clearly palpable.

Many actors in urban society willingly cooperated in these events, and it was suspiciously easy to recruit local institutions to become satellites or extended venues for *Frau Architekt*. In our view, this was a clear indication that the new edition of an old theme came at the right time and was not only (finally!) a burning issue at DAM.

---

12 Lecture by Dörthe Jung in the DAM series „*Stadtplus*": „*Die Stadt + der Feminismus – Wie die Frauenbewegung Frankfurt bewegt(e)*", October 4, 2017, DAM auditorium.

13 Podium discussion with Bascha Mika and Tanja Paulitz, moderated by Uta Zybell, February 2, 2018, DAM Auditorium. See also Mika (2011).

The resonance was impressive. All told, there were approximately 35 events, organized in cooperation with universities, professional organizations, local initiatives, museums, the German Film Institute and the adult education center in Frankfurt. This diverse program attracted over 2000 participants, who by no means hailed from the same academic peer group. For many, *Frau Architekt* exemplifies the fundamental struggles that women must fight in a man's world. In doing so, these events apparently touched a nerve in society—perhaps ignited indirectly by the emerging #MeToo debate—and continue to do so. During the 2019 Hamburg Architecture Sommer, *Frau Architekt* was presented with great success at the local *Museum der Arbeit* (Museum of Work), a museum that does not have a direct connection to architectural issues.[14] Parallel to *Frau Architekt* in Hamburg, exhibitions at two other local venues, the *Museum für Kunst und Gewerbe* (Museum for Art and Industry) and the *Medizinhistorisches Museum* (Medical Historical Museum), were organized. Both also addressed women who challenged traditional gender roles and the construction of professional identity, in the applied arts and in medicine, respectively.

At the beginning of 2020, a digitalized version of the exhibition was created to accompany an international conference, "Women in Design 2020+" in Mumbai at the local Goethe Institute.[15] Towards the end of February 2020, an extraordinarily well attended opening ceremony took place at the *Zentrum Architektur* Zürich (ZAZ or Center Architecture Zürich) in Switzerland.[16] Part of the *Frau Architekt* concept strongly encouraged the local venues that displayed the exhibition to be flexible with the selection and presentation of the 22 portraits, and they were invited to add figures who played a role in their regional or national context. For the ZAZ it made sense to slightly modify the exhibition and to add a "*SAFFA* Room", dedicated to the pioneering Swiss women architects and organizers of the two earlier *SAFFAs* (Swiss Exhibitions of Women's Work), organized in Bern (1928) and Zürich (1958). As in

14 *Frau Architekt. Seit mehr als 100 Jahren: Frauen im Architekturberuf*, Museum der Arbeit Hamburg, June 15–September 8, 2019.

15 *Frau Architekt. For more than 100 years: Women in the Profession of Architecture*, Goethe-Institut Max Mueller Bhavan, Mumbai, January 7–February 20, 2020

16 *Frau Architekt. Seit mehr als 100 Jahren: Frauen im Architekturberuf*, Zentrum Architektur Zürich (ZAZ), February 28–July 19, 2020.

Frankfurt, an extensive and ambitious program of events accompanied the Zürich exhibition and continued well after it had closed in December 2020.[17]

In late summer 2020 *Frau Architekt* was displayed in a reduced form at the *Architektenkammer NRW* (Chamber of Architects of the Federal State of North-Rhine Westphalia or NRW) in Düsseldorf. It was supplemented by a second exhibition, organized by the *Museum für Baukultur* NRW (Museum for Architecture Culture NRW), which presented contemporary projects by women in areas such as urban planning, landscape and interior design, as well as historical building research.[18] Despite the restrictions imposed upon public life due to the pandemic, other venues devised strategies to show *Frau Architekt* in 2021 and 2022 as well.[19]

The response in the media has been huge and, for the most part, positive; throughout Germany, the press—by no means limited to the typical architectural publications or the serious newspapers—embraced the subject. Even mass-market publications devoted coverage to it, signaling a clear indication of its impact and the interest in the issues that it raised. One absolute premiere for DAM: the exhibition *Frau Architekt* was even mentioned in GALA, the German life-style magazine.

Inspiring debate

Nevertheless: Gender is a complex theme and provokes controversial reactions. After viewing the 2017-18 exhibition held at DAM, visitors were encouraged to submit their reactions on slips of paper and then hang them anonymously on a wall by the exit. (Figure 4) Comments ranged from: "I am female, have hands to work with and a head for thinking. What is the

17 See: https://www.zaz-bellerive.ch/programm/archiv, accessed on September 29, 2020.

18 *Frau Architekt. Seit mehr als 100 Jahren: Frauen im Architekturberuf, Haus der Architekten und Architektinnen,* August 12–October 2, 2020; curated and supplemented by the *Museum der Baukultur NRW.*

19 To adapt to conditions during the pandemic, a virtual version of *Frau Architekt* was shown at Goethe-Insitut in Izmir in May 2021. Titled *Kadın Mimar. Türkiye ve Almanya'da mimarlık mesleğinde kadınlar,* it featured portraits of nine German women architects and nine Turkish women architects along with diverse virtual events. See: https://www.goethe.de/ins/tr/de/kul/sup/ekt.html, accessed on April 26, 2021. An adapted version of *Frau Architekt* was shown at Goethe-Institut in Athens (2021); Nikosia (2021-22); and Bucharest (2022).

Figure 3: Entrance (left) and the Frauenzimmer (right), Frau Architekt (DAM). Source: Moritz Bernoully/DAM.

Figure 4: Message wall, Frau Architekt (DAM). Source: Moritz Bernoully/DAM.

difference? And what is really your problem?" to "After five years in the profession I have quit, listened to endless misogynist chit-chat in Cologne and London, and experienced a boss who, in reaction to it, said to me: 'Toughen up, buttercup!' Really now?!" (Figure 5)

Some wandered through the *Frau Architekt* exhibition and felt offended, misunderstood or overwhelmed by feminist ideology. They complained that the special treatment of women was deeply discriminatory. Others, and there were considerably more, felt that they had finally been taken seriously and were encouraged. They more or less represented an opposing argument, that it is not the definition of inequality that is the problem, but inequality in and of itself. Concerning these exchanges, Despina Stratigakos, a Canadian-American architecture historian from State University at Buffalo, New York, USA wrote: "I am glad to hear that the exhibition is provoking debate. That is so much better than silence. And, as Freud said, 'If the patient is not resisting, the cure is not working'."[20]

Despite or precisely because of the polarization: Whether they agreed with it or not, all who came in contact with it had the feeling that *Frau Architekt* was one of the most successful exhibitions that DAM had staged in recent years.

Finally, instead of a few closing words, I leave you with a remark from Anna Heringer. In her 2017 film portrait she declared: "Earlier I was not a feminist, but now I am—architecture has made me one."

Translated by Mary Pepchinski

---

20 Email, Despina Stratigakos to Christina Budde, October 2018.

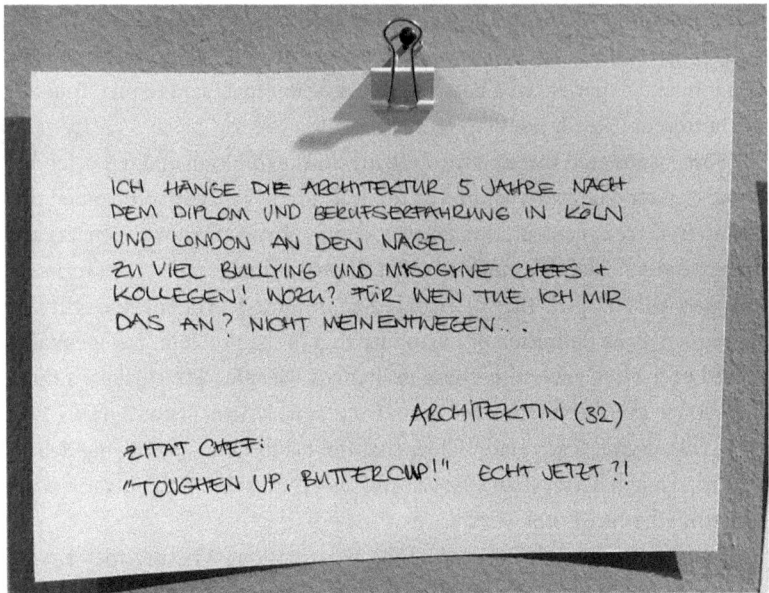

Figure 5: "After five years in the profession I have quit. ..." Message wall, Frau Architekt (DAM). Source: Mary Pepchinski.

Literature

Kaufmann, Hermann/Ihsen, Susanne/Braslavsky, Paula-Irene Villa (2019), *Frauen in der Architektur. Vorstudie zur Entwicklung eines drittmittelfinanzierten Forschungsprojektes über fachkulturell relevante geschlechtergerechte Veränderungen in der Architektur*, online under: www.holz.ar.tum.de/for schung/gender-equitye/doc/1519783/1519783.pdf

Mika, Bascha (2011), *Die Feigheit der Frauen: Rollenfallen und Geiselmentalität— eine Streitschrift wider den Selbstbetrug*, München: C. Bertelsmann Verlag.

Pepchinski, Mary/Budde, Christina/Voigt, Wolfgang/Schmal, Peter C. (eds.) (2017), *Frau Architekt. Seit mehr als 100 Jahren: Frauen im Architekturberuf/ Frau Architekt. Over 100 Years of Women in Architecture*, Ausstellungskatalog/Exhibition Catalogue, Deutsches Architekturmuseum (DAM), Frankfurt-am-Main (30.09.2017-08.03.2018), Tübingen/Berlin: Wasmuth.

Pogrebin, Robin (2016), "I am not the decorator. Female architects speak out," *New York Times*, April 12, 2016 https://www.nytimes.com/2016/04/13/arts/

design/female-architects-speak-out-on-sexism-unequal-pay-and-more.
html, accessed on June 30, 2020.

Internet Sources

Bundesarchitektenkammer   https://www.bak.de/architekten/wirtschaft-ar
beitsmarkt/ausbildung/, accessed on February 20, 2021.

Films

Frau Architekt: Portraits of Women Architects. Director: Sophia Edschmid;
Camera: Holger Priedemuth; Sound: Philipp Kehm. (2017). Film portraits
of: Iris Dullin-Grund; Ingeborg Kuhler; Marie-Theres Deutsch; Susanne
Hofmann; Anna Heringer; Cathrin Schultz und Kathrin Sievers; Aylin
Akgöz und Meike Kimmel.

About *Frau Architekt*
Stéphanie Bouysse-Mesnage in conversation
with Mary Pepchinski

Stéphanie Bouysse-Mesnage, Mary Pepchinski

SBM: How did the idea of creating an exhibition about the history of German women architects occur?

MP: Starting in 2011, I taught seminars at the Technical University of Dresden and the University of Applied Sciences Dresden about women architects in different historical and geographical contexts. My students took advantage of the growing body of secondary literature about these figures, and I believe they read texts in nine languages (Czech, Dutch. English, French, German, Mandarin, Polish, Slovak and Spanish). The stories about these women inspired much critical reflection. In December 2013, I told Wolfgang Voigt, who was then the deputy director of DAM (*Deutsches Architekturmuseum*), about the interest that the seminars had generated among my students. He was intrigued—and suggested we develop an exhibition. In addition, I lectured about the themes emerging from these seminars at different venues, including the inaugural Parity Talks at the ETH Zürich in 2016, and contributed a chapter about them to the British volume, *A Gendered Profession* (J. B. Brown, H. Harriss, R. Morrow, J. Soane (eds.), (2016)). All these experiences contributed to the making of *Frau Architekt*.

SBM: What was your initial idea for the exhibition?

MP: The original concept included the biographies in addition to cross-cutting themes, like women architects in institutions (such as the Bauhaus) or their contributions to building exhibitions. However, time was limited. In the end we—Christina Budde, who was then public education curator at DAM,

Wolfgang Voigt and me—decided to concentrate on the biographies. Nonetheless, if you read the short biographical texts and inspected the displays, you would have discovered supplemental information, such as the impact of the feminist movements of the 1970s and 1980s in the Federal Republic of Germany or the nature of architectural practice during Socialism in the German Democratic Republic.

SBM: The exhibition presented 22 portraits of German female architects who represent different social backgrounds, diverse individual situations (single/ married/with children; women working alone/women with partners), and attitudes about architecture and politics. How did you choose these women?

MP: Basically, we wanted to show a history of 20th century architecture in Germany, but with female protagonists. (Figure 1) By alternate narrative I do not mean one all-encompassing, linear argument, but a collection of disparate stories about issues that are normally considered marginal, namely the lives of women and their buildings. By presenting these stories in DAM—the most important venue to put forth ideas about architecture in Germany today—, we proposed that the marginal was a radical proposition with the potential to transform how we perceive architecture and the architectural professional. Needless to say, our alternate narrative starkly contrasts with the manner in which architectural history is taught in Germany, where there is a focus on a few masculine protagonists and, most importantly, an emphasis on the physical attributes of buildings, such as form and construction.

Geographical diversity was imperative as was the need to shed light on different kinds of protagonists and their contexts. On the one hand, we wanted to take advantage of the excellent new research on figures like Gerdy Troost (1904-2003), who was Hitler's confidant and interior designer; or Lotte Cohn (1893-1983), who hailed from Berlin and became first woman architect in Mandatory Palestine; or Lotte Stam-Beese (1903-1988), who briefly trained at the Bauhaus, worked in Berlin, Brno, Kharkov and Amsterdam in addition to overseeing large urban planning projects in Rotterdam after 1945. On the other, it was important to showcase less well-known women architects, whose lives and oeuvre merit further attention. These include: Therese Mogger (1875-1956), an architect, project developer and writer, who was active in

Figure 1. Frau Architekt, Deutsches Architekturmuseum (DAM), Frankfurt-am-Main, 2017-18. Source: DAM/Moritz Bernoully.

Düsseldorf and Bavaria; Princess Victoria zu Bentheim und Steinfurt (1887-1961), who built rural architecture and restored historic buildings on her family's estates in North-Rhine Westphalia and Bavaria; Verena Dietrich (1941-2004), a Cologne-based educator and a feminist, who designed striking steel structures; and Gertrud Schille (1940-), who developed sophisticated planetaria that were constructed around the world by the Carl Zeiss Company, located in the German Democratic Republic.

In the first decades of the 20th century, women architects sometimes trained in related areas, like the fine and applied arts. For this reason, we included Marlene Moeschke Poelzig (1894-1985), a sculptor, and Lilly Reich (1885-1947), an interior and exhibition designer. In the 1920s and 1930s, these women worked independently and in collaboration with a male architect, such as Hans Poelzig or Mies van der Rohe, respectively. We included them to illustrate what it means to "put women back into history": when we insert them into the story, we do not simply fill up the holes but are forced to write a whole new narrative. In the case of Moeschke Poelzig and Reich, we demonstrated that seminal projects which have been ascribed to a famous man were either designed by a woman or were the result of a collaborative process that engaged the unique talents of both contributors.

As DAM is located in Frankfurt-am-Main, we included the Austrian Grete Schütte-Lihotzky (1897-2000). During the 1920s she worked for Ernst May's New Frankfurt building program, and she remains a compelling figure in this city's historical memory. Although she is associated with the eponymous Frankfurt Kitchen, it was important to demonstrate the contribution of women architects beyond the domestic sphere. Other women in the exhibition—Wera Meyer-Waldeck (1906-1964), Karola Bloch (1905-1994), Lucy Hillebrand (1906-1997), Grit Bauer-Revellio (1924-2013) and Ingeborg Kuhler (1943-)—realized public architecture and Sigrid Kressmann-Zschach (1929-1990), Iris Dullin-Grund (1933-) and Merete Mattern (1930-2007) developed large urban and landscape projects.

And last but not least: We had roughly one year to produce the exhibition and catalogue! As the papers and supplemental professional materials, like models, drawings and letters, of women architects are rarely preserved in archives or, when they do exist, are sometimes attributed to a man, it was necessary to select women whose documents survive and are readily accessible. Luckily the DAM archive contains extensive materials from the estates of Lucy Hillebrand and Verena Dietrich. There were less obvious exhibits there too, like the delicately colored drawings of the expressive interior columns of the *Grosses Schauspielhaus* (1919) in Berlin that had been attributed to Hans Poelzig. Recent scholarship has revealed that several were drawn by Marlene Moeschke Poelzig or were worked on by both Hans and Marlene. We exhibited these drawings—and gave Marlene her long overdue recognition. DAM also owned a portfolio containing drawings of projects from the 1920s by the office of Richard Kauffmann, the Frankfurt-born architect who migrated to Mandate Palestine after the First World War. Lotte Cohn was an early employee of Kauffmann, and fortunately she signed her name—Charlotte Cohn—on several of her designs in this portfolio. These made their way to the walls of the exhibition. Other materials were found in private archives, public collections—or on Ebay and the *Zentralverzeichnis Antiquarischer Bücher* (Central Register of Antiquarian Books). Colleagues at the Technical University of Dresden also directed seminars with students, who researched and built the seven models of architecture by women. These models were on display too.

SBM: I was really interested in reading your article in the exhibition catalogue, "Desire and Reality: A Century of Women Architects in Germany." It enables us to learn about the general context of female contributions to architecture in Germany. I wonder why this analysis and contextualization was not presented in the exhibition? Did you want to present those portraits as an "extract"? Or did you have to restrict exhibition spaces because of technical or budget constraints?

Figure 2. Frau Architekt, Museum der Arbeit, Hamburg, 2019. Local curator: Sandra Schürmann. Source: Mary Pepchinski.

MP: Generally, we felt there was adequate supplemental information in the individual biographies. Also, we did not want the exhibition to have too much textual information—the danger is that one is reading a great deal and not looking at the items on display. Finally, at the center of the first-floor gallery at DAM, where *Frau Architekt* was exhibited, a room was converted into a small cinema showing 7 short films about 9 living women architects, who were born between 1933 and the early 1990s. We hope that you read the catalogue, perused the exhibition and watched the films because the different experiences are intended to be complementary.

SBM: In the past DAM hosted five exhibitions about women architects: Eileen Gray in 1996, Margarete Schütte-Lihotzky in 1997, Verena Dietrich in 2007, Galina Balashova in 2015 and Zaha Hadid 2017. Have there been previous exhibitions about the history of German women architects? In the editors' foreword, you mentioned an exhibition held in the 1980s, organized by Helga Schmidt-Thomsen and Christine Jachmann. Was it the first one? Could you tell me more about this exhibition?

MP: Technically there were only four exhibitions with catalogues about women architects at DAM. In actuality, the Zaha Hadid "exhibition" was a small display of several prints by this architect that are in the DAM archive. They were hung in a very small gallery in conjunction with *Frau Architekt*.

To my knowledge, in 1984 in West Berlin, Helga Schmidt-Thomsen, Christine Jachmann along with the West German section of the *L'Union Internationale des Femmes Architectes* (UIFA), organized the first historical exhibition after the Second World War about women architects in Germany. In 1985-86, an English-language version was shown in the USA for the UIFA meeting in Seattle. These exhibitions produced catalogs that have served as the basis for subsequent historical research. Because the organizers were based in West Berlin, the post-war era focused on women who were active in that city and the Federal Republic of Germany.

In 1912, the first known exhibition of German women architects was included in the mammoth event, *Die Frau im Haus und Beruf* (The Woman in her Home and her Profession), which presented the cultural, professional and charitable endeavors of middle-class and aristocratic German women. It occupied the capacious exhibition halls at the *Zoologischer Garten* in Berlin. Lilly Reich, in addition to two other leading applied artists, Else Oppler-Legband (1875-1965) and Fia Wille (1868-1920), oversaw the planning. Although it was only open for a month, it attracted a half-million visitors. Museums today can only dream of such resonance! It also contained a small display of work by women architects, featuring projects by Emilie Winkelmann (1875-1951), Elisabeth von Knobelsdorff (1877-1959) and Therese Mogger. Shortly thereafter, in 1914, two temporary pavilions for the display of fine and applied arts by middle-class women were erected at trade fairs in Germany: the *Haus der Frau* (Woman's Building) at the Cologne Werkbund Exhibition and the *Haus der Frau* at the Book and Graphic Exhibition in Leipzig. These were a milestone, as women architects designed both pavilions—Margarete Knüppelholz-Roeser (1886-1949) in Cologne and Emilie Winkelmann in Leipzig. Each also housed an exhibit of work by women architects. This practice was revived in the Weimar period with exhibitions such as *Die gestaltende Frau* (The designing Woman) at the Wertheim Department Store in Berlin in 1930.

SBM: To prepare this exhibition, have you been inspired by exhibitions that have been held in other countries about this theme?

MP: When I was studying for my bachelor's degree in art history at Barnard College (the women's college of Columbia University in New York City), Susana Torre curated the exhibition *Women in American Architecture* (1977) at the Brooklyn Museum, also in New York City. At the time, the second wave feminist movement was a force in New York, and women in academia were questioning the canons of art and architectural history. We read the iconic text by Linda Nochlin, "Why have there been no famous women artists?" (1971), which encouraged us to probe the machinations of institutional power to understand women's marginalization in the arts, along with the feminist art criticism of Lucy Lippard. During the late 1970s and early 1980s, when I attended the Graduate School of Architecture Planning Preservation (GSAPP) at Columbia University, I befriended Susana Torre, who was teaching there at the time. Her exhibition was certainly lodged in the back of my mind.

Like the 1977 exhibition, *Frau Architekt* uses a collection of tables as an architectural device. But where Susana Torre's exhibition asked the question, "How did women shape the built environment in the USA?" and included women who played other roles, like critics, *Frau Architekt* focused narrowly on women who had realized buildings or made designs. Nevertheless, it is crucial to keep in mind that *Women in American Architecture* was a product of second wave feminism in the USA. In its striving for exemplary buildings and protagonists, it sometimes turned a blind eye to other meanings and interpretations. One was the uncritical championing of the monumental Women's Building at the 1893 Chicago World's Fair, designed by Sophia Hayden, one of the first female graduates in architecture from the Massachusetts Institute of Technology (MIT) in the USA. Left unsaid was the vigorous exclusion of the contributions of people of color to the 1893 Chicago World's Fair and the Woman's Building in particular, a reflection of the brutal politics of

Figure 3. Frau Architekt, Zentrum Architektur Zürich (ZAZ), Zürich, 2020. Local curator: Evelyn Steiner. Source: Mary Pepchinski.

racial separation in the United States at that time.[1] So, what might appear as a proud symbol of professional success for white, native-born Anglo-American, middle-class women, was a bitter expression of suppression, oppression and discrimination against women of color, immigrant women and other marginalized groups.

---

1 The Pavilion of Haiti was one exception at the 1893 World's Fair. The pamphlet, "The Reason Why the Colored American is Not in the World's Columbian Exposition" by Ida B. Wells was available here. Although there were other instances of African American participation at the fair, such as the six African American women who contributed lectures about developments after emancipation to the World's Congress of Representative Women at the Woman's Building, the overall presence of African Americans was severely restricted. See: Hautzinger (2018); https://worldsfairchicago1893.com/tag/frederick-douglass/, accessed on March 12, 2021; and the discussion of the 1893 Haiti Pavilion in: St. Hubert (2018).

For this reason, *Frau Architekt* also broached politics and social concerns. For example, we show that Lilly Reich not only produced seminal exhibition designs and furniture with Mies van der Rohe, but also marshalled her talents in service of Nazi propaganda. Others, like Lotte Cohn, chose migration; Marie Frommer and Karola Bloch went into exile; Gertrud Schille and Iris Dullin-Grund found unique professional opportunities under East German socialism; and Verena Dietrich discovered her voice through engagement with the feminist movements of the 1970s and 1980s. We did not want to see women as being all the same but elected to present their differences and the circumstances that shaped their professional lives. And perhaps this is one approach that distinguished *Frau Architekt* from the 1977 exhibition in New York.

Susana Torre has also talked about how the giant field of red drawing tables, which formed the main element of the 1977 New York exhibition, was like a giant art object that was inserted into the grand space of the Beaux-Arts exhibition hall at the Brooklyn Museum. Unlike a typical exhibition, artifacts and information were displayed on the red drawing tables. According to Torre, this approach was necessary because if examples of women's work were hung on the walls of this vast gallery, they would appear small and pathetic—and give critics a reason to denigrate the historical contributions of women. Furthermore, Torre emphasizes that the tables represent individual yet *anonymous* women architects. In contrast, I see the tables that we used for *Frau Architekt* as being generic elements that anchor a small depository of documents about *one particular woman*—a mini-retrospective of her life and her work, if you will. Like Torre's tables, they have a spatial purpose, but it is about locating the individual, and not creating one big gesture.

Finally, the adaptability of *Frau Architekt* is worth noting. This exhibition is not an immutable *Gesamtkunstwerk*, as the tables, exhibits and films are meant to be flexible components that can be added to, subtracted from or supplemented to suit a particular context. So far, this concept has proved successful as *Frau Architekt* was adapted for display in Hamburg (Museum der Arbeit, 2019); Zürich (Zentrum Architektur Zürich, 2020) and Düsseldorf (Haus der Architekten, 2020). (Figures 2–4) In addition, under the auspices of Goethe-Institut, a version of *Frau Architekt* has been shown in conjunction with exhibitions of local women architects in several Asian and European cities.[2]

---

2 Goethe-Institut Mumbai (2020); Goethe-Institut Izmir (2021); Goethe-Institut Athens (2021); Goethe-Institut Nikosia (2021-22); and Goethe-Institut Bucharest (2022).

Figure 4. Frau Architekt, Haus der Architekt, Düsseldorf, 2020. Local curator: Ursula Kleefisch-Jobst. Source: Ursula Kleefisch-Jobst.

Literature

Hautzinger, Daniel (2018), "Friedrich Douglass's Defiant Stand at Chicago's World's Fair", wttw, February 14, 2018, https://interactive.wttw.com/playlist/2018/02/14/frederick-douglass-chicago-worlds-fair, accessed on March 12, 2021.

Pepchinski, Mary/Budde, Christina/Voigt, Wolfgang/Schmal, Peter C. (eds.) (2017), *Frau Architekt. Seit mehr als 100 Jahren: Frauen im Architekturberuf/ Frau Architekt. Over 100 Years of Women in Architecture*, Ausstellungskatalog/Exhibition Catalogue, Deutsches Architekturmuseum (DAM), Frankfurt-am-Main (30.09.2017-08.03.2018), Tübingen/Berlin: Wasmuth.

St. Hubert, Hadassah (2018), *Visions of a modern nations: Haiti at the World's Fairs*, Dissertation (2018), University of Miami, Coral Gables Florida, USA.

Torre, Susana (ed.)(1977), *Women in American Architecture*. Exhibition catalogue, The Architectural League of New York/Brooklyn Museum, Brooklyn, New York (February 24-April 17, 1977), New York: Watson-Guptill.

Union internationale des Femmes Architects Sektion Bundesrepublik e.V. (ed.)(1984), *Zur Geschichte der Architektinnen und Designerinnen im 20. Jahrhundert. Eine erste Zusammenstellung*, Berlin: Union internationale des Femmes Sektion Bundesrepublik e.V.

Internet Sources

Chicago World's Fair/Friedrich Douglass https://worldsfairchicago1893.com/
tag/frederick-douglass/, accessed on March 12, 2021.

Women in American Architecture https://archleague.org/exhibitions/wom
en-in-american-architecture-a-historic-and-contemporary-perspec
tive-exhibition/, accessed on Feb. 1, 2021.

Making Difference
Reflections on teaching "Architectures of Gender"

Torsten Lange & Gabrielle Schaad

In this essay we reflect on our experiences of collaboratively conceiving and teaching the tripartite seminar series "Architectures of Gender," held at the Department of Architecture, ETH Zürich as part of our appointment to the Visiting Lectureship of the Theory of Architecture between 2017 and 2019. Doing so, we will first address the particular institutional and disciplinary context in which our course sought to intervene, before sketching out some of its wider ambitions, contents and methods. In closing, we consider the legacy and contribution of our seminar to discourse within the department—given its disappearance from the curriculum after we left the school.

To start, a few words to situate ourselves: One of us trained in architecture, coming to this discipline—using the contemporary jargon of institutional diversity—from a "non-traditional background," and later transitioned to architectural history and theory within the Anglo-Saxon academic system. The other is an art historian with an interest in contemporary spatial practices as well as the relationship between art and architecture, having lived and worked in Japan for several years before teaching at an art and design college prior to joining the architecture faculty of the ETH Zürich. In different ways, our personal and professional histories have shaped our way of navigating this peculiar academic setting, which we joined with a sense of excitement but also bewilderment. Our *modus operandi* as researchers and, foremost, as pedagogues was driven by this productive friction with our day-to-day work environment. Understanding our labor as a form of practice that critically engages with its context and seeks to transform it, we act in a collaborative, transdisciplinary and transversal manner.

Before working together, we were both active members of a large grass-roots initiative called the Parity Group, which came together in 2014 and sought to address the severe underrepresentation of women and general lack of diversity at all levels of the Department of Architecture at the ETH (and beyond). This absence was present throughout this institution, from leadership positions and as role models to the subjects of research and objects of study in an overwhelmingly European, male-focused curriculum. Through its annual symposia and action-oriented workshops—called the Parity Talks (2016–2019)—this transient and large group has spun a dense web of relations to other individuals and collective actors who advocate affirmative change in our discipline.[1] Discussions around pedagogy were part and parcel of its institutional activism from the outset, with the idea of an interdepartmental seminar focusing on issues of gender first circulating "in the air" in 2016.[2]

When we conceived "Architectures of Gender" in the summer 2017, we were not aware that there had been previous efforts to introduce gender as an issue into the curriculum at the ETH. Unbeknownst to us, there was a forgotten history of researching and disseminating the contribution of women to the production environment at this institution. Under the direction of Eliana Perotti and Katia Frey, a research group investigated the architectural theory and pedagogy of Flora Ruchat-Roncati and has been crucial in unforgetting this history.[3] This has been particularly insightful at a time when the department's once progressive past—Ruchat-Roncati was the first woman to be appointed to full professor at the ETH Zürich in 1985, two years after an exhibition showcased the work of the pioneering Swiss female architect, Lux Guyer—came to haunt the school, as criticism and controversies mounted around strategic professorial appointments.[4] Apart from Ruchat-Roncati, whose preserved lecture notes testify to her commitment to showcasing the work of women architects, such as Eileen Gray, the seminal contribution on the part of Petra Stojanik and her elective course *Frauen in der Geschichte des*

---

1   For an account of the Parity Group and its activism until 2018 see: Lange/Malterre-Barthes (2018).

2   To that end, one of the authors and Emily Eliza Scott chaired a roundtable salon on feminist pedagogies at the 13th AHRA international conference Architecture & Feminisms at KTH Stockholm in November 2016. See: Lange/Scott (2017).

3   See their two edited volumes in the series *Theoretikerinnen des Städtebaus* (Women Theorists of Urbanism): Frey/Perotti (2015)(eds.); Frey/Perotti (2019)(eds.).

4   See the monographic issue "Flora Ruchat-Roncati. Architektur als Netzwerk" in *werk, bauen + wohnen*, (2017); and Frey/Perotti (2018).

Bauens (Women in the History of Architecture) must be mentioned as well.[5] Stojanik initially joined the department in the mid-1980s as part of Roncati's team and worked independently as an assistant professor for design from 1993 to 1996. At the same time, the *Institut gta* (*Institut für Geschichte und Theorie der Architektur* or Institute for History and Theory of Architecture) also went through a period of intense retro- and introspection, as 2017 saw its fiftieth anniversary. It, too, had its share of controversy regarding practices like hiring and awarding tenure to women. Its history is marked by the absence of women among its rank of full professors, with Bettina Köhler's short tenure as assistant professor between 1996 and 2002 providing the only exception. A statistical analysis by Sarah Nichols and Ita Heinze-Greenberg, presented as part of the *gta50* exhibition, also exposed the predominance of male figures as dissertation topics in the 198 completed theses. Not a single one was supervised by a woman professor.[6] After Petra Stojanik's important work of documenting women's contribution to the built environment all but disappeared—if not from research, then from teaching, and following the departure of these ground-breaking women from the department around 2000,[7] this means of inquiry has recently been revived by colleagues such as art historian Dora Imhof through her oral history courses and Silvia Claus, former director of the Master of Advanced Study (MAS) in History and Theory of Architecture.[8]

Our course, however, remained distinct from these efforts. Supplementing, rather than contrasting, the "herstory" mode of including women into canonical narratives, "Architectures of Gender" introduced the knowledge developed by gender and queer studies into theory and design studio practices, bringing with it the potential to deconstruct long-accepted notions that form the foundation of this discipline. Across its three iterations, the seminar set out to study architecture's role in the social and material construction of (binary) gender in the modern era. Following contemporary thinkers

---

5 Stojanik (1995). It is also worth noting that figures like the art historians Irene Nierhaus and Dorothee Huber also published essays in the series *Beiträge zum Diplomwahlfach Frauen in der Geschichte des Bauens*, edited by Stojanik between 1994 and 1996.

6 Nichols (2019).

7 Of course, others deserve to be mentioned, as well, such as Barbara Zibell.

8 At the time of writing the website/database of the MAS seminar and research project *Frauen Bauen* was under construction. See: http://www.schweizerarchitektinnen.ch, accessed on March 9, 2021.

such as Paul B. Preciado, we were interested in asking how architecture not only houses gendered bodies, but also—somewhat paradoxically—plays a role in the constitution of those bodies, and their corresponding subjectivities.[9] Michel Foucault's concept of "political technology" proved useful here. With the former he sought to describe the complex protocols, arrangements and apparatuses that not only give stability and meaning to social institutions, but also shape modern subjectivity by acting on, as well as operating through, the body. We see architecture as such a form of technology, where modern self(-hood) and power intersect. Despite the seminar's focus on close readings of theoretical and historical texts, our goal was to cultivate discussion. Rather than resort to simple answers or hide behind "neutrality," we sought to develop an atmosphere of critical questioning. This entailed shifts in perspective in order to destabilise fixed meanings and undo the "invisibility work"[10] that sustains normalization—not only in architectural discourse, but also in the unquestioned customs and codes of everyday behaviour within a predominantly masculine, white, heterosexual, European academic environment. The encounter with a range of texts from different authors and various architectural case studies provided productive openings to re-think the process of mutual co-construction between architecture and its human subject(s).

Making Difference: Revisiting gender, separate spheres, challenging narratives (Fall Semester 2017)

If built structures do not necessarily represent sexual difference, how exactly did they create and maintain separate spheres? Why does modernity's seemingly neutral architecture, modelled after a universal image of the ideal man, create—above all—exclusions? These are some questions that motivated us to propose a seminar on the intricate relationships of specific gender constructs, stereotypes and spatializations. (Figure 1) In order to deconstruct normative programs and protocols, the course aimed at an in-depth understanding of the matter in which unconscious daily behaviour

---

9 Kogan (2010).

10 Boys (2018).

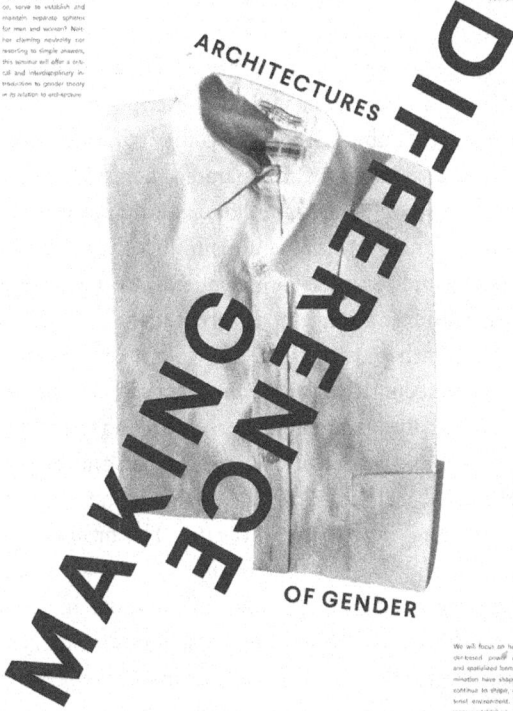

Figure 1: Poster, Seminar: Making Difference. Architectures of Gender. ETH Zürich, Faculty of Architecture, Fall Semester 2017, based on art by Diller Scofidio + Renfro. Poster Design: Blanka Major.

and language re-produce heteronormative space in architectural plans and practices. Acknowledging the relevance of performativity in architecture, we analysed specific types of gender-segregated spaces. To accomplish this, we chose a group of texts whose authors have tried to de-normalize the built environment. These texts enabled us to sharpen our attention to the implicit meanings that are embodied in spaces and descriptions of them as well as to improve our analytical abilities over the course of the seminar, which had three-parts: A) gender, sexuality and separate spheres; B) queer lives de-naturalizing normative space; and C) methodological approaches and the plurality of voices in different waves of feminism since the 1960s. Regarding the theme of gender, sexuality and separate spheres, we acknowledge that spatial segregations manifest a range of different intersectional or discriminatory attitudes. One of them is the stereotype of the biologically rooted, gender binary and sexual identity/orientation, deconstructed since the 1990s by gender theorist Judith Butler, among others.[11] Through the centuries, several moral presumptions and prescriptions have shaped and co-produced a set of behavioural rules, specifying how bodies should inhabit and use private and public spaces.[12] A telling example is the use of bathrooms in Switzerland: Even if almost everybody is quite used to share a toilet with people of different sexes at home, regulations and hence installations in Switzerland—as well as until recently in many Western nations, impose a binary separation in public and semi-public spaces such as restaurants. We took the investigation of the conditions on campus focusing on the Department of Architecture at the ETH. First, the students examined the regulations regarding toilets in public buildings. Then they experimented with the signage of the bathrooms within the faculty building and documented the reactions of the passers-by to these changes. Finally, they counted the number of students and employees, comparing the proportionality of men's, women's, and gender-neutral toilets.

Turning to the question of queer lives and the de-naturalization of normative space, we asked, along with the English philosopher Sara Ahmed: How do the spatialities of a non-heterosexual life look like? After all, what most people perceive through their privileged experience as their "comfort zone" is largely moulded on everyday heteronormative assumptions of gen-

11 Butler (1990), "Subjects of Sex/Gender/Desire," 6–16.
12 Preciado (2004).

der roles.[13] Beyond these "comfort zones," one discovers non-compliant bodies that appropriate specific locations in the urban fabric, transforming them into safe spaces. A screening of Wu Tsang's film *Wildness* (2012) organised with the students at Helden Bar, one of the long-standing, weekly gay-bars in Zürich, offered an excellent opportunity not only to personally connect to the founders of the gay-rights movement in this city, but also to learn about their perspective on urbanism and the transient nature of such "safe spaces." It also allowed students to gain first-hand experience with a non-normative community without objectifying and exoticizing its members.

Regarding the methodological approaches and the plurality of voices in different waves of feminism since the 1960s, it was necessary to discuss the nature of historiography, that is, how the history and criticism of architecture is conceived and communicated. What are the theoretical positions and names of architects who represent what we consider the architectural canon? How do positivist objectivity and a universalist perspective construct the impression of a researcher's seemingly neutral voice? What are the strategies to enhance knowledge that go behind this purported neutrality? How do we build our stories and devise analytical models? In order to do this, do we need to rely on key heroic figures, or can we talk about collectives, constellations and networks instead?

Care work: Ecologies of care and interdependent bodies (Fall Semester 2018)

We continued the series in Winter Semester 2018, centering our seminar on "reproductive labor," which is necessary for all human production, architecture included. (Figure 2) The procreative and nurturing capacity of the female body has too often been treated as a prerequisite for the expropriation of women's unpaid work, in the context of reproduction and more widely. This normalization not only devalues all kinds of care and maintenance at the emotional level but also makes it invisible and pushes it into oblivion. So, we wondered: How has this attitude towards feminine care and reproduction informed planning, from the design of single-family houses to the layout of cities? The critical analysis of philosopher Nancy Fraser provided us

---

13 Ahmed (2004), "(Dis)comfort and Norms," 146–155.

with a framework to answer this question. In decrying the present-day conditions of "late Capitalism," she speaks about a crisis in care work that affects a whole range of interdependent services, in particular, the "global chains of care." [14] Fraser's analysis ties in with earlier critiques of capitalism's dependence on unpaid reproductive work, notably those found in Silvia Federici's early text "Wages against Housework." [15] Addressing this issue from another perspective, Ruth Schwartz-Cowan's socio-anthropological studies trace the (psychological) effects of a supposed technological or industrial revolution in the household on the workload and expectations of "housewives" since the 1920s. Schwartz-Cowan ultimately provides tools for critically discussing not only historical developments but also a means to evaluate the promises of contemporary smart home technologies. [16]

Another issue that Fraser addresses concerns the consequences of the division of labor in two-wage households, where both partners engage in professional activities outside the home, thus requiring someone else to perform the domestic tasks for remuneration. To meet this demand, migrants entrust their children and elderly parents to other family members and then perform domestic work elsewhere in their country or abroad for wealthy families. The majority of these migrants are women. They range from unskilled domestic workers to trained health services personnel. Rather than creating conditions that could facilitate the evolution of the organization and valuation of these personal services, the importation of labor displaces the problem by not addressing the unfair distribution of these tasks within the home. [17] These interdependencies create specific spatializations. In Hong Kong, the ephemeral space that regularly surfaces at outdoor gatherings of domestic workers on their day off from work is one example. In order to reflect on how these issues structure our built environment, we assigned small research projects in Zürich. These included: An investigation into whether and how Zürich's development strategy (Zürich 2040) considered aspects of gender and care; the social and spatial distribution of care work in different communal housing models; Swiss research and development of smart home technologies and automated care solutions; architec-

---

14 Fraser (2016).

15 Federici (1975; reprint 2012).

16 Schwartz-Cowan (1976).

17 Fraser (2016).

tural projects for people with disabilities; the history of the HIV-Lighthouse hospice in Zurich; and the mapping of maintenance regimes and networks in the HIL building, which is home to the ETH Zürich's architecture department on the Hönggerberg campus. The aim of this research was to further develop analytical tools to evaluate architecture through the lens of gender. These projects resulted in stimulating students to reflect on the lifestyles and everyday experiences that unfold in their architectural designs and within buildings. However, we know very well that a more equitable and fair distribution of reproductive tasks, for example, a revaluation or—even more—an appropriate remuneration for all kinds of maintenance and care work, does not depend solely on architectural design. Nevertheless, the architecture we propose reflects our social attitudes and expectations, while it imposes them onto the people who use it.

body_building: Bodies of knowledge / knowledge of bodies (Spring Semester 2019)

Our encounter with non-normative bodies by way of the mini symposium on interdependence[18] and the design of spaces with bodily difference rather than an "ideal user" in mind prompted us to think more deeply about the concept of the body in and through architecture. For this reason, we devoted the entire third semester to questions concerning the gendered body, and its metaphorical and material (re)building in the contemporary era of technologically enhanced living. (Figure 3) While once again cultural and social theories provided the critical framework and tools to understand notions of "difference" and "care" in their spatial dimension, during this semester, histories and philosophies of science and technology took center stage. Above all, Donna Haraway's subversive re-reading of the technocratic figure of the "cyborg" and its emancipatory transformation to counter gender bias, binary

---

18 On the notion of interdependence see Kathryn Abrams' article that discusses the encounter (a stroll through San Francisco's Mission district) between disability activist Sunara Taylor and the philosopher Judith Butler in Astra Taylor's documentary film and later book *The Examined Life* (2008). (Abrams (2011)).

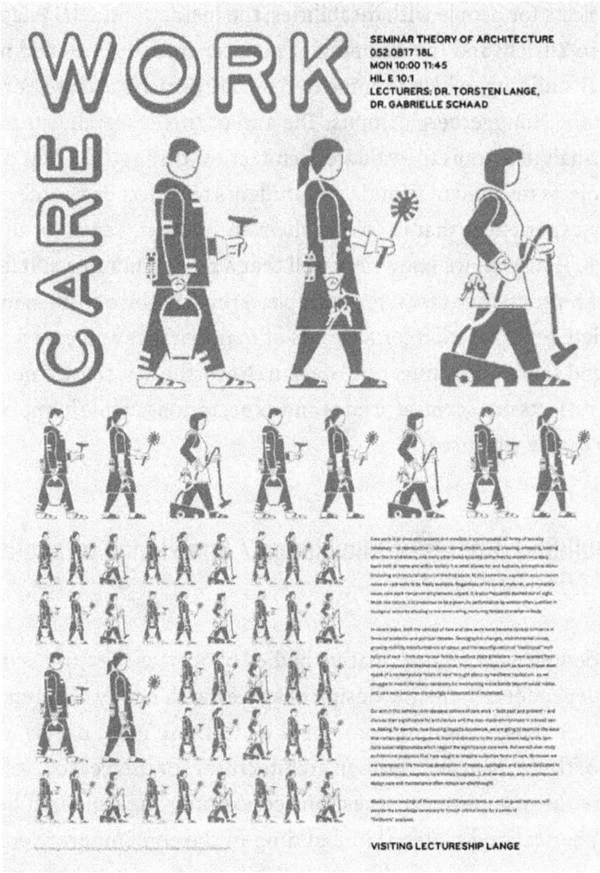

Figure 2: Poster, Seminar: Care Work. Ecologies of care and independent bodies. ETH Zürich, Faculty of Architecture, Fall Semester 2018, based on art by Andreas Siekmann. Poster Design: Blanka Major.

constructions, the "reproductive matrix" and essentialist understandings of nature, became a key reference.[19]

Humanoid figures—half-living fleshy body, half machine—have haunted the (architectural) imaginary and its discourses for a long time, often serving distinctly utopian or dystopian narratives. The same counts for the idea of architecture and technology more broadly as extensions to the body and its capacities. Likewise, if the human body did indeed serve as a model for architecture, the latter has also contributed to the former's construction, especially in the modern era, through techniques of measuring, norms and standards. We therefore explored the following question: How does this relationship change in the present day, as the boundaries between human body and technology increasingly blur, and the presumed integrity of the body becomes subject to debate and alteration?

Taking recent theorisations of "embodiment" in feminist, queer-, critical race- and disability studies as our point of departure, we problematized the body as a historical and cultural construct, and asked: To what extent can its un- and re-building in certain forms of trans* embodiment bear the utopian potential to destabilise associated binary understandings, like nature vs. culture? Which concepts of the body undergird these visions? How did they historically come to be? What drives the desire to leave behind humanistic ideas of the body in favour of a "posthuman" future? and: Is this posthuman future already inscribed in the vibrant material assemblages that constitute our embodied experiences?

To answer these questions, we looked at ways in which modernist architecture declared the "normal" body—a highly artificial construct based on statistical averages drawn from anthropometric data since the nineteenth-century advent of "Human Science"—its aesthetic ideal. Depicted in drawing standards and measured human figures and thus becoming legible to architects and designers, "Man, the measure of all things" turned out to have severe implications for all those who were rendered "nonconforming" by this new "normate template," as Aimi Hamraie has shown—be they female, racialised, or otherwise pathologized human beings.[20] Given this effacing, disabling and levelling character of our modern-day material and built environment, it is not surprising that, since the late-1980s, techno-feminists have seen a great emancipatory

---

19 Haraway (1985).

20 Hamraie (2017).

potential in the advent of cyberspace and virtual reality. It is these disembodied visions and their critique (as phallogocentric) found in the writings of feminist philosophers such as Elizabeth Grosz and Luce Irigaray, who advocated a return to corporeality and lived spatiality, that we turned to next. After considering the experience of living and interacting with machines and (medical) technologies in a shift from prosthetic to augmented bodies—which, needless to say, comes with its own contradictions around standardisation, technical compliance, and fixedness/user-friendliness—we focused on techniques of altering one's own body. We also looked at the spaces in which these self-modifications take place: Marcia Ian's account of female body building practices in a public sports facility and Paul B. Preciado's auto-theoretical story of using "testogel" in the safety of their home. The semester ended with a look to the future. We engaged with Jack Halberstam's reading of Gordon Matta-Clark's "anarchitectural" projects as a blueprint for recent art and spatial practices, those by trans* artists in particular that encourage us to "unbuild gender" in dialogue with the notion of the "posthuman" and considered Laboria Cubonik's call to "denaturalize" as found in the Xenofeminist Manifesto. In addition to Jack Halberstam's guest lecture (Figure 4), a presentation by the architect Joel Sanders introduced us to his recent "Stalled!" project about the design of gender-neutral and inclusive public bathrooms.[21]

Teaching to transgress: In lieu of a conclusion

Over the course of the two-year period, the "Architectures of Gender" seminar series and its occasional side events allowed us to build transversal connections both inside and outside our institution, for example, with design studios like Adam Caruso's "Hidden Interiors" (Fall 2018), which investigated gender, among other issues, to understand the politics of domestic space. The most rewarding of those collaborations, however, was with the Future Clinic for Critical Care, a performance-based event series around questions of care organised by disability scholar and activist Nina Mühlemann, the comedian and performer Edwin Ramirez, in collaboration with artist Jeremy Wade.[22] Together with students and other colleagues, like Li Tavor, we participated

---

21 See https://www.stalled.online, accessed on September 7, 2020; Sanders (2017).
22 See https://www.futureclinic.org, accessed on September 7, 2020.

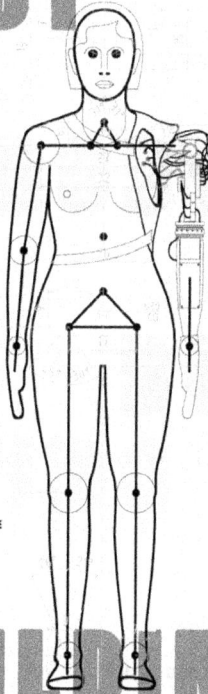

Figure 3: Poster, Seminar: body_building: Bodies of knowledge
/ knowledge of bodies. ETH Zürich, Faculty of Architecture,
Spring Semester 2019, based on art by Thomas Carpenter. Poster
Design: Blanka Major.

as the ETH Critical Care Collective in two events that focused on the theme of home (February 2019) and the institution (November 2019).

Traces of our conversations with students remain visible not only in the "Making Difference" seminar blog, which became a space for participants to test ideas and practice their writing skills.[23] They have also informed the approximately ten elective theses that address different aspects of gender and architecture—from biographical studies (on Lina Bo Bardi and Margarete Schütte-Lihotzky), to historical analyses of modern office and residential buildings against the background of women joining the labour force, to speculative and creative enquiries into the colour pink and the gendered dimension of contemporary public space. In combination with external factors—the growth of the *Frauenstreikbewegung* (women's strike movement), in particular—these conversations have stretched far beyond the ivory tower of the ETH.[24] They amplified the voices of empowered students to engage more actively in the institution and the ongoing debates at the Parity Talks, specifically to speak up about instances of sexism and harassment or the toxic culture of the *crit*, the design consultation with a supervising instructor, and to voice their dissatisfaction with the painfully slow progress in achieving parity in professorships, the invited speakers at public events, as well as diversifying the curriculum.

Whether or not we succeeded in making a difference within this relatively short span of three semesters remains to be seen. Let's work to make sure that those who might stumble upon our modest efforts in twenty or so years will no longer feel that nothing has changed. With bell hooks we believe that "the work of transforming the academy" demands that we "embrace struggle and sacrifice. We cannot be easily discouraged."[25] Ultimately, only in a mutually empowering partnership between students and teachers will the transgression of outmoded patterns be achieved.

---

23 See https://blogs.ethz.ch/making-difference, accessed on September 7, 2020.

24 See Schaad (2020).

25 hooks (1994), 33.

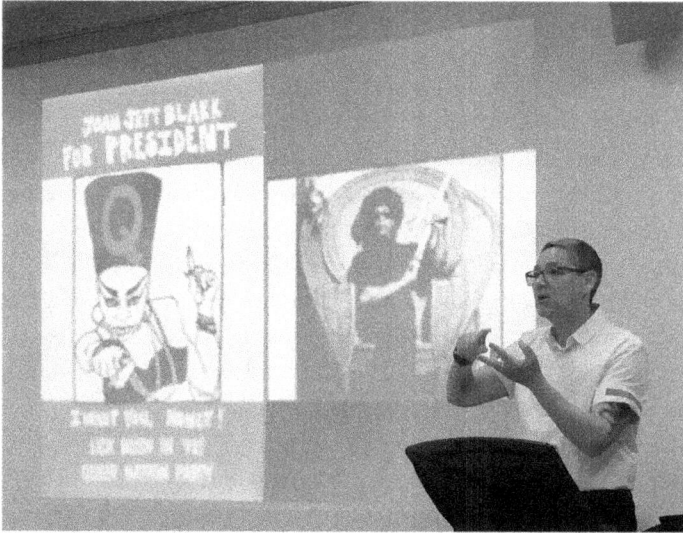

Figure 4: Jack Halberstam, Guest Lecture, ETH Zürich, Faculty of Architecture,
Spring Semester 2019. Source: Torsten Lange/Gabrielle Schaad and Lisa Maillard.

Literature

Abrams, Kathryn (2011), "Performing Interdependence: Judith Butler and
    Sunara Taylor in 'The Examined Life'," *Columbia Journal of Gender and Law*,
    vol. 21, no. 1 (2011), 72–89.

Ahmed, Sara (2004), *The Cultural Politics of Emotion*, Edinburgh: Edinburgh
    University Press, 2nd ed., 146–155.

Boys, Jos (2018), "Invisibility Work? How Starting from Dis/ability Challenges
    Normative Social, Spatial and Material Practices," in: Frichot, Hélène/
    Gabrielsson, Catharina/Runting, Helen (eds.), *Architecture and Feminisms.
    Ecologies, Economies, Technologies*, London and New York: Routledge, 270–
    280.

Butler, Judith (1990), *Gender Trouble. Feminism and the Subversion of Identity*,
    New York: Routledge.

Federici, Silvia (1975; reprint 2012), "Wages Against Housework (1975)," in:
    Revolution at Point Zero. Housework, Reproduction, and Feminist Struggle,
    Brooklyn: Common Notions, 15–22.

Fraser, Nancy (2016), "Contradictions of Capital and Care," *New Left Review*, (July 2016), 99–117.

Frey, Katia/Perotti, Eliana (2015) (eds), *Theoretikerinnen des Städtebaus. Texte und Projekte für die Stadt*, Berlin: Reimer.

Frey, Katia/Perotti, Eliana (2018), "Flora Ruchat-Roncati, First Woman Professor at ETH Zurich. Introducing Women's Standpoint in Architectural Pedagogy," in: Serain, Helena/Franchini, Caterina/Garda, Emilia (2018) (eds.), *Women's Creativity since the Modern Movement (1918-2018). Toward a New Perception and Reception*, Ljubljana: France Stele Institute of Art History, Založba ZRC, 58–66.

Frey, Katia/Perotti, Eliana (2019) (eds.), *Frauen blicken auf die Stadt: Architektinnen, Planerinnen, Reformerinnen*, Berlin: Reimer.

Hamraie, Aimi (2017), *Building Access: Universal Design and the Politics of Disability*, Minneapolis: University of Minnesota Press.

Haraway, Donna (1985), "A Manifesto for Cyborgs: Science, Technology and Socialist Feminism in the 1980s," *Socialist Review*, no. 80 (1985), 65–10.

hooks, bell (1994), *Teaching to Transgress: Education as the Practice of Freedom*, New York: Routledge.

Kogan, Terry S. (2010), "Sex Separation: The Cure-All for Victorian Social Anxiety," in: Molotch, Harvey/Norén, Laura (eds), *Toilet: Public Restrooms and the Politics of Sharing*, New York: New York University Press, 145–164.

Lange, Torsten/Scott, Emily Eliza (2017), "Making Trouble to Stay With: Architecture and Feminist Pedagogies," *Field*, vol. 7, no. 1, 89–100.

Lange, Torsten/Malterre-Barthes Charlotte (2018), "Architects Who Make a Fuss," *Site Magazine*, June 25, 2018, URL: http://www.thesitemagazine.com/read/architectswhomakeafuss, accessed on September 7, 2020.

Nichols, Sarah (2019), "Taking Stock," in: Stalder, Laurent/Avermaete, Tom/Delbeke, Maarten/Heinze-Greenberg, Ita/Ursprung, Philip (eds.), *Founding Myths*, Zürich: gta Verlag, 107–111.

Preciado, Beatriz (Paul)(2004), "Pornotopia," in: Colomina, Beatriz/Brennan, Annmarie/Kim, Jeannie (eds.), *Cold War Hothouses: Inventing Postwar Culture from Cockpit to Playboy*, New York: Princeton Architectural Press, 216–253. „Flora Ruchat-Roncati. Architektur als Netzwerk," (2017), *werk, bauen + wohnen*, no. 12, (2017).

Sanders, Joel (2017), "Stalled! Transforming Public Restrooms", *Footprint Journal*, vol. 11, no. 2 (2017), 109–118.

Schaad, Gabrielle (2020), „A Room of One's Own? – Zur Verzahnung von Geschlechterrollen und Architektur seit dem Industriezeitalter," *widerspruch. Beiträge zu sozialistischer Politik: Frauen*streiken*, no. 74, (2020), 147–158.

Schwartz-Cowan, Ruth (1976), "The 'Industrial Revolution' in the Home: Household Technology and Social Change in the 20th Century," *Technology and Culture*, vol. 17, no. 1, (1976), 1–23.

Stojanik, Petra (1995), „Frauen in der Geschichte des Bauens: ein fragmentarischer Rückblick," *DISP: the planning review*, vol. 31, no. 1 (1995), 3–10.

Internet Sources

Future Clinic https://www.futureclinic.org, accessed on September 7, 2020.

Making Difference https://blogs.ethz.ch/making-difference, accessed on September 7, 2020.

Stalled https://www.stalled.online, accessed on September 7, 2020.

Women architects in Switzerland http://www.schweizerarchitektinnen.ch, accessd on March 19, 2021.

Introducing Gender and Spatial Theory to the Technical University of Darmstadt

Donna J. Drucker

Incorporating gender issues into the course offerings of an engineering department, along with promoting interdisciplinary research and teaching, is a challenge in a traditionally male-oriented field. The elective course "Gender and the Built Environment" was added to the Department of Civil and Environmental Engineering curriculum at the Technical University of Darmstadt (TuDa), Germany in 2013, and it has been taught three times since. This chapter outlines the teaching practices developed for that course and student responses thereto. It shows how students with little previous exposure to either topic discover the ways that "gender [is] lived in and through space and its intersection with other dimensions of identity."[1]

It uses examples from the two major campuses of TuDa, an engineering and science-focused university in the state of Hessen. The university's two primary campuses—one in the city center (*Stadtmitte*) adjacent to a heavily used urban park and a second (*Lichtwiese*) bordering open space on the south-eastern side of the city—both have teachable architectural and spatial issues, together demonstrating "the gendered nature of everyday spaces."[2] Ideas of gender are structured by interactions with other members of the university community and public, the urban environment itself, and mental perceptions of safety and danger. Gender and space co-produce each other in urban environments, and a university campus with public art is an ideal place in which to examine how ideas and embodiments of gender both shape and are shaped by surroundings: a mixture of public and semi-private spaces. Students can then take that local knowledge and explore gender and spatiality in cities

---

1 Johnson (2008), 562.

2 Valentine/Jackson/Mayblin (2014), 404.

that spark their individual interests. While students were interested in representations of gender in public art, those representations did not keep their attention for long. Instead, the class's discussions of everyday experiences and interactions in cities made the abstractions of spatial theory come to life.

Background

The course was held on the TuDa *Lichtwiese* campus, which was built on an abandoned former airfield surrounded with forests and open space. As the university outgrew its buildings in the Darmstadt city center in the late 1960s, the school built a new campus for its engineering and architecture faculties three kilometers southeast of the center.[3] As the campus grew through the 1980s and early 1990s, and professors complained publicly about the isolation of the campus relative to the city center, the architecture professor Heiner Knell energized the idea of a permanent sculpture park.[4] He envisioned that new artwork would enhance the campus buildings and the walking areas around them, and that the artworks would visually connect to the natural landscape and to the buildings.[5]

The university, the art foundation of the state of Hessen and private donors together could afford the artwork in large part because many of the artists were current or former members of the architecture faculty. Wilhelm Loth and Thomas Duttenhoefer were also able to choose the locations of their sculptures.[6] Furthermore, according to Knell, the committee that chose the artwork wanted contemporary art but otherwise had no specific esthetic criteria: "'Figurative' or 'not figurative' was never a question, there was no interest in this topic."[7] Four of the eleven sculptures had human characteristics: Alfred Hrdlicka's "Marsyas II," Waldemar Grzimek's "The Threatened II," Loth's "Large Female Figure in Diamond" and Duttenhoefer's "The Earth."

---

3 Architekten Datz Kullman (2005); Karhausen (2002); Scorzin (2002a).

4 Scorzin (ed.) (2002b).

5 'Große Frauenfigur im Rhombus' (1992); Wannemacher 1993; Scorzin (ed.) (2002b); Karhausen (2002).

6 Knell (1991); Hennecke et al. (2002).

7 Chmilecki/Scholz/Scorzin (2002), 18.

After a sculpture symposium in 1993, no further sculptures were added.[8] The sculpture garden thus provides a readily accessible means of teaching students how gendered objects can affect perceptions of, and interactions with, public space. The sculpture garden, along with the street renaming discussed below, also sheds light on how external gender representations comingle with individual understandings of gendered selves.

Theoretical Framework

The summer 2015 syllabus of "Gender and the Built Environment" included readings from multidisciplinary scholars who have considered the relationship of gender and spatiality. The following discussion focuses on three class activities using discussions and experiences of local space as a means of illustrating the arguments of three scholars: Elizabeth Grosz, Henri Lefebvre, and Dolores Hayden. During the first meeting of "Gender and the Built Environment," students considered Grosz's spatial and feminist theory in her 1992 article "Bodies-Cities" in order to think about the sculptures' implications for gender and spatiality. She argues against two influential philosophical views of the city: first, seeing the interrelationship between bodies and cities as one of historic necessity—people need places to live and work, so they create cities—and second, that cities and their inhabitants share a metaphorical relationship alone: the physical body and the body politic are mirror elements of the same social order. Instead, "the city provides the order and organization that automatically links otherwise unrelated bodies."[9] Therefore, the city is one of the crucial factors in the social production of (sexed) corporeality. In short, "the city must be seen as the most immediately concrete locus for the production and circulation of power."[10] So, the built environment provides the shape and contour of life and for how people interact with each other.

Secondly, students read selections from the 1991 English translation of Lefebvre's 1977 book *The Production of Space*. Lefebvre's "conceptual triad" of

---

8   Feuk (1993); Held (1993); Kuntzsch (1993); „Plastiken für Lichtwiese"(1994); Architekten Datz Kullman (2005).

9   Grosz (1992), 243.

10 Ibid., 250.

space involves three elements: first, spatial practice, "which embraces production and reproduction, and the particular locations and spatial sets characteristic of each social formation."[11] Thus, spatial practice includes all the actions that take place within and between human interactions, animate and inanimate objects, and buildings. Secondly, representations of space "are tied to the relations of production and to the 'order' which those relations impose, and hence to knowledge, to signs, to codes, and to 'frontal' relations."[12] Those representations include signs, printed maps, nowadays geographical information systems and other electronic mapping tools, and other guides to navigation. Thirdly, representational spaces embody "complex symbolisms, sometimes coded, sometimes not, linked to the clandestine or underground side of social life."[13] Representational spaces include individual perceptions, thoughts, memories and meanings that individuals and groups give to spaces. For Lefebvre, spaces are best understood when one is able to comprehend and analyze each of these three elements for them. In October 2013, the university renamed some streets on the *Lichtwiese* campus in honor of the hundredth anniversary of Jovanka Bontschits (1887–1966), the first female student in Germany to complete an engineering degree, who also received a second degree in architecture. This street renaming provided an ideal example for students to apply Lefebvre's three-part concept of space to the campus.

Thirdly, shifting to the *Stadtmitte* campus—where many students also have classes—provided an excellent opportunity for students to apply Dolores Hayden's concept of the "non-sexist city" to the *Stadtmitte* campus and to the immediate surroundings of downtown Darmstadt. Hayden's 1980 article "What Would a Non-Sexist City Be Like?" outlined the various ways that the design of American suburbs around major cities after World War II restricted women's mobility, ability to work outside the home, and general human development.[14] Hayden suggested that the built environment of the suburbs kept women isolated in single-family homes without the economic means to break free of bad marriages or living situations. She argued for reform of the suburbs and identified spatial rearrangements intended to

11 Lefebvre ([1977] 1991), 33.

12 Ibid.

13 Ibid.

14 Hayden (1980).

remove such isolation would require community efforts to work with cities to rezone single-family residential areas as mixed-use areas. Darmstadt is not a suburb but certainly has sexist elements to discuss.

Methods

On the first day of class, after I introduced the work of Elizabeth Grosz in a short lecture, the fifteen students and I took a walk through the sculpture garden to investigate the extent to which the sculptures illustrated her ideas. I asked them to look at three of the four sculptures with human figures with me (Figures 1–4). The first sculpture that we walked to was Thomas Duttenhoefer's 1993 sculpture "The Earth".[15] The figure expresses the artist's hope that viewers would take better care of the earth. Though the statue may indeed inspire students to be better environmental stewards, my class perceived only degradation and ugliness. Next, we examined Waldemar Grzimek's "The Threatened II", a short walk from "The Earth". Grzimek pictured the figure as a visiting music school student, who was unsettled about his relationship, his education, and his finances. If that is the case, "The Threatened II" is threatened by nothing more than his everyday worries.[16] Lastly, we walked to the last stop, Wilhelm Loth's "Large Female Figure in Diamond."[17] "Large Female Figure" was placed parallel to "Ball/Cone" in 1991 in order to link them and other campus sculptures together visually.[18] A contemporary article on the sculpture described one art historian's interpretation of Loth's work (the detailed vagina in particular) as Loth's appreciation of second wave feminism's articulation of a newly sexually assertive form of womanhood.[19]

On the first day of class, students had a mixed reaction to seeing the sculptures. None of them cared for any of the sculptures aesthetically, and

15 Hennecke et al. (2002).

16 „Eine Plastik von Grzimek" (1989); „Der Bedrohte II" (1989); „Hommage an den Bildhauer Waldemar Grzimek" (1989); Karhausen (2002).

17 Baumann et al. (2002); Maxheimer (2003).

18 „Kunstlandschaft" (1991); Knell (1991); „„Große Frauenfigur im Rhombus' Gestellt'" (1991); „Große Frauenfigur im Rhombus von Wilhelm Loth" (1992); Wannemacher (1993).

19 „Große Frauenfigur im Rhombus" (1992).

perhaps they did not want to challenge a professor's perceptions of how the sculptures functioned as representations of gender on the campus. By the end of the period, however, they understood my argument that the statues were problematic (a non-sexist city would be empty of sexist art), even if they did not make associations between the statues and their own lived experiences. The statues were no threat to their health or safety, in the ways that other types of interactions in everyday life in an urban environment could be. Elizabeth Grosz's argument that "a complex feedback relation" exists between bodies and environments was more vivid when interactions took place between living actors.[20] However, these statues alone do not tell the whole story of gendered messages and interpretations of spatiality on campus. They must be examined alongside another set of gendered spatial influences: the recent renaming of the campus streets, and Lefebvre's theory helps do that.

During the second class period, I asked students to restate Lefebvre's theory (which I had assigned them to read) in their own words and to apply it to the renaming of the streets. Concerning spatial practice, the students did not think that changing the names of streets to honor the first female student, graduate, and professor would change people's behaviors in those spaces, beyond the need to change university business cards, letterhead stationery, and websites. As regards spatial representations, they could use their computers, tablets and mobile phones to see if the street names had been revised in online maps and navigational systems. They found that most of the names had changed, and that the university had made a sweeping announcement to that effect. Lastly, regarding representations of space, the students thought through the different ways that the street name changes would rework people's thoughts and memories of these streets. They concluded that the street renaming would serve as a constant present-day reminder of the historical presence of women at the university—not one that people would reflect on with much depth, perhaps, but a reminder, nonetheless. However, the reasons that these seven individuals were chosen muted the renaming's feminist potential. While three streets were renamed for women—including Bontschits who achieved recognition in the university's history through a combination of hard work and historical happenstance—, the four men whose names are now street names were all former TuDa professors honored

---

20 Grosz (1992), 242.

Figure 1: Thomas Duttenhoefer, "The Earth"
(1993), Technical University of Darmstadt,
Germany. Source: Donna J. Drucker.

Figure 2: Waldemar Grzimek, "The Threatened II"
(1984), Technical University of Darmstadt, Germany.
Source: Donna J. Drucker.

for international academic achievements alone. It was a missed opportunity to honor female professors who had attained equal success.

What, then, are the experiences of the living women on the campus in the present? The third and last example of teaching gender and space, which examines problems on and around the *Stadtmitte* campus, helps answer that question. I asked the students to describe Hayden's "non-sexist city" in their own words, and then to consider the ways that Darmstadt was and was not a sexist city. They did not focus on Hayden's concerns about married women with families in suburbs but rather on the broader issues of safety, freedom and mobility that she raised. Male and female students had different experiences of the city. A female student mentioned that she did not walk by a certain bar near campus because of the verbal harassment that she received from male patrons shouting out of the windows. A male student visiting from Turkey stated that an introductory presentation for study-abroad students to the university included a warning that female students—but not male students—should avoid walking through the *Herrngarten*, a park in the city, at night. Another female student spoke of unwanted touching on the trams and buses when she was traveling to and from campus. Yet another female student pointed out the poor lighting on the *Lichtwiese* campus at night and stated her concerns about safety when walking alone to the bus, train or tram stops. Altogether, the students concluded that Darmstadt was mostly a non-sexist city, but that there was room to improve both actual security and perceptions thereof, especially regarding public transit.

These three examples of pedagogy for gender and spatiality show that TuDa students have a keen sense of how ideas and experiences of gender operate in everyday life. Overall, the students were convinced that people living in gendered bodies—themselves and the people they encounter every day—affected their own gendered movements and those of others. They were less convinced that static, non-living representations of gendered bodies and names, like those in the sculpture garden and on campus streets, had a measurable impact on the living.

Conclusion

From the research that other scholars have conducted and the above reflections on teaching the intersectionality of gender and space, it is clear that the creation of gendered spatiality is a set of multifaceted, ongoing "co-constructed event[s]."[21] The interplay of gendered persons and ideas, not to mention other concepts of identity, embodiment and selfhood, is happening constantly at multiple levels of spatiality over time. Not only is it true that "genders are mutually constituted by the performer and by the viewer in a particular space," so too are other forms of identity that affect ideas and perceptions of spatiality, power and control.[22]

At TuDa, research and teaching experiences demonstrate the multiple levels of gendered power that are enacted in various forms in different spaces across campuses and the city. Retiring the two artworks in the sculpture garden that show women as torsos alone and replacing them with sculptures that represent women as wholes would be a good place to start. However, honoring the craft of the living sculptors and the memory of the deceased may keep them in place. Perhaps my own experience of being one of the few female professors on campus, and seeing the sculptures every day, heightened my sense of the need for full-bodied representation. Rumors may continue to structure the *Herrngarten* as a risky place for women to walk after dark, when in fact the public spaces of trains, trams, buses and streets also contain potential threats to safety. Perhaps streets around the *Stadtmitte* or the other three smaller TuDa campuses will someday be renamed in honor of women professors with achievements equal to any of their male peers. In the meantime, I will continue to teach, and students will continue to learn, the deep interconnectedness of gender and spatiality that structures their academic work and everyday life.

---

21 Doan (2010), 642.

22 Ibid, 645.

Figure 3: Wilhelm Loth, "Large Female Figure in Diamond" (1989), Technical University of Darmstadt, Germany. Source: Donna J. Drucker.

Figure 4: Fritz Koenig, "Ball/Cone" (1970) with Wilhelm Loth's "Large Female Figure in Diamond' (1989) in the background, Technical University of Darmstadt, Germany. Source: Donna J. Drucker.

Acknowledgements

This excerpt of Donna J. Drucker, "Bringing Gender and Spatial Theory to Life at a German Technical University," *Gender, Place and Culture* 23 (no. 11, 2016): 1560–71, is reprinted with permission of Taylor and Francis, Ltd.

Literature

Architekten Datz Kullman (2005). *Planungswerkstatt Standort Lichtwiese*. Mainz: Architekten Datz Kullman. TuD/THD; Bauten Lichtwiese II Folder, Universitätsarchiv Technische Universität Darmstadt, Darmstadt, Germany.

„Kunstlandschaft" (1991), *Darmstädter Echo*, December 7, 1991.

Baumann, Nina/Runge, Stephanie/Schunder, Martina/Scorzin., Pamela C. (2002), „Wilhelm Loth: Große Frauenfigur im Rhombus," in: Scorzin, Pamela C. (ed.), *Skulpturengarten Lichtwiese*, Darmstadt: Technische Universität Darmstadt, 56–63.

Chmilecki, Martin/ Scholz, Thomas/Scorzin, Pamela C. (2002), „Heiner Knell im Gesprach über den Skulpturengarten Lichtwiese," in: Scorzin, Pamela C. (ed.), *Skulpturengarten Lichtwiese*, Darmstadt: Technische Universität Darmstadt, 18–19.

Doan, Petra L. (2010). "The Tyranny of Gendered Spaces—Reflections from beyond the
Gender Dichotomy," *Gender, Place, and Culture* 17 (5), 635–654.

Feuk, Jörg (1993), „Wegweiser in Lichtwiese," *Frankfurter Rundschau*, July 20, 1993.

Grosz, Elizabeth (1992), "Bodies-Cities," in: Colomina, Beatriz (ed.), *Sexuality and Space*, London: Routledge, 241–253.

Hayden, Dolores (1980), "What Would a Non-Sexist City Be Like? Speculations on Housing, Urban Design, and Human Work," *Signs: Journal of Women in Culture and Society* 5 (S3), 170–187.

Held, Roland (1993), „Kunst und Nature: Schweigend, aber Beredt," *Darmstädter Echo*, August 3, 1993.

Hennecke, Christian/Hubert, Ute/Lassota, Jeanette/Scorzin, Pamela C. (2002), „Thomas Duttenhoefer: Die Erde," in: Scorzin, Pamela C. (ed.),

Skulpturengarten Lichtwiese, Darmstadt: Technische Universität Darmstadt, 64–67.

Johnson, Louise C. (2008), "Re-placing Gender? Reflections on 15 Years of Gender, Place and Culture," *Gender, Place, and Culture* 15 (6), 561–574.

Karhausen, Eva (2002), „Erweiterung der Universität Lichtwiese: Das Konzept der Landschaftsgestaltung," in: Scorzin, Pamela C. (ed.), *Skulpturengarten Lichtwiese*, Darmstadt: Technische Universität Darmstadt, 14–17.

Kuntzsch, Brigitte (1993), „Skulpturensymposium an der TH Darmstadt," Darmstadt: Darmstädter Kulturannual.

„Große Frauenfigur im Rhombus von Wilhelm Loth." (1992), Darmstadt: Darmstädter Kulturannual.

„Große Frauenfigur im Rhombus: Kunstwerk für den Skulpturengarten der TH Darmstadt." (1992), *TUD-Intern*, January 30, 1992.

„,Große Frauenfigur im Rhombus' Gestellt: weitere Kunstwerke im THD Skulpturengarten" (1991), *Darmstädter Wochenblatt*, December 12, 1991.

Lefebvre, Henri ([1977] 1991), *The Production of Space.* (translated by Nicholson-Smith, Donald), Oxford: Blackwell.

Maxheimer, Sibylle (2003), „Der Nabel ist die Nase," *Darmstädter Echo*, January 8, 2003.

Scorzin, Pamela C. (2002a), „Der Skulpturengarten auf der Lichtwiese der Technischen Universität Darmstadt," in: Scorzin, Pamela C. (ed.), *Skulpturengarten Lichtwiese*, Darmstadt: Technische Universität Darmstadt, 8–13.

Scorzin, Pamela C. (2002b)(ed.), *Skulpturengarten Lichtwiese*, Darmstadt: Technische Universität Darmstadt.

„Eine Plastik von Grzimek: ,Der Bedrohte II' an der Lichtwiese" (1989), *Darmstädter Echo*, July 20, 1989.

„Plastiken für Lichtwiese" (1994), *Frankfurter Allgemeine Zeitung*, July 19, 1994.

„Der Bedrohte II" (1989), *TUD-Intern*, October 19, 1989.

„Hommage an den Bildhauer Waldemar Grzimek" (1989), *Frankfurter Allgemeine Zeitung*, July 21, 1989.

Valentine, Gill/Jackson, Lucy/Mayblin, Lucy (2014), "Ways of Seeing: Sexism the Forgotten Prejudice?," *Gender, Place, and Culture* 21 (4), 401–414.

Wannemacher, Annette (1993), „Von einer Skulptur zur nächsten: Der Kunstgarten auf der Lichtwiese wird um eine Frauenfigur von Wilhelm Loth bereichert," *Darmstädter Echo*, December 13, 1993.

Archives

University Archive, Technical University of Darmstadt, Darmstadt, Germany

A Gendered Profession
Reflections on an experiment

Harriet Harriss and Ruth Morrow

Introduction

In 2016 we co-edited a book, entitled, *A Gendered Profession: the question of representation in placemaking*, together with James Brown and James Soane. This short essay offers some pithy reflections upon the drivers for this project, how they evolved, what has happened since and what we feel is next. (Figures 1–2)

For a profession that professes to serve the needs of wider society through the production of buildings and spaces, continuing gender imbalance in architectural education and practice is a difficult subject. Difficult, because as we discovered, it has been stagnant for some thirty years. In 2016, ninety-two percent of female architects in the UK reported that having children would put them at a disadvantage in architecture: a five percent increase on the previous year. That so many women feel that their profession is prejudiced against them is shocking enough, but the lack of reliable statistics that report male architects' opinions on fatherhood in the profession is equally telling. Given that only five percent of retiring UK architects are female, a professional culture, where the preferred image of the "masters" remains almost exclusively male and where its "mistresses" leave early, demotivated by the lack of promotion prospects and leadership roles is continually reinforced.[1]

---

1 Only 2/100 of the world's leading architecture firms are directed by women. Source: https://www.dezeen.com/2017/11/16/survey-leading-architecture-firms-reveals-shocking-lack-gender-diversity-senior-levels/, accessed on Feb. 1, 2021.

It was statistics such as this that prompted us; editors, James Brown, Harriet Harriss, Ruth Morrow and James Soane to curate a book on the subject of whether an alternative strategy could be envisioned, although with some caveats. While our editorial profile combined cismale/cisfemale and LGBTQ perspectives on the problem, we are aware that we are all caucasian, northern Europeans, and have, therefore, a framing of the problem that is contextualised by wider regional, racial and economic inequalities. We took the view that feminist thinking is a meaningful mechanism to respond to all forms of inequality caused by modern capitalism. Specifically, we pointed to a generation of inclusive feminist critique that is characterized by a willingness to confront inequalities far beyond "traditional" and outdated gender-binaries. This new critique recognises that the forces disadvantaging some over others have structural rather than social origins, although this does not exonerate the profession of architecture from its evident imbalances. After the Second World War, architecture was a public profession that rallied around its obligation to fulfill a social need, whereas today, the mainstream of our profession has capitulated its servitude to capitalism, evidenced through the shift in its code of conduct. What we only partially succeeded in considering is whether the meaningful and effective responses to gender inequality in architecture that were proposed within the book, could be just as effective at responding to other forms of inequality in architecture too.

Gendered co-authorship

As we watch feminism's "fourth wave" unfold, we have met all too often with the stubborn misconception that feminism is only for and about women. The conversation has to be collectively critical: women cannot dictate a solution to men, just as men cannot dictate a solution to women. However, one could argue that it is a failure of our profession to resolve its own internal inequalities, and a failure of those in positions of leadership and influence, to address the culture that supports inequalities head on. At stake is more than just the lack of female representation. Sexism and gendered practices in architecture condemn all of us to a set of expectations around stereotypical behaviour. Male architects suffer from the same ingrained mechanisms of gender stereotyping that prejudices women, obliging us to place professional commitments above those to our family, children *and* ourselves.

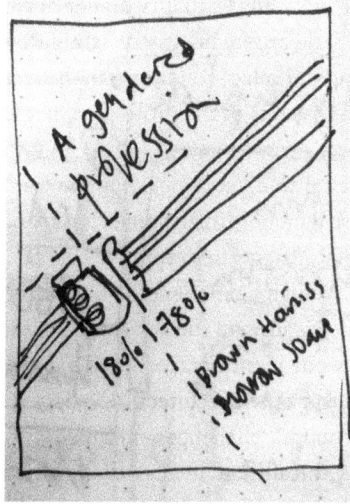

Figure 1: Sketch for the cover of A Gendered Profession, 2015.
Source: Harriet Harriss.

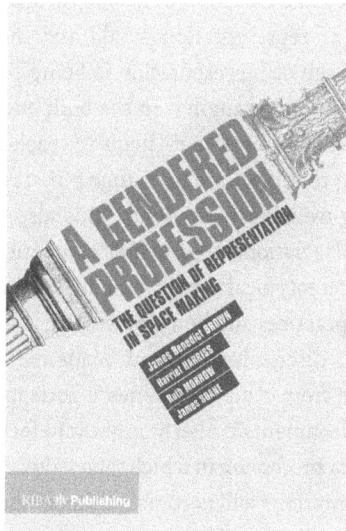

Figure 2: A Gendered Profession. The Question of Representation
in Architecture. J. Brown, H. Harriss, R. Morrow, J. Soane (eds.)
(2016). Source: London: RIBA Publishing.

And for those whose gender and sexuality do not fit comfortably within the binary conception of male or female, gay or straight, we find that the progress made in improving workplace conditions in the architect's studio has yet to be matched in other aspects of the profession, not least the construction site.

It is therefore critical to dispute not only the traditional binary definition of gender, but also a mono-dimensional concept of gender along a spectrum, one that ultimately categorises everyone between the same binary. We need to think beyond women's experiences of architectural education, practice and culture; gender is instead the key for a broader and more inclusive understanding of how our identity affects our experience of life and work. In order to recast the role of the architect in society it is imperative to take on the political and economic challenges entwined within the gender debate, and hence to practice ethically and inclusively. It is critical to recognise that we operate within relative frameworks. As we age, climb the ladder of progression, grow as an architect—we change too, more often than we might like to think.

Through the writing and editing process, we recognised that any attempt to address the issue of representation would and should be inconclusive and emerging. This issue of representation is being played out not only in books such as this, but, more tangibly, in the built environment around us. We also questioned why it seems so difficult to teach architects about gendered spaces, arguing that if we are to change our starchitect culture, then we must change how we educate students. This also requires us to scrutinise the "master-pupil" relationship, and how competition and long working hours can reaffirm stereotypical "hegemonic masculinity" arguing for new and different labour practices and hours of work that suit both genders; that resist traditionalism, discrimination and academic capitalism. Whether architecture can learn from other disciplines' efforts in order to create more gender equitable environments is also brought into focus, concluding with a statement of hope for a profession in which tacit values and judgments made on stereotypical assumptions will become a thing of the past.

An unsolicited momentum

The *Gendered Profession* book launch took place on Tuesday 8th November 2016 at the Royal College of Art in London, the same day Donald Trump was elected President of the United States of America. Whilst we quaffed student union wine with co-authors and colleagues, we were unaware that we were only hours away from what has amounted to a devastating blow to the progress that had been made towards gender equality and its continuing corrosion thereafter. Having highlighted what we thought of as slow progress and referred to as a "calcification" of the gender debate in our introduction, we were now confronted with the sense that the foundations upon which we could make such an assured evaluation were now crumbling beneath us. Since that day, Trump's many legislative attacks on women's rights, the #MeToo movement, the Shitty Men in Architecture list and the Kavanaugh narrative have made clear that none of the progress, that had been fought and won before the book was even imagined, can be taken for granted. Instead, we have conceded progress for protection and, as that has fallen, only protest remains. (Figure 3)

Fighting back, but differently

Although the queer-positive, sex-positive, trans-inclusive, body-positive, and digitally driven tactics of fourth wave feminism have provided a rapid and often effective response to the corrosion of women's rights, determining preventative tactics requires a more inconspicuous and less immediate approach. It requires a willingness to address the structural rather than the symptomatic and to offer strategies for change rather than damning diagnostics. When we began the book, we recognised the role of capitalism in imposing inequalities upon architecture, but what we failed to really address was the extent to which architecture's inequalities are deeply rooted within its culture. To paraphrase Audre Lorde, the American writer, feminist and activist, we cannot dismantle the master's house with the master's tools. Subsequently, to "fix" any of architecture's inequalities, from the homophobia on site to gendered pay differentials, requires us to challenge (as a reflection of society's) architecture's core values, by questioning its curricula and teaching, its practice processes and its outcomes. Indeed, one argument

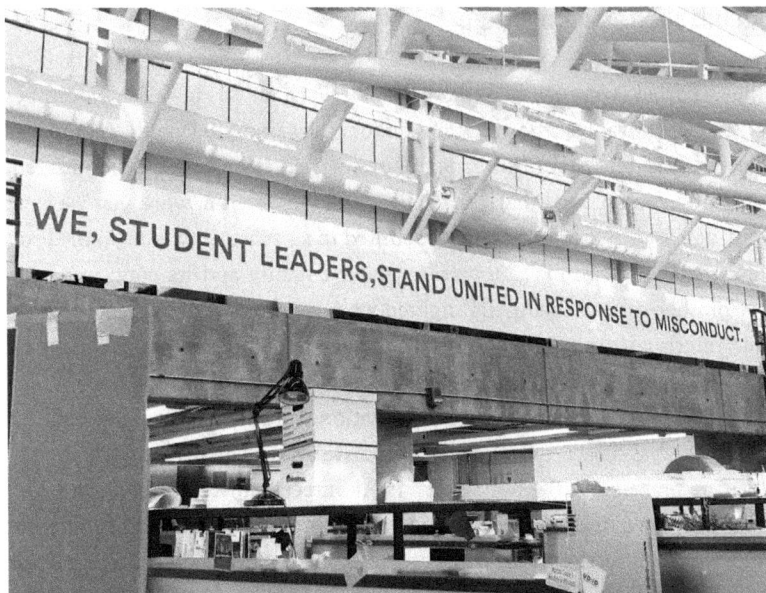

Figure 3: "We, student leaders, stand united in response to misconduct." Shitty Men List Protest, Graduate School of Design (GSD), Harvard University, Cambridge, Mass., USA, 2018. Source: Malia Teske.

made within the book is that sometimes what we think of as male privilege is at times a trap. And for those who understand the source of their exclusion and marginalisation, rather than seek to gain entry to an exclusive club with which they share few values, they might instead relish the freedom of a place where there are few precedents and no norms to measure up to. And that if we *choose* (and that's the critical component here—that it's *our* choice) to occupy this space then we are free to ignore or indeed upturn the conventions or traditions that seek to bind us. Architecture, then, is whatever we want it to be.

Next steps?

Perhaps now, post-book, in our more radical moments, we recognise that across our own careers, tinkering with given structures has brought about only small changes that have been slow to arrive and tough to gain. Con-

sequently we have become convinced that in order to make significant difference we have to disengage from those given structures and simply create
our own. To do so we will need to reposition ourselves to some core societal
concepts that create the difficulties that women (and others) face. We foreground two such concepts, chosen because they are so integral to material
and creative practices, such as architecture.

The first concept is Time. Women fall outside normative time cultures.
Demands on their time can be fragmented and unpredictable. Their temporal rhythms do not sync with the "commodified clock time of capitalist culture." In this way women's time tends to be undervalued and fails to connect
to mainstream power structures. Being visibly present in the workplace is
connected to status and conveys a sense of being "on top of things". Part-time
workers are therefore stigmatised as lacking commitment and reliability. In
the past, women have felt encouraged by feminism to work full time—to
assert their right to work—yet they have done so within a concept of time
that is ill-fitting and where they struggle to balance their time across work,
caring needs and their own developmental needs. But whilst it's clearly the
social construct of time that is amiss, it is individual women who feel at fault
for not managing their time effectively.

Parlour, the Australian project on women, equity and architecture, published guides aimed at improving the architecture profession for women.[2]
Of their eleven guides, three dealt directly with the work/time relationship
(Long-hours culture, Part-time work and Flexibility). They offer some prag-
matic ways to bring about change in the Architecture Profession but clearly
there is a need to build more progressive time concepts.

Some clues as to how this is to be done lie in the work of Kathi Weeks
in *The Problem with Work: Feminism, Marxism, Antiwork Politics and Postwork
Imaginaries*, where she critiques the "pro-work suppositions" of feminism
and questions whether work is in fact an inevitable activity at a time when
there is insufficient work to go around.[3] She argues for a reduction in work-
hours without a reduction in pay, as much to enhance people's productive/
creative practices and experiences, as to provoke a reconceptualisation of the
role and value of work in society. It's a provocative call, yet by considering the
idea of less work or indeed no work, it allows us also to think of play and its

---

2 https://archiparlour.org, accessed on Feb. 1, 2021.
3 Weeks (2011).

value to society. Indeed, within the creative practice of architecture, we recognise the need to combine creativity and rigor: where maintaining an open and playful attitude is critical when tackling complex problems and where there are moments when it may be best practice to take time to reach decisions rather than rushing pell-mell into an ill-thought resolution. Indeed, we are starting to accept that in professional roles, the cognitive aspect of the work continues beyond the office, on the school run, in the surgery waiting room, etc., and that part-time in such jobs means only "part-time-present" not "part-time-engagement." There is clearly an upside to part-time work that we have failed to fully understand and a marked urgency to re-conceptualize our work/time relationships, to reconsider the balance of up time, down time, thinking-time, playtime and taking time.

The second concept is Technology. One only has to scan the literature to see how infrequently Feminism and Technologies of the Built Environment are referenced. When it comes to technology and innovation, women's efforts have naturally been focused on industries where they have been employed or in those areas that affect their daily lives. As one indicator of this, we tend to see women patenting technologies in textiles and home appliance sectors but rarely in construction. Of course, historically, technology has been gendered, where certain knowledge and skill domains dominated by women are considered as "craft" and only gain significance and become named as "technological" once they are appropriated by men. The term "technology" itself can be off-putting—even today where it is synonymous with information, gaming or virtual technology, the number of women active remains significantly lower than their male counterparts. Feminists, however,have begun to unravel our relationship to technology—at least in theory—expanding the definition and creating new narratives. By taking the focus off "the thing of it," placing more emphasis on tacit interactions and diverse and underrepresented knowledges can lead to inclusive material ecologies. The next step is to look for existing methods and to generate new examples where theory becomes practice. To some extent the book did that, but we need to look for further examples of where technology has been re-appropriated to suit the practice of others outside of the mainstream. (Figure 4)

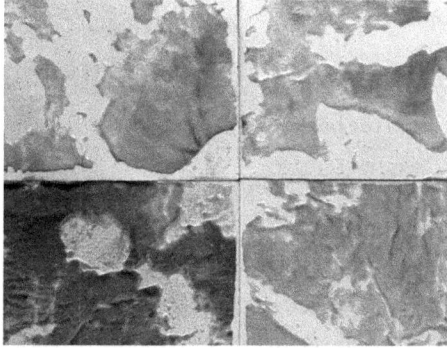

*Figure 4: Making Hard Things Soft: Velvet and
Concrete Patented Technologies from Tactility Factory,
Belfast. Source: Trish Belford and Ruth Morrow.*

Concluding comments

The book sought to offer a diagnostic check on our profession. But the condition is on-going, and the case is definitely not closed. The infrastructure of both education and practice requires systems which routinely perform a diversity and inclusion health check on the profession: one that not only monitors the problem but prescribes solutions too. Whilst we all seem too willing to admit that an inclusive discussion on the subject of architecture and gender is needed, one that can address some of the injustices facing our discipline, we see so few attempts to initiate these forums, platforms and policies for change, even on a personal level, with colleagues at work.

We remain resolute in our conviction towards the importance of feminist texts on gender, no matter how quickly they date. Because in those dark times, when we as individuals doubt our value, it is these texts, whether in hand or online, that support, make sense of and depersonalise the challenges and exclusion that we face.

We are under no illusion that the gender question will ever go away but instead point to the principles and practices of what is now the potential beginning of the Fifth Wave of Feminism: that an attitude of inclusion is more than an act of publicly calling out the problem, but one characterised by taking strategic and tactical ACTION!

Acknowledgments

We extend our appreciation to our co-editors, James Brown and James Soane, and all authors within the book.

Literature

Brown, James/Harriss, Harriet/Morrow, Ruth/Soane, James (eds.)(2016), *A Gendered Profession. The question of representation in placemaking*, London: RIBA Publishing.

Weeks, Kathi (2011), *The Problem with Work: Feminism, Marxism, Antiwork Politics, and Postwork Imaginaries*, Durham: Duke University Press.

Internet Sources

Parlour https://archiparlour.org, accessed on Feb. 1, 2021

Authors

Christina Budde is the former curator for public education at the *Deutsches Architekturmuseum* (DAM). She co-edited *Von Häusern und Menschen: Architekturvermittlung im Museum* (About Houses and People: Communicating Architecture in the Museum) (2010) and *Architektur ganztags: Spielräume für baukulturelle Bildung* (Architecture all-day long: Opportunities for architectural education) (2014). In 2017-18, she co-edited the *Frau Architekt* catalogue which accompanied the exhibition she co-curated at DAM.

Stéphanie Bouysse-Mesnage, an architect and architecture historian, is completing a dissertation about women architects from the late 19th century until 1975 in France. In 2021 she co-organized the *Gender dynamics and practices in architecture, urbanism and landscape architecture* conference in Paris.

Elizabeth Darling, reader in architectural history at Oxford Brookes University, investigates gender, space and reform in the 1890s–1940s and interwar English modernism. She is the co-editor of *AA Women in Architecture 1917-2017* (2017) which accompanied the exhibition she co-curated at the Architectural Association.

Sigal Davidi is an architect and architecture historian. Her research focuses on the relations between gender and aging, immigration, nationality and the modern architecture of pre-state Israel. Her book, *Building a New Land: Women Architects and Women's Organizations in Mandatory Palestine*, appeared in Hebrew in 2020.

Donna J. Drucker teaches English at the Technical University of Darmstadt. A historian of the intersection of science and technology with gender and sexuality, her books include *The Classification of Sex* (2014), winner of the 2015 Bullough Prize; *Contraception* (2020); and *Fertility Technologies* (forthcoming).

Katia Frey is a senior researcher at the *Zürcher Hochschule für Angewandte Wissenschaften* (ZHAW). She works on urban history, with special emphasis on social, cultural, theoretical and gender issues. She co-edited *Theoretikerinnen des Städtebaus* (Women Theorists of Urbanism) (2015) and *Frauen blicken auf die Stadt* (Women looking at the City) (2019).

Harriet Harriss (Ph.D.), architect and dean of the Pratt School of Architecture in Brooklyn, New York, focuses on social justice and climate crisis pedagogies. Her recent co-edited book, *Architects After Architecture* (2020), considers the multi-sector impact of an architectural qualification.

Kathleen James-Chakraborty, professor of art history at the University College Dublin, is the author of: *Modernism as Memory: Building Identity in the Federal Republic of Germany* (2018); *Architecture since 1400* (2014; Chinese edition: 2017); and *German Architecture for a Mass Audience* (2000).

Karl Kiem is professor emeritus of architectural history and historic preservation at Siegen University. His essay about the architecture of Victoria zu Bentheim und Steinfurt appeared in the catalogue of the 2017-18 *Frau Architekt* exhibition at the *Deutsches Architekturmuseum* (DAM).

Annette Krapp directs the art education program at the Arp Museum Bahnhof Rolandseck. Her dissertation about the architect Maria Schwarz was published as *Die Architektin Maria Schwarz* (The woman architect Maria Schwarz) in 2015.

Elke Krasny is professor for art and education at the Academy of Fine Arts Vienna. Krasny's scholarship and curatorial labor focuses on social and ecological justice and emancipatory practices in art, architecture, urbanism, contemporary transnational feminisms and remembrance activism.

Torsten Lange, lecturer at Lucerne University of Applied Sciences and Arts (HSLU), was a research fellow in 2019 at the Canadian Centre for Architecture, Montréal with the project "Queer Ecologies of Care." He is co-editor of *archithese reader: Critical Positions in Search of Postmodernity, 1971–1976* (2022).

Edina Meyer-Maril was the senior lecturer at the Department of Art History at Tel Aviv University until her retirement in 2013. Her research focuses on European architects who emigrated to Eretz Israel/Israel; the architecture of synagogues and *Volkshäuser*; and Orientalism in fine arts and architecture.

Ruth Morrow is professor of biological architecture at Newcastle University. Previously she was the first woman professor of architecture on the island of Ireland. Between 2009 and 2018, she directed Tactility Factory, an innovative company creating award-winning building products.

Irene Nierhaus was professor for art history and aesthetic theory at Bremen University until her retirement in 2021. She directs the research project *wohnen+/—ausstellen* (living+/—displaying) at the Mariann Steegmann Institute, Kunst & Gender at Bremen University.

Mary Pepchinski was professor for architecture and society at the Technical University of Dresden until her retirement in 2021. She co-edited *Ideological Equals. Women Architects in Socialist Europe* (2016) and was the scientific advisor to the 2017-18 *Frau Architekt* exhibition and catalogue at the *Deutsches Architekturmuseum* (DAM).

Eliana Perotti, lecturer at the *Zürcher Hochschule für Angewandte Wissenschaften* (ZHAW), researches urban history and architecture, focusing on gender studies, colonial studies, cultural studies and sustainability. She co-edited *Theoretikerinnen des Städtebaus* (Women Theorists of Urbanism) (2015) and *Frauen blicken auf die Stadt* (Women looking at the City) (2019).

Kerstin Renz is an architecture historian and moderator in Stuttgart, Germany. She was visiting professor for architecture history at the University of Kassel and senior researcher at the Technical University of Stuttgart. Her latest publication, *Testfall der Moderne* (Test case of Modernity)(2017), focuses on international transfers of architectural knowledge

Gabrielle Schaad is a post-doctoral researcher at the Technical University of Munich and a research associate at Zürich University of the Arts. She is the co-editor of *archithese reader: Critical Positions in Search of Postmodernity, 1971–1976* (2022) and the author of *Shizuko Yoshikawa* (2018).

Mariann Simon, retired professor of architecture history and theory at Szent István University, Faculty of Landscape Architecture and Urbanism, Budapest, is the author of *Valami más* (The Other) (2003) and *Újrakezdések/ Restarts* (2016) and the co-editor of *Ideological Equals. Women Architects in Socialist Europe* (2016).

Wolfgang Voigt is the former deputy director of the *Deutsches Architektur-museum* (DAM) in Frankfurt-am-Main. His research interests include Paul Schmitthenner's architecture and professional circle and queer spaces and queer architects in historical contexts. In 2017-18 he co-edited the *Frau Architekt* catalogue which accompanied the exhibition he co-curated at DAM.

Lynne Walker is a senior research fellow at the Institute of Historical Research, University of London and has written extensively on gender, space and architecture. She is the co-editor of *AA Women in Architecture 1917-2017* (2017) which accompanied the exhibition she co-curated at the Architectural Association.

GPSR Authorized Representative: Easy Access System Europe, Mustamäe tee
50, 10621 Tallinn, Estonia, gpsr.requests@easproject.com